MICROSOFT®

Access 2000

Comprehensive Course

Mastering and Using

Updated Edition

H. Albert Napier
Philip J. Judd

COURSE
TECHNOLOGY

Thomson Learning™

25 THOMSON PLACE, BOSTON, MA 02210

Australia • Canada • Mexico • Singapore • Spain • United Kingdom • United States

ISBN: 0-619-05150-7

1 2 3 4 5 6 7 RRD 03 02 01 00

Managing Editor: Melissa Ramondetta
Project Manager/Editor: Ollie Rivers
Marketing Manager: Kim Wood
Consulting Editor: Betsy Newberry, Custom Editorial Productions, Inc.
Production Editor: Kristen Guevara
Production Services: GEX Publishing Services
Graphic Designer: Brenda Grannan, Grannan Graphics

What's New in Access 2000

Office

- ► Different Office 2000 suites
- ► Personalized menus and toolbars
- ► Multi-language support
- ► Web-based analysis tools
- ► Improved Office Assistant
- ► Online collaboration with NetMeeting and Web discussions from inside Office applications
- ► E-mail from inside Office applications
- ► Collect and Paste and Office Clipboard toolbar
- ► New Open and Save As dialog box features
- ► Saving directly to Web server
- ► New Clip Gallery format and new clips

Access

- ► Switchboard
- ► Cascade Update and Cascade Delete
- ► Data Access Pages
- ► Macro builder
- ► Encrypting and decrypting a database
- ► Add-ins (Database Splitter, Analyzer)
- ► Convert database to prior Access version
- ► Improved Database window (Objects Bar)
- ► Conditional formatting
- ► Subdatasheets
- ► Drag-and-drop to Excel
- ► Hyperlink handling

Napier & Judd

In their over 48 years of combined experience, Al Napier and Phil Judd have developed a tested, realistic approach to mastering and using application software. As both academics and corporate trainers, Al and Phil have the unique ability to help students by teaching them the skills necessary to compete in today's complex business world.

H. Albert Napier, Ph.D. is the Director of the Center on the Management of Information Technology and Professor in the Jones Graduate School of Administration at Rice University. In addition, Al is a principal of Napier & Judd, Inc., a consulting company and corporate trainer in Houston, Texas, that has trained more than 90,000 people in computer applications.

Philip J. Judd is a former instructor in the Management Department and the Director of the Research and Instructional Computing Service at the University of Houston. Phil now dedicates himself to corporate training and consulting as a principal of Napier & Judd, Inc.

Philip J. Judd

H. Albert Napier, Ph.D.

Preface

At Course Technology, we believe that technology will change the way people teach and learn. Today there are millions of people using personal computers in their everyday lives—both as tools at work and for recreational activities. As a result, the personal computer has revolutionized the ways in which people interact with each other. The Napier and Judd series combines the following distinguishing features to allow people to do amazing things with their personal computers.

Distinguishing Features

All the textbooks in the *Mastering and Using* series share several key pedagogical features:

Case Project Approach. In their more than twenty years of business and corporate training and teaching experience, Napier and Judd have found that learners are more enthusiastic about learning a software application if they can see its real-world relevance. The textbook provides bountiful business-based profiles, exercises, and projects. It also emphasizes the skills most in demand by employers.

Comprehensive and Easy to Use. There is thorough coverage of new features. The narrative is clear and concise. Each unit or chapter thoroughly explains the concepts that underlie the skills and procedures. We explain not just the *how*, but the *why*.

Step-by-Step Instructions and Screen Illustrations. All examples in this text include step-by-step instructions that explain how to complete the specific task. Full-color screen illustrations are used extensively to provide the learner with a realistic picture of the software application feature.

Extensive Tips and Tricks. The author has placed informational boxes in the margin of the text. These boxes of information provide the learner with the following helpful tips:

▶ Quick Tip. Extra information provides shortcuts on how to perform common business-related functions.

▶ Caution Tip. This additional information explains how a mistake occurs and provides tips on how to avoid making similar mistakes in the future.

▶ Menu Tip. Additional explanation on how to use menu commands to perform application tasks.

▶ Mouse Tip. Further instructions on how to use the mouse to perform application tasks.

▶ Internet Tip. This information incorporates the power of the Internet to help learners use the Internet as they progress through the text.

▶ Design Tip. Hints for better presentation designs (found in only the PowerPoint book).

End-of-Chapter Materials. Each book in the *Mastering and Using* series places a heavy emphasis on providing learners with the opportunity to practice and reinforce the skills they are learning through extensive exercises. Each chapter has a summary, commands review, concepts review, skills review, and case projects so that the learner can master the material by doing. For more information on each of the end-of-chapter elements see page ix of the How to Use this Book section in this preface.

Appendices. *Mastering and Using* series contains three appendices to further help the learner prepare to be successful in the classroom or in the workplace. Appendix A teaches the learner to work with Windows 98. Appendix B teaches the learner how to use Windows Explorer; Appendix C illustrates how to format letters; how to insert a mailing notation; how to format envelopes (referencing the U.S. Postal Service documents); how to format interoffice memorandums; and how to key a formal outline. It also lists popular style guides and describes proofreader's marks.

Microsoft Office User Specialist (MOUS) Certification. The logo on the cover of this book indicates that these materials are officially certified by Microsoft Corporation. This certification is part of the MOUS program, which validates your skills as a knowledgeable user of Microsoft applications. Upon completing the lessons in the book, you will be prepared to take a test that could qualify you as either a core or expert user. To be certified, you will need to take an exam from a third-party testing company called an Authorization Certification Testing Center. Call **1-800-933-4493** to find the location of the testing center nearest you. Tests are conducted at different dates throughout the calendar year. To learn more about the MOUS program, you can visit Microsoft's Web site at *www.mous.net*.

SCANS. In 1992, the U.S. Department of Labor and Education formed the Secretary's Commission on Achieving Necessary Skills, or SCANS, to study the kinds of competencies and skills that workers must have to succeed in today's marketplace. The results of the study were published in a document entitled *What Work Requires of Schools: A SCANS Report for America 2000*. The in-chapter and end-of-chapter exercises in this book are designed to meet the criteria outlined in the SCANS report and thus help prepare learners to be successful in today's workplace.

Instructional Support

All books in the *Mastering and Using* series are supplemented with the following items:

Instructor's Resource Package. This printed instructor's manual contains lesson plans with teaching materials and preparation suggestions, along with tips for implementing instruction and assessment ideas; a suggested syllabus for scheduling semester, block, and quarter classes; and SCANS workplace know how. The printed manual is packaged with an Electronic Instructor CD-ROM. The Electronic Instructor CD-ROM contains all the materials found in the printed manual as well as:

- ► Career Worksheets
- ► Evaluation Guidelines
- ► Hands-On Solutions
- ► Individual Learning Strategies
- ► Internet Behavior Contract
- ► Lesson Plans
- ► Portfolio Guidelines
- ► PowerPoint Presentations

- ► SCANS Correlations
- ► Scheduling (including Block Scheduling)
- ► Solution Files
- ► Student Data Files
- ► Student Lesson Plans
- ► Teacher Training Notes
- ► Test Questions
- ► Transparency Graphics Files

Course Test Manager: Testing and Practice at the Computer or on Paper Course Test Manager is cutting-edge, Windows-based testing software that helps instructors design and administer practice tests and actual examinations. Course Test Manager can automatically grade the tests students take at the computer and can generate statistical information on individual as well as group performance.

MyCourse.com MyCourse.com is an online syllabus builder and course-enhancement tool. Hosted by Course Technology, MyCourse.com is designed to reinforce what you already are teaching. It also adds value to your course by providing content that corresponds with your text. MyCourse.com is flexible: choose how you want to organize the material, by date or by class session; or don't do anything at all, and the material is automatically organized by chapter. Add your own materials, including hyperlinks, assignments, announcements, and course content. If you're using more than one textbook, you can even build a course that includes all your Course Technology texts—in one easy-to-use site! Start building your own course today…just go to *www.mycourse.com/instructor*

Learner Support

Activity Workbooks. The workbook includes additional end-of-chapter exercises over and above those provided in the main text.

Data CD-ROM. To use this book, the learner must have the data CD-ROM (also referred to as the Data Disk). Data Files needed to complete exercises in the text are contained on this CD-ROM. These files can be copied to a hard drive or posted to a network drive.

How to Use This Book

Learning Objectives — A quick reference of the major topics learned in the chapter

Case profile — Realistic scenarios that show the real world application of the material being covered

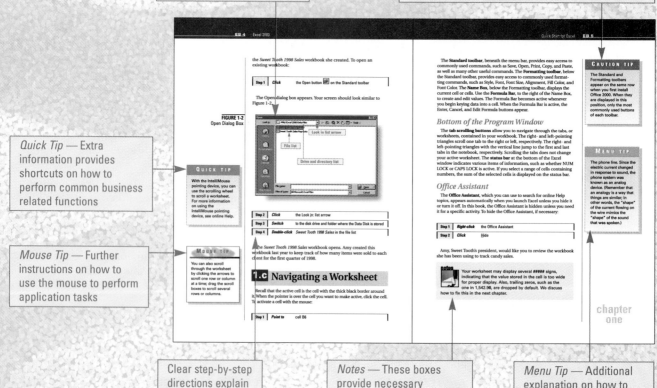

Excel 2000

Quick Start for Excel

Chapter Overview

In this chapter, you learn about the components of the Excel workbook window. You open an existing workbook, create a new workbook, enter and revise data, and save your work. You also learn about Excel's "workhorses"–formulas and functions.

LEARNING OBJECTIVES

► Explore the Excel components
► Locate and open an existing workbook
► Navigate a worksheet
► Enter text, dates, and numbers
► Select cells
► Edit cell content
► Clear contents and formatting of cells
► Use Undo and Redo
► Enter formulas and functions
► Save workbooks
► Close workbooks and Exit Excel

Case profile

Amy Lee runs a rapidly growing candy business called Sweet Tooth. Today, her confections are sold to retail outlets in many states. Because Sweet Tooth is growing so rapidly, the company has hired you to computerize the company records. In this chapter, you use Excel to track how many items were sold at each location.

chapter one

Chapter Overview — A concise summary of what will be learned in the chapter

Full color screen illustrations provide a realistic picture to the user

Caution Tip — This additional information explains how a mistake occurs and provides tips on how to avoid making similar mistakes in the future

Quick Tip — Extra information provides shortcuts on how to perform common business related functions

Mouse Tip — Further instructions on how to use the mouse to perform application tasks

Clear step-by-step directions explain how to complete the specific task

Notes — These boxes provide necessary information to assist you in completing the exercises

Menu Tip — Additional explanation on how to use menu commands to perform application tasks

End-of-Chapter Material

Summary — Reviews key topics discussed in the chapter

Commands Review — Provides a quick reference and reinforcement tool on multiple methods for performing actions discussed in the chapter

Concepts Review — Multiple choice and true or false questions help assess how well the reader has learned the chapter material

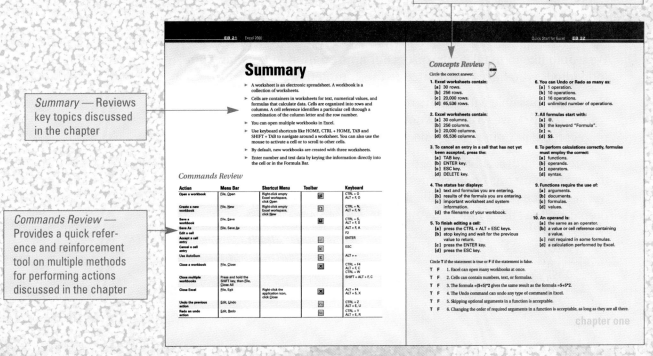

Skills Review — Hands-on exercises provide the ability to practice the skills just learned in the chapter

Case Projects — Asks the reader to synthesize the material they learned in the chapter and complete an office assignment

Internet Case Projects — Allow the reader to practice using the World Wide Web

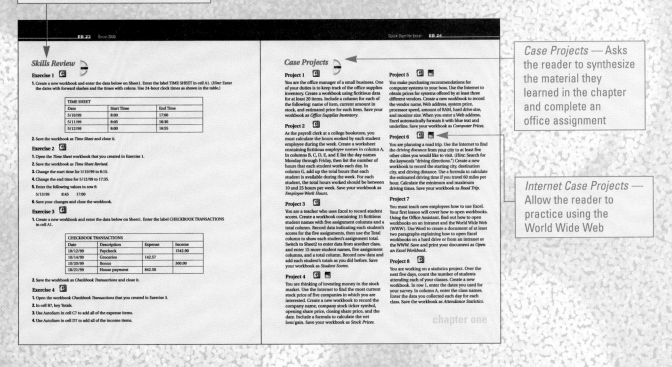

Acknowledgments

We would like to thank and express our appreciation to the many fine individuals who have contributed to the completion of this book.

No book is possible without the motivation and support of an editorial staff. Therefore, we wish to acknowledge with great appreciation the project team at Course Technology.

We are very appreciative of the personnel at Napier & Judd, Inc., who helped prepare this book. We acknowledge, with great appreciation, the assistance provided by Ollie Rivers and Nancy Onarheim in preparing the Office unit and Appendices for this book.

H. Albert Napier
Philip J. Judd

Contents

ACCESS UNIT ——————————————————————— AB 1

Microsoft
Office 2000

Getting Started with Microsoft Office 2000

Chapter Overview

Microsoft Office 2000 provides the ability to enter, record, analyze, display, and present any type of business information. In this chapter you learn about the capabilities of Microsoft Office 2000, including its computer hardware and software requirements and elements common to all its applications. You also learn how to open and close those applications and get help.

LEARNING OBJECTIVES

► Describe Microsoft Office 2000
► Determine hardware and software requirements
► Identify common Office elements
► Start Office applications
► Get help in Office applications
► Close Office applications

For more information on how to prepare for the MOUS certification exam, check out the MOUS certification grids located on the data CD-ROM under the MOUS correlation folder for each book.

chapter one

1.a What Is Microsoft Office 2000?

Microsoft Office 2000 is a software suite (or package) that contains a combination of software applications you use to create text documents, analyze numbers, create presentations, manage large files of data, create Web pages, and create professional-looking marketing materials. Table 1-1 lists four editions of the Office 2000 suite and the software applications included in each.

Applications	Premium	Professional	Standard	Small Business
Word	X	X	X	X
Excel	X	X	X	X
PowerPoint	X	X	X	
Access	X	X		
Outlook	X	X	X	X
Publisher	X	X		X
FrontPage	X			

TABLE 1-1
Office 2000 Editions

The **Word 2000** software application provides you with word processing capabilities. **Word processing** is the preparation and production of text documents such as letters, memorandums, and reports. **Excel 2000** is software you use to analyze numbers with worksheets (sometimes called spreadsheets) and charts, as well as perform other tasks such as sorting data. A **worksheet** is a grid of columns and rows in which you enter labels and data. A **chart** is a visual or graphic representation of worksheet data. With Excel, you can create financial budgets, reports, and a variety of other forms.

PowerPoint 2000 software is used to create **presentations,** a collection of slides. A **slide** is the presentation output (actual 35mm slides, transparencies, computer screens, or printed pages) that contains text, charts, graphics, audio, and video. You can use PowerPoint slides to create a slide show on a computer attached to a projector, to broadcast a presentation over the Internet or company intranet, and to create handout materials for a presentation.

Access 2000 provides database management capabilities, enabling you to store and retrieve a large amount of data. A **database** is a collection of related information. A phone book or an address book are common examples of databases you use every day. Other databases include a price list, school registration information, or an inventory. You can query (or search) an Access database to answer specific questions about the stored data. For example, you can determine which customers in a particular state had sales in excess of a particular value during the month of June.

chapter
one

Outlook 2000 is a **personal information manager** that enables you to send and receive e-mail, as well as maintain a calendar, contacts list, journal, electronic notes, and an electronic "to do" list. **Publisher 2000** is desktop publishing software used to create publications, such as professional-looking marketing materials, newsletters, or brochures. Publisher wizards provide step-by-step instructions for creating a publication from an existing design; you also can design your own publication. The **FrontPage 2000** application is used to create and manage Web sites. **PhotoDraw 2000** is business graphics software that allows users to add custom graphics to marketing materials and Web pages.

A major advantage of using an Office suite is the ability to share data between applications. For example, you can include a portion of an Excel worksheet or chart in a Word document, use an outline created in a Word document as the starting point for a PowerPoint presentation, import an Excel worksheet into Access, merge names and addresses from an Outlook Address Book with a Word letter, or import a picture from PhotoDraw into a newsletter created in Publisher.

1.b Hardware and Software Requirements

You must install Office 2000 applications in Windows 95, Windows 98, or Windows NT Workstation 4.0 with Service Pack 3.0 installed. The applications will not run in the Windows 3.x or the Windows NT Workstation 3.5 environments.

Microsoft recommends that you install Office on a computer that has a Pentium processor, at least 32 MB of RAM, a CD-ROM drive, Super VGA, 256-color video, Microsoft Mouse, Microsoft IntelliMouse, or another pointing device, and at least a 28,800-baud modem. To access certain features you should have a multimedia computer, e-mail software, and a Web browser. For detailed information on installing Office, see the documentation that comes with the software.

1.c Identifying Common Office Elements

Office applications share many common elements, making it easier for you to work efficiently in any application. A **window** is a rectangular area on your screen in which you view a software application, such as Excel. All the Office application windows have a similar look and arrangement of shortcuts, menus, and toolbars. In addition, they share many features, such as a common dictionary to use for spell checking your work and identical menu commands, toolbar buttons, shortcut menus, and keyboard shortcuts that enable you to perform tasks such as copying data from one location to another. Figure 1-1 shows the common elements in the Office application windows.

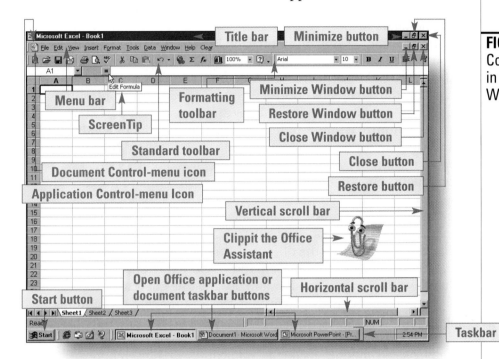

FIGURE 1-1
Common Elements in Office Application Windows

Title Bar

The application **title bar** at the top of the window includes the application Control-menu icon, the application name, the filename of the active document, and the Minimize, Restore (or Maximize), and Close buttons.

The **application Control-menu** icon, located in the left corner of the title bar, displays the Control menu. The Control menu commands manage the application window, and typically include commands such as: Restore, Move, Size, Minimize, Maximize, and Close. Commands that are currently available appear in a darker color. You can view the Control menu by clicking the Control-menu icon or by holding down the ALT key and then pressing the SPACEBAR key.

The **Minimize** button, near the right corner of the title bar reduces the application window to a taskbar button. The **Maximize** button, to the right of the Minimize button, enlarges the application window to fill the entire screen viewing area above the taskbar. If the window is already maximized, the Restore button appears in its place. The **Restore** button reduces the application window size. The **Close** button, located in the right corner of the title bar, closes the application and removes it from the computer's memory.

CAUTION TIP

In order to save hard disk space, Office installs many features and components as you need them. Shortcuts, toolbar buttons, and menu commands for these features appear in the application window or dialog boxes, indicating that the feature is available.

chapter
one

Menu Bar

The **menu bar** is a special toolbar located below the title bar and contains the menus for the application. A **menu** is list of commands. The menus common to Office applications are File, Edit, View, Insert, Format, Tools, Window, and Help. Each application may have additional menus.

The **document Control-menu** icon, located below the application Control-menu icon, contains the Restore, Move, Size, Minimize, Maximize, and Close menu commands for the document window. You can view the document Control menu by clicking the Control-menu icon or by holding down the ALT key and pressing the HYPHEN (-) key.

The **Minimize Window** button reduces the document window to a title-bar icon inside the document area. It appears on the menu bar below the Minimize button in Excel and PowerPoint. (Word documents open in their own application window and use the title bar Minimize button.)

The **Maximize Window** button enlarges the document window to cover the entire application display area and share the application title bar. It appears on the title-bar icon of a minimized Excel workbook or PowerPoint presentation. (Word documents open in their own application window and use the title bar Maximize button.) If the window is already maximized, the Restore Window button appears in its place.

The **Restore Window** button changes the document window to a smaller sized window inside the application window. It appears to the right of the Minimize Window button in Excel and PowerPoint. (Word documents open in their own application window and use the title bar Restore button.)

The **Close Window** button closes the document and removes it from the computer's memory. It appears to the right of the Restore Window or Maximize Window button. (In Word, the Close Window button appears only when one document is open. Otherwise, Word uses the title bar Close button.)

Default Toolbars

The **Standard** and **Formatting toolbars,** located on one row below the menu bar, contain a set of icons called buttons. The toolbar buttons represent commonly used commands and are mouse shortcuts used to perform tasks quickly. In addition to the Standard and Formatting toolbars, each application has several other toolbars available. You can customize toolbars by adding or removing buttons and commands.

When the mouse pointer rests on a toolbar button, a **ScreenTip** appears identifying the name of the button. ScreenTips, part of online Help, describe a toolbar button, dialog box option, or menu command.

Scroll Bars

The **vertical scroll bar,** on the right side of the document area, is used to view various parts of the document by moving, or scrolling, the document up or down. It includes scroll arrows and a scroll box. The **horizontal scroll bar**, near the bottom of the document area, is used to view various parts of the document by scrolling the document left or right. It includes scroll arrows and a scroll box.

Office Assistant

The **Office Assistant** is an animated graphic you can click to view online Help. The Office Assistant may also anticipate your needs and provide advice in a balloon-style dialog box when you begin certain tasks, such as writing a letter in Word.

Taskbar

The **taskbar,** located across the bottom of the Windows desktop, includes the Start button and buttons for each open Office document. The **Start button,** located in the left corner of the taskbar, displays the Start menu or list of tasks you can perform and applications you can use.

You can switch between documents, close documents and applications, and view other items, such as the system time and printer status, with buttons or icons on the taskbar. If you are using Windows 98, other toolbars—such as the Quick Launch toolbar—may also appear on the taskbar.

1.d Starting Office Applications

You access the Office applications through the Windows desktop. When you turn on your computer, the Windows operating system software is automatically loaded into memory. Once the process is complete, your screen should look similar to Figure 1-2.

notes The desktop illustrations in this book assume you are using Windows 98 with default settings. Your desktop may not look identical to the illustrations in this book. For more information on using Windows 98 see Appendix A or information provided by your instructor.

chapter
one

FIGURE 1-2
Default Windows 98
Desktop

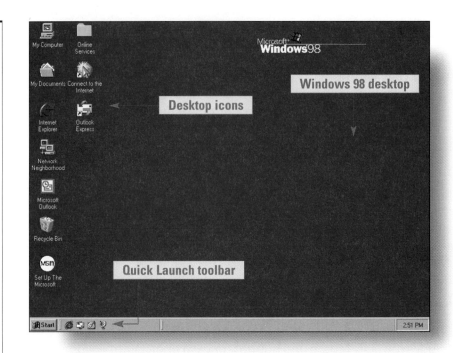

MOUSE TIP

This book uses distinct instructions for mouse operations. **Point** means to place the mouse pointer on the specified command or item. **Click** means to press the left mouse button and then release it. **Right-click** means to press the right mouse button and then release it. **Double-click** means to press the left mouse button twice very rapidly. **Drag** means to press and hold down the left mouse button and then move the mouse on the mouse pad. **Right-drag** means to press and hold down the right mouse button and then move the mouse on the mouse pad. **Scroll** means to use the application scroll bar features or the IntelliMouse scrolling wheel.

You begin by opening the Excel application. To use Start button to open Excel:

Step 1	*Click*	the Start button [Start] on the taskbar
Step 2	*Point to*	Programs
Step 3	*Click*	Microsoft Excel on the Programs menu

The Excel software is placed into the memory of your computer and the Excel window opens. Your screen should look similar to Figure 1-1.

You can open and work in more than one Office application at a time. When Office is installed, the Open Office Document command and the New Office Document command appear on the Start menu. You can use these commands to select the type of document on which you want to work rather than first selecting an Office application. To create a new Word document without first opening the application:

Step 1	*Click*	the Start button [Start] on the taskbar
Step 2	*Click*	New Office Document
Step 3	*Click*	the General tab, if necessary

The dialog box that opens should look similar to Figure 1-3.

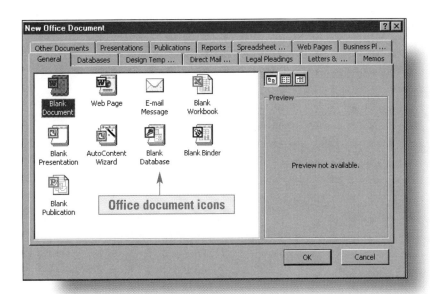

FIGURE 1-3
General Tab in
the New Office
Document Dialog Box

QUICK TIP

A **dialog box** is a window that contains options for performing specific tasks. The New Office Document dialog box contains **icons** (or pictures) for creating a blank Word document, Web page (in Word), e-mail message (using Outlook or Outlook Express), Excel workbook, PowerPoint presentation, Access database, or Publisher publication. The available icons depends on the Office applications you have installed.

To create a blank Word document:

| Step 1 | *Click* | the Blank Document icon to select it, if necessary |
| Step 2 | *Click* | OK |

The Word software loads into your computer's memory, the Word application opens with a blank document, and a taskbar button appears for the document. Your screen should look similar to Figure 1-4.

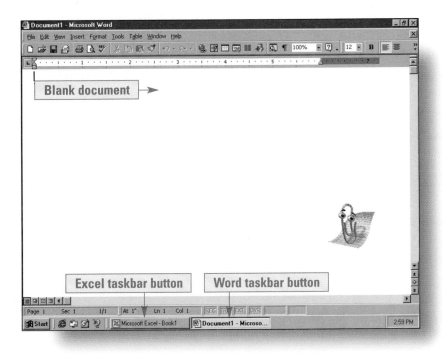

FIGURE 1-4
Word Application Window

chapter
one

Next you open a blank presentation. To open the PowerPoint application and a blank presentation:

Step 1	*Open*	the New Office Document dialog box using the Start menu
Step 2	*Double-click*	the Blank Presentation icon
Step 3	*Click*	OK in the New Slide dialog box to create a blank title slide, as shown in Figure 1-5

FIGURE 1-5
Blank PowerPoint Presentation

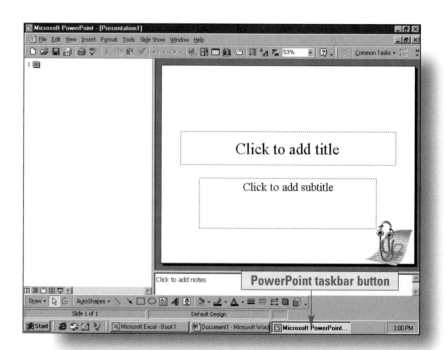

You can also open an Office application by opening an existing Office document from the Start menu. To open an existing Access database:

Step 1	*Click*	the Start button **Start** on the taskbar
Step 2	*Click*	Open Office Document
Step 3	*Click*	the Look in: list arrow in the Open Office Document dialog box
Step 4	*Switch*	to the disk drive and folder where the Data Files are stored
Step 5	*Double-click*	*International Sales* to open the Access application and database, as shown in Figure 1-6

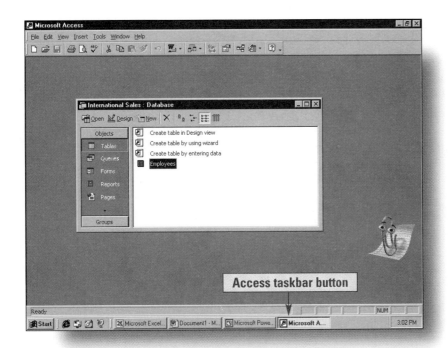

FIGURE 1-6
International Sales
Database in
Access Window

You can switch between open Office documents by clicking the appropriate taskbar button. To switch to the Excel workbook and then the Word document:

Step 1	*Click*	the Excel button on the taskbar
Step 2	*Observe*	that the Excel window and workbook are visible
Step 3	*Click*	the Word Document1 button on the taskbar
Step 4	*Observe*	that the Word window and document are visible

1.e Getting Help in Office Applications

There are several ways to get help in any Office application. You can display the Office Assistant, get context-sensitive help, or launch your Web browser and get Web-based help from Microsoft.

Using the Office Assistant

The **Office Assistant** is an interactive, animated graphic that appears in the Word, Excel, PowerPoint, and Publisher application windows. When you activate the Office Assistant, a balloon-style dialog box

> **QUICK TIP**
>
> If multiple windows are open, the **active window** has a dark blue title bar. Inactive windows have a light gray title bar.

chapter
one

opens containing options for searching online Help by topic. The Office Assistant may also automatically offer suggestions when you begin certain tasks. As you begin to key a personal letter to Aunt Isabel, the Office Assistant automatically asks if you want help writing the letter. To begin the letter:

Step 1	*Verify*	the Word document is the active window
Step 2	*Click*	the Microsoft Word Help button 🔲 on the Standard toolbar, if the Office Assistant is not visible
Step 3	*Key*	Dear Aunt Isabel: (including the colon)
Step 4	*Press*	the ENTER key

The Office Assistant and balloon appear. Your screen should look similar to Figure 1-7.

FIGURE 1-7
Office Assistant Balloon

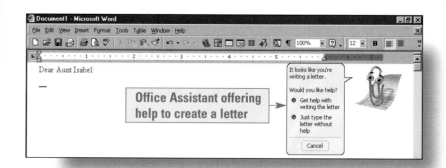

The Office Assistant balloon contains three options you can click with the mouse. If you click the "Get help with writing the letter" option, the Letter Wizard dialog box opens. A **wizard** is a series of dialog boxes you can use to complete a task step-by-step. If you click the "Just type the letter without help" option or the Cancel option, the balloon closes.

| Step 5 | *Click* | Cancel to close the balloon |

If you prefer to use the Microsoft Help window to access online Help, you can choose to show or hide the Office Assistant or you can turn off the Office Assistant completely. To hide the Office Assistant:

| Step 1 | *Right-click* | the Office Assistant |
| Step 2 | *Click* | <u>H</u>ide |

You can activate the Office Assistant at any time to search online help for specific topics or to customize the Office Assistant. Custom options affect all Office applications. To review the Office Assistant customization options:

Step 1	*Click*	the Microsoft Word Help button [?] on the Standard toolbar
Step 2	*Click*	the Office Assistant to view the balloon, if necessary
Step 3	*Click*	Options in the Office Assistant balloon
Step 4	*Click*	the Options tab, if necessary

The dialog box that opens should look similar to Figure 1-8.

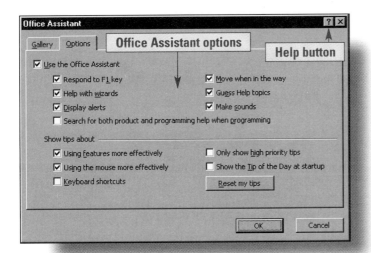

MENU TIP

You can hide the Office Assistant by clicking the Hide the Office Assistant command on the Help menu. You can redisplay the Office Assistant by clicking the Show the Office Assistant on the Help menu.

FIGURE 1-8
Options Tab in the Office Assistant Dialog Box

To learn about dialog box options, you can use the dialog box Help button or you can right-click an option. To view the ScreenTip help:

Step 1	*Drag*	the Office Assistant out of the way, if necessary
Step 2	*Right-click*	the Keyboard shortcuts option
Step 3	*Click*	What's This? to view a ScreenTip help message for this option
Step 4	*Press*	the ESC key to close the ScreenTip help message

MOUSE TIP

You can drag the Office Assistant to a new location with the mouse pointer.

The default Office Assistant image is Clippit. But you can select from a gallery of animated images. To view the Office Assistant image options:

Step 1	*Click*	the Gallery tab

Step 2	*Click*	the <u>N</u>ext> and <<u>B</u>ack buttons to view different image options
Step 3	*Click*	Cancel to close the dialog box without changing any options

You can use the Office Assistant to search an application's online Help. Suppose you want to learn how to turn off the Office Assistant. To search online Help:

Step 1	*Click*	the Office Assistant to activate the balloon
Step 2	*Key*	turn off the Office Assistant in the text box
Step 3	*Press*	the ENTER key to view a list of help options in the balloon dialog box
Step 4	*Click*	the Hide, show, or turn off the Office Assistant option

The Microsoft Word Help window opens and contains information about how to manage the Office Assistant. Your screen should look similar to Figure 1-9.

FIGURE 1-9
Microsoft Word
Help Window

You can scroll the Help window to view all the information. You can click the Show button to view the <u>C</u>ontents, <u>A</u>nswer Wizard, and <u>I</u>ndex tabs that access other help topics. If you have Internet access, you can view a Microsoft Help Web page from inside the Help window. To view the additional tabs:

Step 1	*Click*	the Show button in the Help window, if necessary, to display the Contents, Answer Wizard, and Index tabs
Step 2	*Click*	the Close button ☒ in the upper-right corner of the window

Using the Help Menu

The Help menu provides commands you can use to view the Office Assistant or Help window, show or hide the Office Assistant, connect to the Microsoft Web site, get context-sensitive help for a menu command or toolbar button, detect and repair font and template files, and view licensing information for the Office application. To review the Help menu commands:

Step 1	*Click*	Help
Step 2	*Observe*	the menu commands
Step 3	*Click*	in the document area outside the menu to close the Help menu

Using What's This?

You can get context-sensitive help for a menu command or toolbar button using the What's This? command on the Help menu. This command changes the mouse pointer to a help pointer, a white mouse pointer with a large black question mark. When you click a toolbar button or menu command with the help pointer, a brief ScreenTip help message appears describing the command or toolbar button. To a ScreenTip help message for a toolbar button:

Step 1	*Press*	the SHIFT + F1 keys
Step 2	*Observe*	that the help mouse pointer with the attached question mark
Step 3	*Click*	the Save button 🖫 on the Standard toolbar
Step 4	*Observe*	the ScreenTip help message describing the Save button
Step 5	*Press*	the ESC key to close the ScreenTip help message

chapter
one

1.f Closing Office Applications

There are many ways to close the Access, Excel and PowerPoint applications (or the Word application with a single document open) and return to the Windows desktop. You can: (1) double-click the application Control-menu icon; (2) click the application Close button; (3) right-click the application taskbar button and then click the Close command on the shortcut menu; (4) press the ALT + F4 keys; or (5) click the Exit command on the File menu to close Office applications (no matter how many Word documents are open). To close the Excel application from the taskbar:

| Step 1 | *Right-click* | the Excel button on the taskbar |
| Step 2 | *Click* | Close |

You can close multiple applications at one time from the taskbar by selecting the application buttons using the CTRL key and then using the shortcut menu. To close the PowerPoint and Access applications:

Step 1	*Press & Hold*	the CTRL key
Step 2	*Click*	the PowerPoint button and then the Access button on the taskbar
Step 3	*Release*	the CTRL key and observe that both buttons are selected (pressed in)
Step 4	*Right-click*	the PowerPoint or Access button
Step 5	*Click*	Close

Both applications close, leaving only the Word document open. To close the Word document using the menu:

Step 1	*Verify*	that the Word application window is maximized
Step 2	*Click*	File
Step 3	*Click*	Exit
Step 4	*Click*	No in the Office Assistant balloon or confirmation dialog box to close Word without saving the document

Summary

- ► The Word application provides word processing capabilities for the preparation of text documents such as letters, memorandums, and reports.

- ► The Excel application provides the ability to analyze numbers in worksheets and for creating financial budgets, reports, charts, and forms.

- ► The PowerPoint application is used to create presentation slides and audience handouts.

- ► You can use Access databases to organize and retrieve collections of data.

- ► Publisher provides tools for creating marketing materials, such as newsletters, brochures, flyers, and Web pages.

- ► The Outlook application helps you send and receive e-mail, maintain a calendar, "to do" lists, organize the names and addresses of contacts, and perform other information management tasks.

- ► One major advantage of Office suite applications is the ability to integrate the applications by sharing information between them.

- ► Another advantage of using Office suite applications is that they share a number of common elements, such as window elements, shortcuts, toolbars, menu commands, and other features.

- ► You can start Office suite applications from the Programs submenu on the Start menu and from the Open Office Document or New Office Document commands on the Start menu.

- ► You can close Office applications by double-clicking the application Control Menu icon, clicking the application Close button on the title bar, right-clicking the application button on the taskbar, pressing the ALT + F4 keys, or clicking the Exit command on the File menu.

- ► You can get help in an Office application by clicking commands on the Help menu, pressing the F1 or SHIFT + F1 keys, or clicking the Microsoft Help button on the Standard toolbar.

chapter one

Concepts Review

Circle the correct answer.

1. ScreenTips do not provide:
[a] the name of a button on a toolbar.
[b] help for options in a dialog box.
[c] context-sensitive help for menu commands or toolbar buttons.
[d] access to the Office Assistant.

2. To manage a Web site, you can use:
[a] Outlook.
[b] FrontPage.
[c] PhotoDraw.
[d] Publisher.

3. The title bar contains the:
[a] document Control-menu icon.
[b] Close Window button.
[c] Standard toolbar.
[d] application and document name.

4. The Excel application is best used to:
[a] prepare financial reports.
[b] maintain a list of tasks to accomplish.
[c] create newsletters, brochures, and flyers.
[d] create custom graphics.

Circle **T** if the statement is true or **F** if the statement is false.

T F 1. You use Publisher to create newsletters and brochures.
T F 2. Excel is used to create presentation slides.
T F 3. The default Office Assistant graphic is Clippit.
T F 4. Access is used to create and format text.

Skills Review

Exercise 1

1. Identify each common element of Office application windows numbered in Figure 1-10.

FIGURE 1-10
Excel Application Window

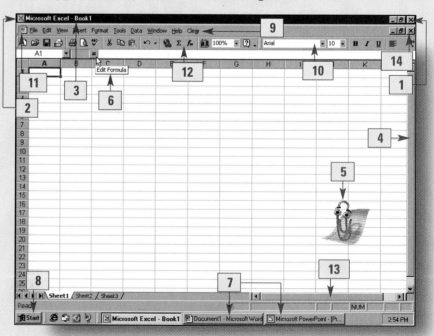

Exercise 2

1. Open the Word application using the <u>P</u>rograms command on the Start menu.
2. Close the Word application using the taskbar.

Exercise 3

1. Open the Excel application and then the PowerPoint application using the Programs command on the Start menu.
2. Open the Access application and the *International Sales* database using the Open Office Document command on the Start menu.
3. Switch to the PowerPoint application using the taskbar button and close it using the Close button on the title bar.
4. Close the PowerPoint and Access applications at the same time using the taskbar.

Exercise 4

1. Create a new, blank Word document using the New Office Document command on the Start menu.
2. Create a new, blank Excel workbook using the New Office Document command on the Start menu.
3. Switch to the Word document using the taskbar and close it using the title bar Close button.
4. Close the Excel workbook using the taskbar button.

Exercise 5

1. Open the Word application using the Start menu.
2. Show the Office Assistant, if necessary, with a command on the Help menu.
3. Hide the Office Assistant with a shortcut menu.
4. Show the Office Assistant with the Microsoft Word Help button on the Standard toolbar.
5. Search online Help using the search phrase "type text." Open the Type text help page.
6. Click the underlined text typing text to view a help page of subtopics. Scroll and review the help page.
7. Close the Help window. Hide the Office Assistant with a shortcut menu.

Case Projects

Project 1

You are the secretary to the marketing manager of High Risk Insurance, an insurance brokerage firm. The marketing manager wants to know how to open and close the Excel application. Write at least two paragraphs describing different ways to open and close Excel. With your instructor's permission, use your written description to show a classmate several ways to open and close Excel.

Project 2

You work in the administrative offices of Alma Public Relations, and the information management department just installed Office 2000 Professional on your computer. Your supervisor asks you to write down and describe some of the Office Assistant options. Open the Options tab in the Office Assistant dialog box. Review each option using the dialog box Help button or the What's This? command. Write at least three paragraphs describing five Office Assistant options.

Project 3

As the new office manager at Hot Wheels Messenger Service, you are learning to use the Word 2000 application and want to learn more about some of the buttons on the Word toolbars. Open Word and use the What's This? command on the Help menu to review the ScreenTip help for five toolbar buttons. Write a brief paragraph for each button describing how it is used.

Project 4

As the acquisitions director for Osiris Books, an international antique book and map dealer, you use Publisher to create the company's catalogs and brochures. A co-worker, who is helping you with a new brochure, opened Publisher and did not know why the Catalog window appeared. She has asked you for an explanation. Open the Publisher application and review the Catalog window. Close the Catalog window leaving the Publisher window open. Use the Office Assistant to find out more about the Catalog by searching online Help using the keyword "catalog." Write your co-worker a short note explaining how the Catalog is used.

chapter one

Working with Menus and Toolbars

Chapter Overview

Office 2000 tries to make your work life easier by learning how you work. The personalized menus and toolbars in each application remember which commands and buttons you use, and add and remove them as needed. In this chapter, you learn how to work with the personalized menus and toolbars, how to customize the menu bar and toolbars, and how to view and customize the Office Shortcut Bar.

LEARNING OBJECTIVES

► **Work with personalized menus and toolbars**
► **View, hide, dock, and float toolbars**
► **Customize the menu bar and toolbars**
► **View and customize the Office Shortcut Bar**

chapter two

2.a Working with Personalized Menus and Toolbars

A **menu** is a list of commands you use to perform tasks in the Office applications. Some commands also have an associated image, or icon, shown to the left of a command. A **toolbar** contains a set of icons (the same icons you see on the menus) called **buttons** that you click with the mouse pointer to quickly execute a menu command.

When you first open Excel, Word, or PowerPoint, the menus on the menu bar initially show only a basic set of commands and the Standard and Formatting toolbars contain only a basic set of buttons. These short versions of the menus and toolbars are called **personalized menus and toolbars**. As you work, the commands and buttons you use most frequently are stored in the personalized settings. The first time you select a menu command or toolbar button that is not part of the basic set, it is added to your personalized settings and appears on the menu or toolbar. If you do not use a command for a while, it is removed from your personalized settings and no longer appears on the menu or toolbar. To view the personalized menus and toolbars in PowerPoint:

Step 1	*Click*	the Start button [🔊Start] on the taskbar
Step 2	*Click*	the New Office Document command on the Start menu
Step 3	*Click*	the General tab in the New Office Document dialog box
Step 4	*Double-click*	the Blank Presentation icon
Step 5	*Click*	OK in the New Slide dialog box to create a blank title slide for the presentation
Step 6	*Click*	Tools on the menu bar
Step 7	*Observe*	the short personalized menu containing only the basic commands, as shown in Figure 2-1

FIGURE 2-1
Personalized Tools Menu

chapter
two

If the command you want to use does not appear on the short personalized menu, you can expand the menu by pausing for a few seconds until the menu expands, clicking the expand arrows at the bottom of the menu, or double-clicking the menu name.

Step 8	*Pause*	until the menu automatically expands, as shown in Figure 2-2

FIGURE 2-2
Expanded Tools Menu

QUICK TIP

You can also use keyboard shortcuts to perform tasks in Office applications. Many of these keyboard shortcuts are shown on the menus to the right of the menu command.

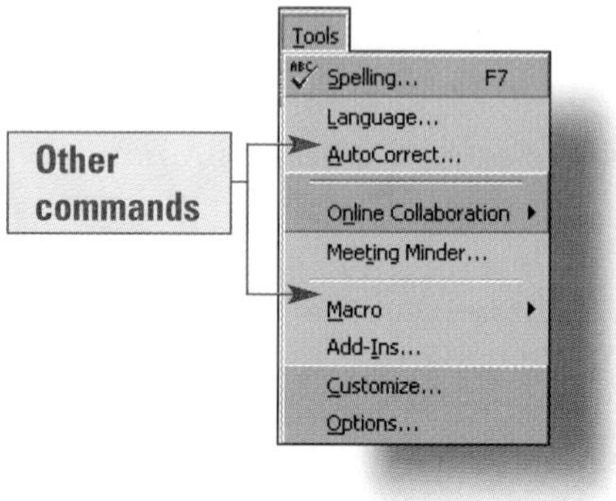

You move a menu command from the expanded menu to the personalized menu, simply by selecting it. To add the AutoCorrect command to the short personalized Tools menu:

Step 1	*Click*	AutoCorrect
Step 2	*Click*	Cancel in the AutoCorrect dialog box to cancel the dialog box
Step 3	*Click*	Tools on the menu bar
Step 4	*Observe*	the updated personalized Tools menu contains the AutoCorrect command, as shown in Figure 2-3

FIGURE 2-3
Updated Personalized Tools Menu

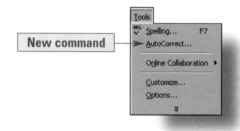

When you first open Word, Excel, or PowerPoint, the Standard and Formatting toolbars appear on one row below the title bar and some default buttons are hidden. You can resize a toolbar to view a hidden button by dragging its **move handle**, the gray vertical bar at the left edge of the toolbar, with the **move pointer,** a four-headed black arrow. To resize the Formatting toolbar:

Step 1	*Move*	the mouse pointer to the move handle on the Formatting toolbar
Step 2	*Observe*	that the mouse pointer becomes a move pointer
Step 3	*Drag*	the Formatting toolbar to the left until nine Formatting toolbar buttons are visible
Step 4	*Observe*	that you see fewer buttons on the Standard toolbar

The buttons that don't fit on the displayed area of a toolbar are collected in a More Buttons list. To view the remaining the Standard toolbar default buttons:

| Step 1 | *Click* | the More Buttons list arrow on the Standard toolbar |
| Step 2 | *Observe* | the default buttons that are not visible on the toolbar, as shown in Figure 2-4 |

| Step 3 | *Press* | the ESC key to close the More Buttons list |

If you want to display one of the default buttons on a personalized toolbar, you can select it from the More Buttons list. To add the Format Painter button to the personalized Standard toolbar:

Step 1	*Click*	the More Buttons list arrow on the Standard toolbar
Step 2	*Click*	the Format Painter button 
Step 3	*Observe*	that the Format Painter button is turned on and added to the personalized Standard toolbar, as shown in Figure 2-5

CAUTION TIP

When updating the personalized Standard or Formatting toolbar with a new button, a button that you have not used recently might move to the More Buttons list to make room for the new button.

FIGURE 2-4
More Buttons List

C

chapter
two

FIGURE 2-5
Updated Personalized
Standard Toolbar

FIGURE 2-5
Updated Personalized
Standard Toolbar

| Step 4 | *Click* | the Format Painter button on the Standard toolbar to turn it off |

If you want to view all the menu commands instead of a short personalized menu and all the default toolbar buttons on the Standard and Formatting toolbars, you can change options in the Customize dialog box. To show all the toolbar buttons and menu commands:

Step 1	*Click*	Tools
Step 2	*Click*	Customize
Step 3	*Click*	the Options tab, if necessary

The dialog box that opens should be similar to Figure 2-6.

FIGURE 2-6
Options Tab in the
Customize Dialog Box

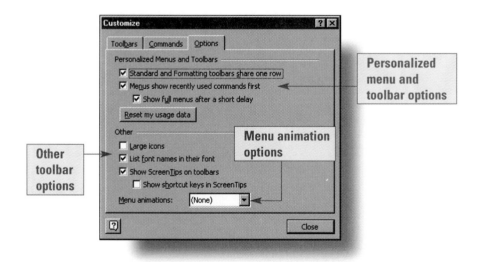

QUICK TIP

If you do not want the short personalized menus to expand automatically when you pause, remove the check mark from the Show full menus after a short delay check box. Then, to show the full menu, double-click the menu or click the expand arrows at the bottom of the menu.

Step 4	*Click*	the Standard and Formatting toolbars share one row check box to remove the check mark and reposition the Formatting toolbar below the Standard toolbar
Step 5	*Click*	the Menus show recently used commands first check box to remove the check mark and show the entire set of commands for each menu
Step 6	*Click*	Close to close the dialog box

Step 7	*Observe*	the repositioned Standard and Formatting toolbars
Step 8	*Click*	Tools to view the entire set of Tools menu commands
Step 9	*Press*	the ESC key

You can return the menus and toolbars to their initial (or **default**) settings in the Customize dialog box. To reset the default menus and toolbars:

Step 1	*Open*	the Options tab in the Customize dialog box
Step 2	*Click*	the Standard and Formatting toolbars share one row check box to insert a check mark
Step 3	*Click*	the Menus show recently used commands first check box to insert a check mark
Step 4	*Click*	Reset my usage data
Step 5	*Click*	Yes to confirm you want to reset the menus and toolbars to their default settings
Step 6	*Close*	the Customize dialog box
Step 7	*Observe*	that the Tools menu and Standard toolbar are reset to their default settings

2.b Viewing, Hiding, Docking, and Floating Toolbars

Office applications have additional toolbars that you can view when you need them. You can also hide toolbars when you are not using them. You can view or hide toolbars by pointing to the Toolbars command on the View menu and clicking a toolbar name or by using a shortcut menu. A **shortcut menu** is a short list of frequently used menu commands. You view a shortcut menu by pointing to an item on the screen and clicking the right mouse button. This is called right-clicking the item. The commands on shortcut menus vary—depending on where you right-click—so that you view only the most frequently used commands for a particular task. An easy way to view or hide toolbars is with a shortcut menu. To view the shortcut menu for PowerPoint toolbars:

| Step 1 | *Right-click* | the menu bar, the Standard toolbar, or the Formatting toolbar |
| Step 2 | *Observe* | the shortcut menu and the check marks next to the names of currently visible toolbars, as shown in Figure 2-7 |

C A U T I O N   T I P

When you choose the Menus show recently used commands first option, it affects all the Office applications, not just the open application.
Resetting the usage data to the initial settings does not change the location of toolbars and does not remove or add buttons to toolbars you have customized in the Customize dialog box.

chapter
two

FIGURE 2-7
Toolbars Shortcut Menu

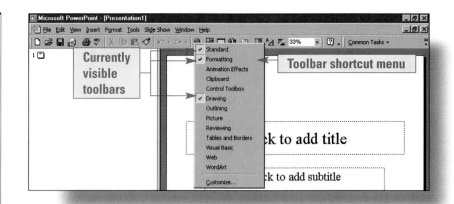

| Step 3 | *Click* | Tables and Borders in the shortcut menu |
| Step 4 | *Observe* | that the Tables and Borders toolbar appears on your screen |

The Tables and Borders toolbar, unless a previous user repositioned it, is visible in its own window near the middle of your screen. When a toolbar is visible in its own window it is called a **floating toolbar** and you can move and size it with the mouse pointer just like any window. When a toolbar appears fixed at the screen boundaries, it is called a **docked toolbar**. The menu bar and Standard and Formatting toolbars are examples of docked toolbars. In PowerPoint, the Drawing toolbar is docked above the status bar. You can dock a floating toolbar by dragging its title bar with the mouse pointer to a docking position below the title bar, above the status bar, or at the left and right boundaries of your screen. To dock the Tables and Borders toolbar below the Standard and Formatting toolbars:

| Step 1 | *Position* | the mouse pointer on the blue title bar in the Tables and Borders toolbar window |
| Step 2 | *Drag* | the toolbar window slowly up until it docks below the Standard and Formatting toolbars |

Similarly, you float a docked toolbar by dragging it away from its docked position toward the middle of the screen. To float the Tables and Borders toolbar:

| Step 1 | *Position* | the mouse pointer on the Tables and Borders toolbar move handle until it becomes a move pointer |
| Step 2 | *Drag* | the Tables and Borders toolbar down toward the middle of the screen until it appears in its own window |

When you finish using a toolbar, you can hide it with a shortcut menu. To hide the Tables and Borders toolbar:

| Step 1 | *Right-click* | the Tables and Borders toolbar |
| Step 2 | *Click* | Tables and Borders to remove the check mark and hide the toolbar |

2.c Customizing the Menu Bar and Toolbars

Recall that you can add a button to a personalized toolbar by clicking the More Buttons list arrow on the toolbar and then selecting a button from the list of default buttons not currently visible. You can also add and delete buttons and commands on the menu bar or other toolbars with options in the Customize dialog box. To customize the menu bar:

Step 1	*Right-click*	any toolbar (the menu bar, Standard toolbar, or Formatting toolbar)
Step 2	*Click*	Customize
Step 3	*Click*	the Commands tab, if necessary

The dialog box on your screen should look similar to Figure 2-8.

You add a button on the menu bar to route the active presentation to other users on the network via e-mail.

FIGURE 2-8
Commands Tab in the Customize Dialog Box

MOUSE **TIP**

You can add hyperlinks (the path to another document) to toolbar buttons. For more information, see online Help.

Step 4	*Verify*	that File is selected in the Categories: list
Step 5	*Click*	Routing Recipient in the Commands: list (scroll the list to view this command)
Step 6	*Click*	Description to view the ScreenTip
Step 7	*Press*	the ESC key to close the ScreenTip
Step 8	*Drag*	the Routing Recipient command to the right of Help on the menu bar
Step 9	*Click*	Close to close the dialog box and add the Routing Recipient button to the menu bar
Step 10	*Position*	the mouse pointer on the Routing Recipient icon to view the ScreenTip, as shown in Figure 2-9

FIGURE 2-9
Button Added to Menu Bar

You can remove a button from a toolbar just as quickly. To remove the Routing Recipient button from the menu bar:

Step 1	*Open*	the Customize dialog box
Step 2	*Drag*	the Routing Recipient button from the menu bar into the dialog box
Step 3	*Close*	the dialog box
Step 4	*Close*	the PowerPoint application and return to the Windows desktop

QUICK **TIP**

You can reset toolbars back to their original buttons and create new custom toolbars with options on the Toolbars tab in the Customize dialog box.
    You can view toolbar buttons in a larger size (for high-resolution monitors), show keyboard shortcuts in the button's ScreenTip, and add animation to menus with options in the Options tab in the Customize dialog box. **Menu animation** refers to the movement the menu makes as it opens on your screen.

2.d Viewing and Customizing the Office Shortcut Bar

The **Office Shortcut Bar** is a toolbar that you can open and position on your Windows desktop to provide shortcuts to Office applications and tasks. It can contain buttons for the New Office Document and Open Office Document commands on the Start menu, shortcut buttons to create various Outlook items like the New Task button, and buttons to open Office applications installed on your computer.

You can view and use the Office Shortcut Bar as needed or you can choose to have it open each time you start your computer. To view the Office Shortcut Bar:

Step 1	**Click**	the Start button [Start] on the taskbar
Step 2	**Point to**	Programs
Step 3	**Point to**	Microsoft Office Tools
Step 4	**Click**	Microsoft Office Shortcut Bar
Step 5	**Click**	No in the Microsoft Office Shortcut Bar dialog box to not open the Office Shortcut Bar each time you start your computer

The Office Shortcut Bar may appear docked in the upper-right corner or along the right edge of your Windows desktop. Your screen may look similar to Figure 2-10.

| Step 6 | **Right-click** | the Office Shortcut Bar Control-menu icon |

The Office Shortcut Bar Control-menu contains commands you can use to customize or close the Office Shortcut Bar. If your Shortcut Bar does not already contain buttons to open the individual Office applications, you may want to customize it for the Office applications you use frequently. To open the Customize dialog box:

| Step 1 | **Click** | Customize |
| Step 2 | **Click** | the Buttons tab |

The dialog box on your screen should look similar to Figure 2-11.

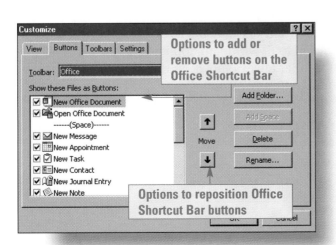

CAUTION TIP

The activities in this section assume that the Office Shortcut Bar does not open automatically when you start your computer or contain Office application buttons.

FIGURE 2-10
Office Shortcut Bar

QUICK TIP

The AutoHide command hides the Office Shortcut Bar and displays only a thin border where the Office Shortcut Bar resides. When you position the mouse pointer on the thin border, the Office Shortcut Bar appears. When you move the mouse pointer away from the border, the Office Shortcut Bar hides again.

FIGURE 2-11
Buttons Tab in the Customize Dialog Box

chapter
two

QUICK TIP

You can enlarge the Shortcut Bar buttons by clicking the Large Buttons check box; this inserts a check mark on the View tab in the Customize dialog box. You can place the Shortcut Bar in its own window, and then move and size the window by clicking the Auto Fit into Title Bar area check box; this removes the check mark on the View tab in the Customize dialog box.

The shortcut button for a particular application or file is visible on the Office Shortcut Bar if a check mark appears in the check box to the left of the application icon in the Show these Files as Buttons: list. To add a shortcut button that opens the Word application:

Step 1	*Scroll*	the Show these Files as Buttons: list to view the check boxes for the Office applications
Step 2	*Click*	the Microsoft Word check box to insert a check mark
Step 3	*Observe*	that a button for the Word application immediately appears on the Office Shortcut Bar

You can easily reposition a button on the Office Shortcut Bar by moving the item into the Show these Files as Buttons: list. To reposition the Word button to the right of the Open Office Document button:

Step 1	*Click*	the Microsoft Word application name to select it in the list
Step 2	*Click*	the Move up arrow until the Microsoft Word application and check box appear immediately below the Open Office Document icon and check box
Step 3	*Observe*	that the Word button on the Office Shortcut Bar is repositioned

You can also delete an application button from the Office Shortcut Bar. To remove the Word application button:

Step 1	*Click*	the Microsoft Word check box to remove the check mark
Step 2	*Move*	the Microsoft Word check box back to its original position above the Excel check box by selecting it and clicking the Move down arrow
Step 3	*Click*	OK

The Office Shortcut Bar may be in the upper-right corner of your screen and sized to fit within an application title bar. This means that Office Shortcut Bar always shows on top of the active application's title bar with small buttons. You can enlarge the buttons and place the Shortcut Bar in its own window so you can move it elsewhere on the screen. You can also hide and redisplay the Shortcut Bar as needed. To close the Office Shortcut Bar:

| Step 1 | *Right-click* | the Office Shortcut Bar Control-menu icon |
| Step 2 | *Click* | Exit |

Summary

▶ When you first start Word, Excel, or PowerPoint, you see personalized menus containing basic commands. As you use different commands, they are automatically added to the personalized menu. Commands that are not used for some time are removed from the personalized menus.

▶ When you first start Word, Excel, or PowerPoint, the Standard and Formatting toolbars share one row below the menu bar. You can reposition the Formatting toolbar to view more or fewer toolbar buttons. The remaining default toolbar buttons that are not visible on the toolbars can be added from the More Buttons list.

▶ FrontPage and Access also provide the personalized menus and toolbars options.

▶ You can turn off or reset the personalized menus and toolbars in the Options tab of the Customize dialog box.

▶ You can hide or view toolbars as you need them by using a shortcut menu.

▶ Toolbars can be docked at the top, bottom, or side of the screen or they can remain floating on the screen in their own window.

▶ You can customize toolbars by adding or deleting buttons and commands, displaying larger-sized buttons, and turning on or off the display of ScreenTips, or adding keyboard shortcut keys to ScreenTips.

▶ The menu bar is a special toolbar that can be customized just like other toolbars.

▶ The Office Shortcut Bar is a customizable toolbar you can position on the desktop and contains shortcuts for opening Office documents and applications.

chapter two

Commands Review

Action	Menu Bar	Shortcut Menu	Toolbar	Keyboard
To display or hide toolbars	View, Toolbars	Right-click a toolbar, click the desired toolbar to add or remove the check mark	☒	ALT + V, T
To customize a toolbar	View, Toolbars, Customize	Right-click a toolbar, click Customize		ALT + V, T, C

Concepts Review

Circle the correct answer.

1. A menu is:
[a] a set of icons.
[b] a list of commands.
[c] impossible to customize.
[d] never personalized.

2. The Options tab in the PowerPoint Customize dialog box does not include an option for:
[a] turning on or off ScreenTips for toolbar buttons.
[b] turning on or off Large icons for toolbar buttons.
[c] adding animation to menus.
[d] docking all toolbars.

3. A toolbar is:
[a] a list of commands.
[b] always floating on your screen.
[c] a set of icons.
[d] never docked on your screen.

4. When you right-click an item on your screen, you see:
[a] the Right Click toolbar.
[b] animated menus.
[c] expanded menus.
[d] a shortcut menu.

Circle **T** if the statement is true or **F** if the statement is false.

T   F   1. The Standard and Formatting toolbars must remain on the same row.

T   F   2. When updating docked personalized toolbars, some buttons may be automatically removed from view to make room for the new buttons.

T   F   3. Resetting your usage data affects your toolbars regardless of their size or position.

T   F   4. You cannot add animation to menus.

Skills Review

Exercise 1

1. Open the Word application.

2. Open the Options tab in the Customize dialog box and reset the usage data, have the Standard and Formatting toolbars share one row, and the menus show recently used commands first.

3. Add the Show/Hide button to the personalized Standard toolbar using the More Buttons list.

4. Add the Font color button to the personalized Formatting toolbar using the More Buttons list.

5. Open the Customize dialog box and reset your usage data in the Options tab.

6. Close the Word application.

Exercise 2

1. Open the Excel application.

2. Open the Options tab in the Customize dialog box and reset the usage data, have the Standard and Formatting toolbars share one row, and the menus show recently used commands first.

3. View the personalized Tools menu.

4. Add the AutoCorrect command to the personalized Tools menu.

5. Reset your usage data.

6. Close the Excel application.

Exercise 3

1. Open the Office Shortcut Bar. (Do not set it to automatically open when you start your computer.)

2. Customize the Office Shortcut Bar to add the Word, Excel, and PowerPoint shortcut buttons or remove them if they already appear.

3. Customize the Office Shortcut Bar to have large buttons and position it in its own window vertically at the right side of the desktop.

4. AutoFit the Office Shortcut Bar to the title bar with small buttons.

5. Remove the Word, Excel, and PowerPoint application shortcut buttons or add them back, if necessary.

6. Close the Office Shortcut Bar.

Exercise 4

1. Open the Word application.

2. Add the Clear command icon from the Edit category to the menu bar.

3. Reset the menu bar back to its default from the Toolbars tab in the Customize dialog box.

4. Close the Word application.

Exercise 5

1. Open the Excel application.

2. View the Drawing, Picture, and WordArt toolbars using a shortcut menu.

3. Dock the Picture toolbar below the Standard and Formatting toolbars.

4. Dock the WordArt toolbar at the left boundary of the screen.

5. Close the Excel application from the taskbar.

6. Open the Excel with the New Office Document on the Start menu. (*Hint:* Use the Blank Workbook icon.)

7. Float the WordArt toolbar.

8. Float the Picture toolbar.

chapter two

9. Hide the WordArt, Picture, and Drawing toolbars using a shortcut menu.

10. Close the Excel application.

Case Projects

Project 1

As secretary to the placement director for the XYZ Employment Agency, you have been using Word 97. After you install Office 2000, you decide you want the menus and toolbars to behave just like they did in Word 97. Use the Office Assistant to search for help on "personalized menus" and select the appropriate topic from the Office Assistant list. (*Hint:* You may need to view all the topics presented in the Office Assistant balloon.) Review the Help topic you select and write down the steps to make the personalized menus and toolbars behave like Word 97 menus and toolbars.

Project 2

You are the administrative assistant to the controller of the Plush Pets, Inc., a stuffed toy manufacturing company. The controller recently installed Excel 2000. She prefers to view the entire list of menu commands rather than the personalized menus and asks for your help. Use the Office assistant to search for help on "full menus" and select the appropriate topic in the Office Assistant balloon. Review the topic and write down the instructions for switching between personalized menus and full menus.

Project 3

As administrative assistant to the art director of MediaWiz Advertising, Inc. you just installed

PowerPoint 2000. Now you decide you would rather view the complete Standard and Formatting toolbars rather than the personalized toolbars and want to learn a quick way to do this. Use the Office Assistant to search for help on "show all buttons" and select the appropriate topic from the Office Assistant balloon. Review the topic and write down the instructions for showing all buttons using the mouse pointer. Open an Office application and use the mouse method to show the complete Standard and Formatting toolbars. Turn the personalized toolbars back on in the Customize dialog box.

Project 4

You are the training coordinator for the information technology (IT) department at a large international health care organization, World Health International. The information technology department is planning to install Office 2000 on computers throughout the organization within the next two weeks. Your supervisor, the IT manager, asks you to prepare a short introduction to the Office 2000 personalized menus and toolbars to be presented at next Monday's staff meeting. He wants you to emphasize the advantages and disadvantages of using the personalized menus and toolbars. Write down in at least two paragraphs the advantages and disadvantages of using the personalized menus and toolbars.

Working With Others Using Online Collaboration Tools

Chapter Overview

I n today's workplace many tasks are completed by several co-workers working together as part of a team called a workgroup. Office applications provide tools to assist workgroups in sharing information. In this chapter you learn about scheduling and participating in online meetings and conducting Web discussions with others in your workgroup.

LEARNING OBJECTIVES

▶ Schedule an online meeting
▶ Participate in Web discussions

chapter three

3.a Scheduling an Online Meeting

Many organizations assign tasks or projects to several workers who collaborate as members of a **workgroup**. Often these workgroup members do not work in the same office or some members travel frequently, making it difficult for the group to meet at one physical location. Office applications, together with Microsoft NetMeeting conferencing software, provide a way for workgroup members to participate in online real-time meetings from different physical locations—just as though everyone were in the same meeting room. In an online meeting, participants can share programs and documents, send text messages, transfer files, and illustrate ideas.

You can schedule an online meeting in advance using Outlook or you can invite others to participate in an online meeting right now by opening NetMeeting directly from Word, Excel, PowerPoint, and Access and calling others in your workgroup. To participate in an online meeting, invitees must have NetMeeting running on their computers.

Calling Others from Office Applications Using NetMeeting

Suppose you are working on an Excel workbook and want to discuss the workbook with another person in your workgroup. You know that they are running NetMeeting on their computer. You can call them while working in the workbook. To open NetMeeting and place a call from within Excel:

Step 1	*Click*	the Start button [Start] on the taskbar
Step 2	*Click*	the Open Office Document command on the Start menu
Step 3	*Double-click*	the *International Food Distributors* workbook located on the Data Disk
Step 4	*Click*	Tools
Step 5	*Point to*	Online Collaboration
Step 6	*Click*	Meet Now to open NetMeeting and the Place A Call dialog box

The directory server and list of names and calling addresses in the Place A Call dialog box on your screen will be different, but the dialog box should look similar to Figure 3-1.

FIGURE 3-1
Place A Call Dialog Box

The person who initiates the meeting call is called the **host**. The person or persons receiving the call are called **participants**. Because you are initiating a call about the open Excel workbook, you are the host for this meeting. You can select a specific directory server and then select the participant to call from a list of persons logged onto the server or select someone from the list of frequently called NetMeeting participants. The *host* now calls a participant in the list:

Step 1	*Right-click*	the name of the person in the list specified by your instructor and click Call

NetMeeting dials the participant. Depending on the participant's NetMeeting configuration, he or she can automatically accept the call or manually accept or ignore the call. If the NetMeeting configuration is set up to manually answer calls, an announcement appears on the participant's screen, allowing him or her to click a button to accept or decline the call.

For the activities in this chapter, the participant's NetMeeting software is configured to automatically accept incoming calls. When the call is accepted, the *International Food Distributors* workbook and the Online Meeting toolbar automatically display on the participant's screen, even if the participant does not have Excel installed. Only the host needs to have the application installed and the file available. Both the *host's* and the *participant's* screens should look similar to Figure 3-2.

The host has **control** of the *International Foods Distributors* workbook when the meeting starts, which means the host can turn on or off collaboration at any time, controlling who can edit the document. When collaboration is turned on, any one participant can control the workbook for editing. When collaboration is turned off,

chapter
three

FIGURE 3-2
Host's and Participant's Screens

QUICK TIP

Only the host of the meeting can use all the features on the Online Meeting toolbar.

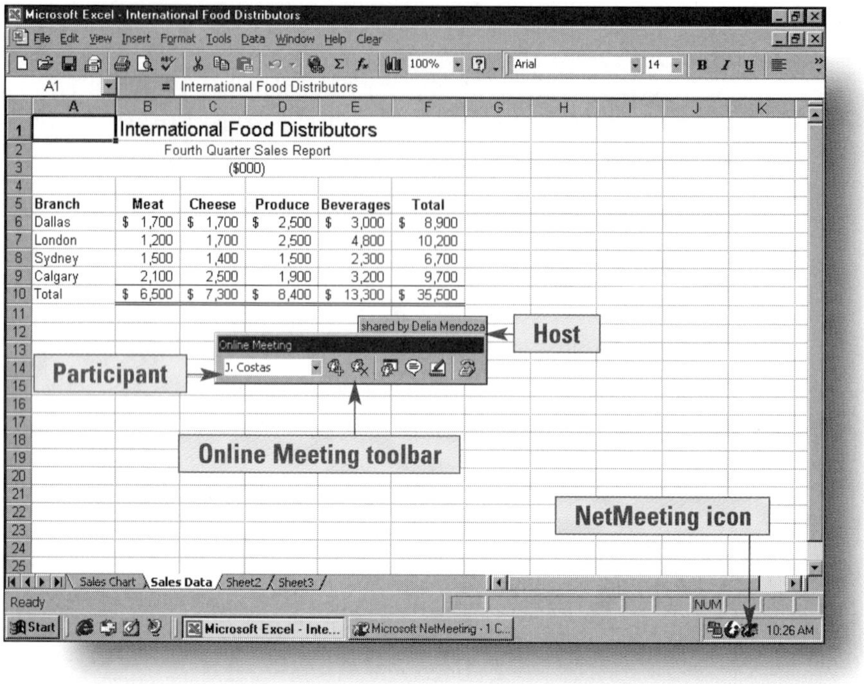

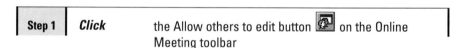

only the host can edit the workbook but all participants can see it. The *host* now turns on collaboration:

Step 1	***Click***	the Allow others to edit button on the Online Meeting toolbar

The first time a participant wants to take control of the workbook, they double-click it. The host can regain control of the workbook at any time simply by clicking it. To regain control of the workbook after the first time they control it, a participant also clicks it. The initials of the person who currently controls the workbook appear beside the mouse pointer. The *participant* takes control of the workbook for the first time to edit it:

Step 1	***Double-click***	the workbook to take control and place your user initials beside the mouse pointer
Step 2	***Click***	Tools
Step 3	***Click***	Options
Step 4	***Click***	the View tab
Step 5	***Click***	the Gridlines check box to remove the check mark
Step 6	***Click***	OK to turn off the gridlines in the workbook

CAUTION TIP

When someone else controls a document during an online meeting, you cannot use your mouse pointer to access commands or edit the document until you regain control of it.

The *host* regains control of the workbook:

| Step 1 | *Click* | the workbook to regain control and place your initials beside the mouse pointer |
| Step 2 | *Turn on* | the gridlines on the View tab in the Options dialog box |

The **Whiteboard** is a tool that participants can use to illustrate their thoughts and ideas. Only the host can display the Whiteboard during an online meeting that originates from within an Office application. All participants can draw on the Whiteboard at the same time only when the host turns off collaboration. The *host* turns off collaboration:

Step 1	*Click*	the workbook to regain control, if necessary
Step 2	*Click*	the Allow others to edit button  to turn off collaboration
Step 3	*Click*	the Display Whiteboard button 🖉 on the Online Meeting toolbar

Your screen should look similar to Figure 3-3.

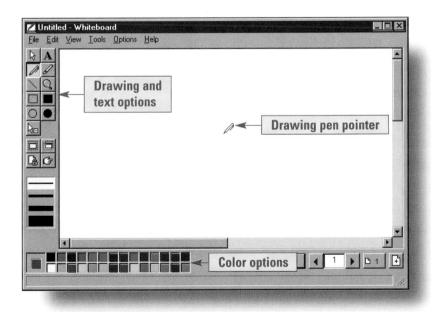

FIGURE 3-3
Whiteboard Window

All participants, including the host, add text, draw shapes, add color, and insert additional pages in the Whiteboard window. The host can save and print Whiteboard pages. The host and participant explore using the drawing, text, and color options for the Whiteboard. First, the *host* selects a color and draws a shape:

chapter
three

| Step 1 | *Click* | Red in the color options |
| Step 2 | *Draw* | a shape by dragging the drawing pen pointer in the Whiteboard drawing area |

The *participant* now takes control of the drawing pen, selects a color, and draws a shape:

| Step 1 | *Click* | the Whiteboard to take control of the drawing pen |
| Step 2 | *Click* | Blue in the color options and draw a shape |

The *host* and the *participant*:

| Step 1 | *Continue* | to share the Whiteboard and explore the different Whiteboard options |
| Step 2 | *Click* | the Close button ☒ on the Whiteboard window title bar to close the Whiteboard |

Each participant can disconnect from the meeting at any time by clicking the End Meeting button on the Online Meeting toolbar. The host can also disconnect any participant by first selecting the participant from the Participants List button and then clicking the Remove Participants button on the Online Meeting toolbar. The host can also end the meeting, which disconnects all the participants. The *host* ends the meeting:

| Step 1 | *Click* | the End Meeting button 🗐 on the Online Meeting toolbar |
| Step 2 | *Close* | the Excel application and workbook from the taskbar without saving changes |

Scheduling Online Meetings in Advance Using Outlook

As a host, you can schedule online meetings in advance using Outlook directly or from inside other Office applications. Suppose you are putting the finishing touches on a PowerPoint presentation and want to schedule an online meeting in advance with other workgroup members. You can do this from inside the PowerPoint application. To open a PowerPoint presentation and invite others to an online meeting:

Step 1	*Open*	the PowerPoint application and the *International Food Distributors* presentation located on the Data Disk using the Open Office Document command on the Start menu
Step 2	*Click*	<u>T</u>ools
Step 3	*Point to*	O<u>n</u>line Collaboration
Step 4	*Click*	<u>S</u>chedule Meeting

The Outlook Meeting window opens, similar to Figure 3-4.

This window provides all the options for setting up the meeting. You address the message to one or more e-mail addresses, key the subject of the meeting, and select the directory server where the meeting will be held. You also select the date and time of the meeting. The current document is selected as the Office document to be reviewed and a meeting reminder is set to be delivered to the host and attendees 15 minutes prior to the scheduled meeting.

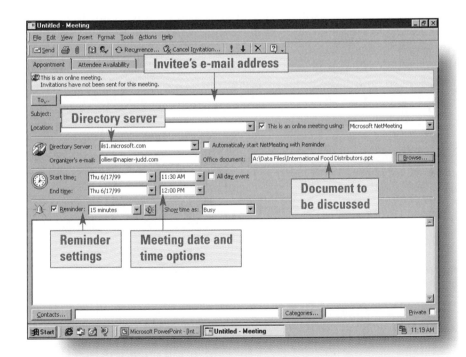

FIGURE 3-4
Outlook Meeting Window

As long as all invitees are using Outlook for their scheduling, you can determine the best time to schedule the meeting by clicking the Attendee Availability tab and inviting others from the Outlook global address book. To review the Attendee Availability tab:

| Step 1 | *Click* | the Attendee Availability tab |

| Step 2 | *Observe* | the meeting scheduling options you can use to compare each invitee's free and busy times from their Outlook calendars and select the best meeting time |
| Step 3 | *Click* | the Appointment tab |

You send the completed meeting invitation by clicking the Send button on the Standard toolbar. Each invitee receives an e-mail message with the meeting information. They can choose to accept, decline, or tentatively accept the invitation by clicking a button inside the message window. If they accept, an Outlook appointment item is added to their calendar. Because you are the host, an appointment item is automatically added to your Outlook calendar. If invitees accept, decline, or accept tentatively, you receive an e-mail notification of their attendance choice and your meeting appointment item is updated to show who is attending and who declined.

Fifteen minutes prior to the scheduled online meeting (if Outlook is running on your computer) a meeting reminder message opens on your screen. If you are the meeting's host, you click the Start this NetMeeting button in the reminder window to begin the meeting. If you are an invited participant, you click the Join the Meeting button in the reminder window to join the meeting or you click the Dismiss this reminder to ignore the meeting invitation.

To close the message window without sending a message:

Step 1	*Click*	the Close button [X] on the message window title bar
Step 2	*Click*	No
Step 3	*Close*	the PowerPoint application and presentation

3.b Participating in Web Discussions

Web discussions provide a way for workgroup members to review and provide input to the same document by associating messages, called **discussion items**, with the document. Discussion items are saved in a database separate from the associated document. This enables the group to consider multiple discussion items related to the same document; it also allows the document to be edited without affecting any discussion items. Discussion items are **threaded**, which means that replies to an item appear directly under the original item. Discussion items are saved as they are entered and are available immediately when the associated document is opened.

QUICK TIP

For more information on scheduling meetings using Outlook, see Outlook online Help.

CAUTION TIP

Special software called Office Server Extensions must be installed on a Web server before discussion items can be created and stored there. For more information on Office Server Extensions software, see the documentation that accompanies Office or online Help.

Suppose you are working on a Word document and want to solicit input from others in your workgroup. Instead of sending a copy to everyone in the workgroup or routing a single copy to everyone, you decide to use the Web discussion feature. To start a Web discussion:

Step 1	*Open*	the Word application and the *Dallas Warehouse Audit* document located on the Data Disk using the Open Office Document command on the Start menu
Step 2	*Click*	Tools
Step 3	*Point to*	Online Collaboration
Step 4	*Click*	Web Discussions

After you connect to your discussion server, the Web Discussions toolbar opens docked above the status bar. See Figure 3-5.

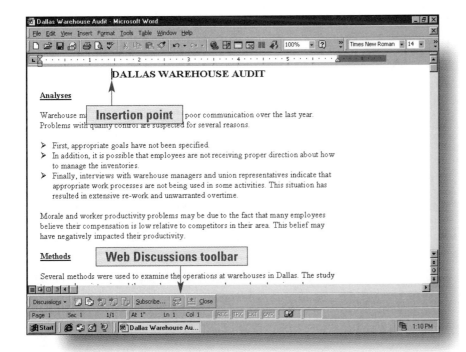

FIGURE 3-5
Document with Web Discussions Toolbar

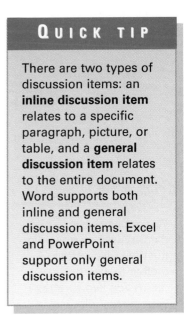

QUICK TIP

There are two types of discussion items: an **inline discussion item** relates to a specific paragraph, picture, or table, and a **general discussion item** relates to the entire document. Word supports both inline and general discussion items. Excel and PowerPoint support only general discussion items.

First, you add a general discussion item identifying the issues to be discussed in the document. To add a general discussion item:

Step 1	*Press*	the CTRL + HOME keys to move the keying position (called the insertion point) to the top of the document
Step 2	*Click*	the Insert Discussion about the Document button  on the Web Discussions toolbar

The dialog box that opens should look similar to Figure 3-6.

chapter
three

FIGURE 3-6
Enter Discussion Text
Dialog Box

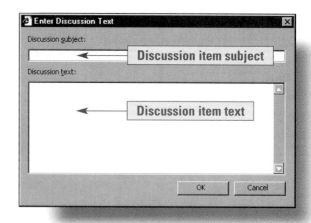

Step 3	*Key*	Problems in Dallas in the Discussion <u>s</u>ubject: text box
Step 4	*Press*	the TAB key to move the insertion point (the keying position) to the Discussion <u>t</u>ext: text box
Step 5	*Key*	We have only three weeks to resolve the problems in Dallas.
Step 6	*Click*	OK

The Discussion pane opens and contains information about the active document, the text of the discussion item, and an Action button. You use the Action button to reply to, edit, or delete a discussion item. Your screen should look similar to Figure 3-7.

FIGURE 3-7
Document with
Discussion Pane

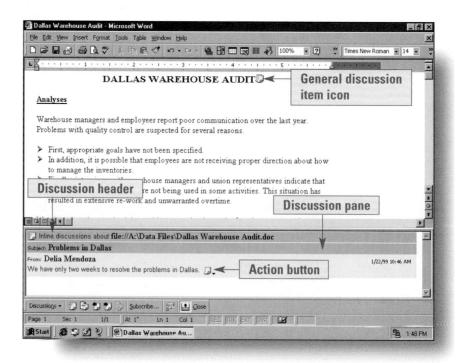

MOUSE TIP

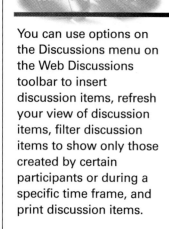

You can use options on the Discussions menu on the Web Discussions toolbar to insert discussion items, refresh your view of discussion items, filter discussion items to show only those created by certain participants or during a specific time frame, and print discussion items.

Next you add an inline discussion item to a specific paragraph. To close the Discussion pane and add an inline discussion item:

Step 1	*Click*	the Show/Hide Discussion Pane button ⬆ on the Web Discussions toolbar
Step 2	*Click*	at the end of the first bulleted item ending in "specified." to reposition the insertion point
Step 3	*Click*	the Insert Discussion in the Document button 📄 on the Web Discussions toolbar
Step 4	*Key*	Goals in the Discussion subject: text box
Step 5	*Key*	Doesn't Yong's group have responsibility for setting warehouse goals? in the Discussion text: text box
Step 6	*Click*	OK

The inline discussion item icon appears at the end of the bulleted text and the Discussion pane opens. Your screen should look similar to Figure 3-8.

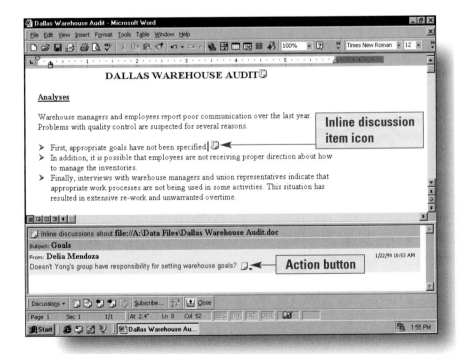

FIGURE 3-8
Inline Discussion Item

| Step 7 | *Click* | the Show/Hide Discussion Pane button ⬆ on the Web Discussions toolbar to close the Discussion pane |

CAUTION TIP

You can modify a document that contains threaded discussions. If you make changes in an area that is not associated with a discussion item, the inline and general discussions are not affected. If you change or delete part of the document associated with a discussion item, any inline discussions are deleted but general discussions are not affected. If you move, rename, or delete a document, all inline and general discussions are lost.

chapter
three

Others in the workgroup can now open the *Dallas Warehouse Audit* document, log on to the discussion server, and review the inline and general discussion items. They can reply to existing items and create new items. They can edit or delete any discussion items they create. Now assume you are a different member of the workgroup and you just opened the *Dallas Warehouse Audit* document, logged on to the discussion server, and want to participate in the discussion. To thread a reply to the inline discussion item at the end of the bulleted list:

Step 1	*Press*	the CTRL + HOME keys to move the insertion point to the top of the document
Step 2	*Click*	the Next button [icon] twice on the Web Discussions toolbar to select the second discussion item and open the Discussion pane
Step 3	*Click*	the Action button in the Discussion pane
Step 4	*Click*	Reply
Step 5	*Key*	Yong's group is currently understaffed and behind schedule. in the Discussion text: text box
Step 6	*Click*	OK to thread your reply immediately below the original discussion item
Step 7	*Close*	the Discussion pane

When discussion items are no longer useful, you can delete them. To open the Discussion pane and delete the discussion items:

Step 1	*Click*	the Show General Discussions [icon] button on the Web Discussions toolbar to open the Discussion Pane
Step 2	*Click*	the Action button
Step 3	*Click*	Delete
Step 4	*Click*	Yes to confirm the deletion
Step 5	*Click*	the Next button [icon] on the Web Discussions toolbar
Step 6	*Delete*	the first inline discussion item
Step 7	*Delete*	the second inline action item
Step 8	*Click*	Close on the Web Discussions toolbar to close the discussions session
Step 9	*Close*	the Word application and the document without saving any changes

---

CAUTION TIP

Selecting and deleting the discussion item icons in a document does not remove the discussion items from the server.

QUICK TIP

Users can subscribe to an e-mail notice of changes to folders and documents stored on a server that also has the Office Server Extension software installed. When you subscribe to a folder or document, you can be notified when a new document is added to the folder, when a document is modified, renamed, moved, or deleted, or whenever a discussion item is added to or deleted from a document. You select the notification period: Within a few minutes, Once a day, or Once a week. For more information on Web Subscriptions, see online Help.

Summary

► You can work with others to complete tasks using Office applications' online collaboration tools: NetMeeting and Web Discussions.

► You can use the NetMeeting conferencing software directly from inside Office applications to host or participate in an online meeting.

► During an online meeting using NetMeeting, participants can take turns editing the current document when the meeting's host turns on collaboration.

► When collaboration is turned off, participants in a NetMeeting online meeting can use the Whiteboard.

► You can chat in real-time during an online meeting and, with a sound card and camera, both see and hear other attendees.

► You can schedule a meeting in advance, either using Outlook or from inside Office applications.

► Another way to work with others on a document is to participate in a Web discussion by associating text comments, called discussion items, with a specific document.

► Inline discussion items relate to specific paragraphs, pictures, or tables in a document. General discussion items relate to the entire document. Only the Word application supports inline discussion items.

Commands Review

Action	Menu Bar	Shortcut Menu	Toolbar	Keyboard
Schedule a meeting using NetMeeting inside Office applications	Tools, Online Collaboration, Meet Now			ALT + T, N, M
Schedule a meeting in advance using Outlook inside Office applications	Tools, Online Collaboration, Schedule Meeting			ALT + T, N, S
Participate in Web Discussions from inside Office applications	Tools, Online Collaboration, Web Discussions			ALT + T, N, W

chapter three

Concepts Review

SCANS

Circle the correct answer.

1. Workgroup members:
 [a] always work in the same physical location.
 [b] never travel on business.
 [c] always work independently of each other.
 [d] often work in different physical locations or travel frequently.

2. A participant in an online meeting:
 [a] can turn collaboration on and off.
 [b] controls access to the Whiteboard.
 [c] can save and print to their own hard drive or printer.
 [d] is the person receiving the call.

3. The first time a participant takes control of a document during an online meeting, the participant must:
 [a] open the Chat window.
 [b] click the document.
 [c] double-click the document.
 [d] press the CTRL + HOME keys.

4. NetMeeting participants use the Whiteboard to:
 [a] key real-time text messages.
 [b] share and edit documents.
 [c] add inline discussion items.
 [d] illustrate their ideas and thoughts.

Circle **T** if the statement is true or **F** if the statement is false.

T   F   1. To participate in an online meeting, invitees must be running NetMeeting on their computer.

T   F   2. When collaboration is turned on, the host of an online meeting always maintains control of the active document.

T   F   3. To gain control of a document during collaboration, participants must double-click it.

T   F   4. The active document can be printed and saved to any participant's printer, hard disk, or server during an online meeting.

notes
You must be connected to the appropriate directory and discussion servers and have NetMeeting and Outlook running with Exchange server to complete these exercises. Your instructor will provide the server and e-mail address information and any NetMeeting and Outlook instructions needed to complete these exercises.

Skills Review

SCANS

Exercise 1

1. Open the Word application and the *Dallas Warehouse Audit* document located on the Data Disk.

2. Invite three other people to an online meeting now.

3. Take turns making changes to the document.

4. End the meeting. Close the Word application and document without saving any changes.

Exercise 2

1. Open the Excel application and the *International Food Distributors* workbook located on the Data Disk.

2. Invite four other people to an online meeting next Thursday at 2:00 PM.

3. Open Outlook and read their automatic meeting reply messages.

4. Open the Outlook appointment item created for the message and view the updated attendee information.

5. Delete the appointment item and send a message to all attendees canceling the meeting.

6. Close Outlook. Close the Excel application and workbook without saving any changes.

Exercise 3

1. Open the PowerPoint application and the *International Food Distributors* presentation located on the Data Disk.

2. Create a general Web discussion item using the text "This is an important presentation."

3. Close the Web discussion and the PowerPoint application and presentation without saving any changes.

Exercise 4

1. Open the PowerPoint application and the *International Food Distributors* presentation located on the Data Disk.

2. Reply to the general discussion item using the text "What is the project due date?"

3. Print the discussion items using a command on the Discussions menu.

4. Delete the general discussion items created for the *International Food Distributors* presentation.

5. Close the Web discussion and the PowerPoint application and presentation without saving any changes.

Case Projects

Project 1

As assistant to the accounting manager at Wilson Art Supply, you are asked to find out how to select a discussion server. Open the Word application and use the Office Assistant to search for discussion server topics using the keywords "Web discussions" and select the appropriate topic from the Office Assistant balloon. Review the topic and write down the instructions for selecting a discussion server.

Project 2

You work in the marketing department at International Hair Concepts, a company that imports professional hairdresser supplies. Your department is going to start scheduling online meetings to collaborate on Word documents and you want to be prepared for potential problems. Open the Word application and use the Office Assistant to find the "troubleshoot online meetings" topic. Write down a list of potential problems and their possible solutions.

Project 3

A co-worker at Merton Partners, a public relations firm, mentions that you can subscribe to documents and folders stored on a Web server and then be notified when changes are made to them. Using Word online Help to search for Web discussion topics; review the topic, "About subscribing to a document or folder on a Web server." Write a paragraph about how subscribing to documents and folders could help you in your work.

Project 4

The Women's Professional Softball Teams annual tournament is in two months and 30 teams from around the world will participate. The director wants to review the schedule (created in Word) at one time with the team representatives in the United States, England, France, Holland, Germany, China, Argentina, Mexico, and Australia. Write at least two paragraphs recommending an online collaboration tool and explaining why this is the best choice.

chapter three

Introduction to the Internet and the World Wide Web

Chapter Overview

Millions of people use the Internet to shop for goods and services, listen to music, view artwork, conduct research, get stock quotes, keep up-to-date with current events, and send e-mail. More and more people are using the Internet at work and at home to view and download multimedia computer files containing graphics, sound, video, and text. In this chapter you learn about the origins of the Internet, how to connect to the Internet, how to use the Internet Explorer Web browser, and how to access pages on the World Wide Web.

LEARNING OBJECTIVES

- ► Describe the Internet and discuss its history
- ► Connect to the Internet
- ► Recognize the challenges to using the Internet
- ► Use Internet Explorer
- ► Use directories and search engines

chapter four

4.a What Is the Internet?

To understand the Internet, you must understand networks. A **network** is simply a group of two or more computers linked by cable or telephone lines. The linked computers also include a special computer called a **network server** that is used to store files and programs that everyone on the network can access. In addition to the shared files and programs, networks enable users to share equipment, such as a common network printer. See Figure 4-1.

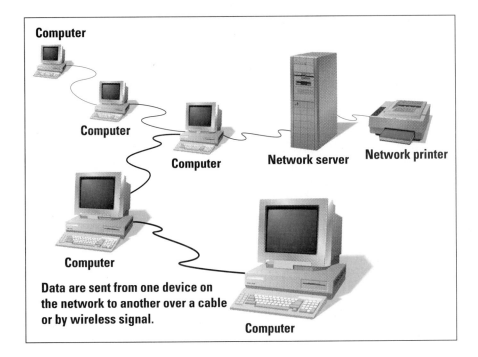

Computer

Computer

Computer

Network server   Network printer

Computer

Data are sent from one device on the network to another over a cable or by wireless signal.

Computer

FIGURE 4-1
Computer Network

The **Internet** is a worldwide collection of computer networks that enables users to view and transfer information between computers. For example, an Internet user in California can retrieve (or **download**) files from a computer in Canada quickly and easily. In the same way, an Internet user in Australia can send (or **upload**) files to another Internet user in England. See Figure 4-2.

The Internet is not a single organization, but rather a cooperative effort by multiple organizations managing a variety of computers.

A Brief History of the Internet

The Internet originated in the late 1960s, when the United States Department of Defense developed a network of military computers called the **ARPAnet**. Quickly realizing the usefulness of such a network,

chapter
four

FIGURE 4-2
The Internet

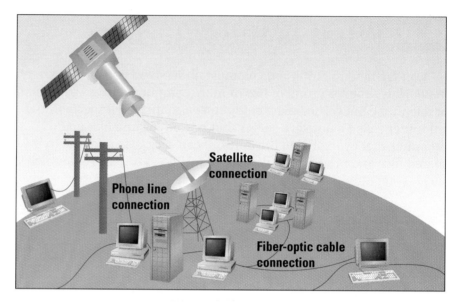

FIGURE 4-2
The Internet

researchers at colleges and universities soon began using it to share data. In the 1980s the military portion of the early Internet became a separate network called the **MILNET**. Meanwhile the National Science Foundation began overseeing the remaining non-military portions, which it called the **NSFnet**. Thousands of other government, academic, and business computer networks began connecting to the NSFnet. By the late 1980s, the term Internet became widely used to describe this huge worldwide "network of networks."

Services Available on the Internet

You find a wide variety of services on the Internet. Table 4-1 explains just some of the options. In this chapter, you learn about using a Web browser and accessing pages on the World Wide Web. Your instructor may provide additional information on other Internet services in the list.

CAUTION TIP

During peak day and evening hours, millions of people are connecting to the Internet. During these hours, you may have difficulty connecting to your host computer or to other sites on the Internet.

4.b Connecting to the Internet

To connect to the Internet you need some physical communication medium connected to your computer, such as network cable or a modem. You also need a special communication program that allows your computer to communicate with computers on the Internet and a Web browser program, such as Microsoft Internet Explorer 5, that allows you to move among all the Internet resources. See Figure 4-3.

Category	Name	Description
Communication	E-mail	Electronic messages sent or received from one computer to another
	Newsgroups	Electronic "bulletin boards" or discussion groups where people with common interests (such as hobbyists or members of professional associations) post messages (called **articles**) that participants around the world can read and respond to
	Mailing Lists	Similar to Newsgroups, except that participants exchange information via e-mail
	Chat	Online conversations in which participants key messages and receive responses on their screen within a few seconds
File Access	FTP	Sending (uploading) or receiving (downloading) computer files via the File Transfer Protocol (FTP) communication rules
Searching Tools	Directories	Tools that help you search for Web sites by category
	Search Engines	Tools to help you find individual files on the Internet by searching for specific words or phrases
World Wide Web (Web)	Web Site	A subset of the Internet that stores files with Web pages containing text, graphics, video, audio, and links to other pages

TABLE 4-1
Internet Services

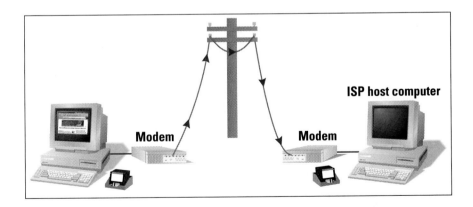

FIGURE 4-3
Internet Connection

chapter
four

Internet Service Providers

After setting up your computer hardware (the network cable or modem) and installing the Internet Explorer Web browser, you must make arrangements to connect to a computer on the Internet. The computer you connect to is called a **host**. Usually, you connect to a host computer via a commercial Internet Service Provider, such as America Online or another company who sells access to the Internet. An **Internet Service Provider (ISP)** maintains the host computer, provides a gateway or entrance to the Internet, and provides an electronic "mail box" with facilities for sending and receiving e-mail. See Figure 4-4.

FIGURE 4-4
Internet Service Providers

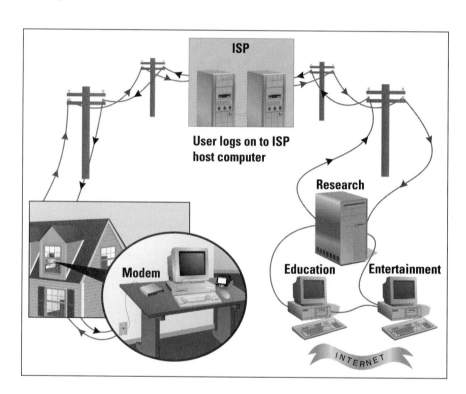

Commercial ISPs usually charge a flat monthly fee for unlimited access to the Internet and e-mail services. Many commercial ISPs generally supply the communication program and browser program you need to access the Internet.

Internet Addresses

A unique Internet address or IP address that consists of a series of numbers identifies each host computer on the Internet. Computers on the Internet use these IP address numbers to communicate with each other, but you will probably need to use one only when you install dial-up networking instructions on your computer. The more important address is the host computer's descriptive address. This address specifies the individual computer within a level of organization, or **domain**, on the Internet. For example, a host computer in the math department at a university might be identified as: *raven.math.uidaho.edu* where "raven" identifies the specific computer, "math" identifies the department, "uidaho" identifies the university, and the suffix "edu" identifies that the address is for an educational institution. You'll find that the descriptive host name is much easier to use and remember than the IP address. Table 4-2 identifies the top-level domain (or highest organizational unit on the Internet) names you see as you work with Internet resources. Other top-level domain names are under consideration but not yet in use.

Top-Level Domain	Organization
.com	Commercial enterprise
.gov	Government institution
.edu	Educational institution
.mil	Military institution
.net	Computer network
.org	Other organizations

TABLE 4-2
Top-Level Domains

User Names

When you make arrangements to access the Internet via an ISP, you also set up a user name that identifies your account with the ISP. Your user name consists of a name you select and the host's descriptive name. User names can be full names, first initial and last names, nicknames, or a group of letters and numbers. For example, the user name for Beth Jackson who accesses the Internet via a commercial ISP named Decon Data Systems might be: *Beth_Jackson@decon.net* where "Beth_Jackson" is the user's name, and "decon.net" is the descriptive name for the ISP's host computer.

4.c Challenges to Using the Internet

Using the Internet to send e-mail, read and post articles to newsgroups, chat online, send and receive files, and search for information is fun and exciting. However, because people use the Internet all over the world, there is a seemingly endless source of data and information available. The sheer size of the Internet can sometimes be intimidating.

Another potential difficulty is the time it takes for messages and files to travel between computers on the Internet. Communication speeds

chapter
four

can be improved by using high-speed modems and special telephone lines. Faster Internet communication via cable is also becoming more widely available.

You should also be aware that the Internet is a cooperative effort, with few widely accepted presentation standards. As a result, the presentation of information on the Internet is varied and inconsistent. Some Web sites are well-designed and easy to use, while some are not. The Internet is a dynamic environment that changes daily with new host computers and Web sites being added and existing ones being removed. This means new or different information is available constantly. Also, old or outdated information may still be available on Web sites that are not properly maintained.

Also, there may be questions about the accuracy of information you find on the Internet. Remember that the Internet is a largely unregulated environment with few, if any, controls over what information is published on the Web or contained in files at FTP sites. It is a good idea to get supporting information from another source before using any information you find on the Internet to make critical business decisions.

Another challenge to using the Internet is the lack of privacy and security for your e-mail and file transmissions. Information sent from one computer to another can travel through many computer systems and networks, where it could be intercepted, copied, or altered. When you access a page on the World Wide Web, it is possible that information such as your e-mail address, which Web pages you view, the type of computer, operating system, and browser you are using, and how you linked to that page can be captured without your knowledge. If you are concerned, you can take advantage of security software that prevents this type of information from being captured.

Certain browser and server programs on Internet computers can encrypt (or scramble) information during transmission and then decrypt (or unscramble) it at its destination. Commercial activities, such as buying an item via credit card or transferring money between bank accounts, can occur in this type of secure environment. However, be advised that much Internet activity takes place in an insecure environment. Government regulations, as well as technological methods to assure privacy and security on the Internet, continue to be developed.

4.d Using Internet Explorer

A **Web browser** is a software application that helps you access Internet resources, including Web pages stored on computers called Web servers. A **Web page** is a document that contains hyperlinks (often called links) to other pages; it can also contain audio and video clips. A **hyperlink** is text or a picture that is associated with the location (path and filename) of another page. To open the Internet Explorer Web browser:

QUICK TIP

Many college and university libraries have Web sites with excellent tips on how to use and evaluate information on the Internet.

INTERNET TIP

To change the start page for the Internet Explorer Web browser, click the Internet Options command on the View menu and then click the General tab. Define the start page by keying the URL in the Address: text box or clicking the Use Current, Use Default, or Use Blank buttons. For more information on designating a start page, see Internet Explorer online Help.

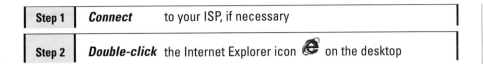

| Step 1 | **Connect** | to your ISP, if necessary |
| Step 2 | **Double-click** | the Internet Explorer icon 🅔 on the desktop |

When the Web browser opens, a Web page, called the **start page**, loads automatically. The start page used by the Internet Explorer Web browser can be the Microsoft default start page, a blank page, or any designated Web page. Figure 4-5 shows the home page for the publisher of this book as the start page.

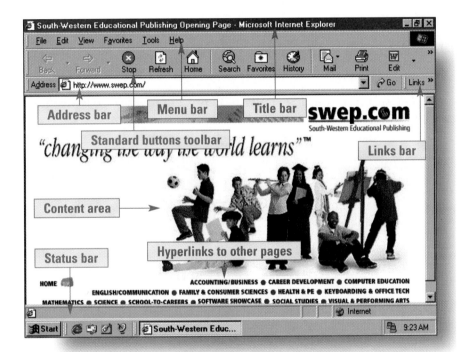

FIGURE 4-5
Internet Explorer Web Browser

Loading a Web Page

Loading a Web page means that the Web browser sends a message to the computer (called a Web server) where the Web page is stored, requesting a copy of the Web page. The Web server responds by sending a copy of the Web page to your computer. In order to load a Web page, you must either know or find the page's **URL** (Uniform Resource Locator)—the path and filename of the page that is the Web page's address. One way to find the URL for a Web page is to use a search engine or directory or you might find a particular company's URL in one of the company's advertisements or on their letterheads and business cards. Examples of URLs based on an organization's name are:

South-Western Educational Publishing   *www.swep.com*
National Public Radio   *www.npr.org*
The White House   *www.whitehouse.gov*

chapter
four

You can try to "guess" the URL based on the organization's name and top-level domain. For example, a good guess for the U.S. House of Representatives Web page is *www.house.gov.*

You can key a URL directly in the Address bar by first selecting all or part of the current URL and replacing it with the new URL. Internet Explorer adds the "http://" portion of the URL for you. To select the contents of the Address bar and key the URL for the U.S. House of Representatives:

Step 1	*Click*	the contents of the Address bar
Step 2	*Key*	www.house.gov
Step 3	*Click*	the Go button or press the ENTER key

In a few seconds, the U.S. House of Representatives page loads. Your screen should look similar to Figure 4-6.

QUICK TIP

When you start keying the URL of a Web page you have previously loaded, the AutoComplete feature automatically adds a suggested URL to the Address bar. You can continue by keying over the suggested URL or you can accept the suggested URL by pressing the ENTER key.

FIGURE 4-6
U.S. House of
Representatives Web Page

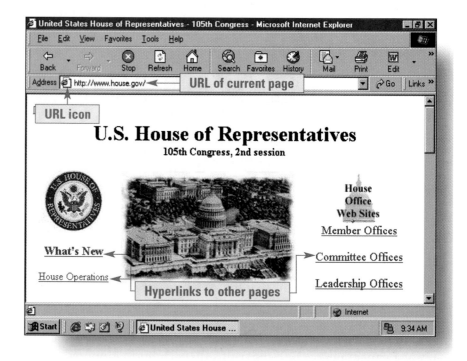

MENU TIP

You can key a URL in the Open dialog box by first clicking the Open command on the File menu.

You can create a favorite by clicking the Favorites command on the menu bar and then clicking Add to Favorites, by right-clicking the background (not a link) on the current Web page and clicking Add to Favorites, or by right-clicking a link on the current Web page and clicking Add to Favorites.

Creating Favorites

Web pages are constantly being updated with new information. If you like a certain Web page or find a Web page contains useful information and plan to revisit it, you may want to save its URL as a **favorite**. Suppose you want to load the U.S. House of Representatives home page frequently. You can create a favorite that saves the URL in a file on your hard disk. Then at any time, you can quickly load this Web page by clicking it in a list of favorites maintained on the Favorites menu.

The URLs you choose to save as favorites are stored in the Favorites folder on your hard disk. You can specify a new or different folder and you can change the name of the Web page as it appears in your list of favorites in this dialog box. To add the U.S. House of Representatives Web page as a favorite:

Step 1	*Click*	Favorites
Step 2	*Click*	Add to Favorites
Step 3	*Click*	OK
Step 4	*Click*	the Home button 🏠 to return to the default start page

One way to load a Web page from a favorite is to click the name of the favorite in the list of favorites on the Favorites menu. To load the U.S. House of Representatives home page from the Favorites menu:

Step 1	*Click*	Favorites
Step 2	*Click*	the U.S. House of Representatives favorite to load the page
Step 3	*Click*	the Home button 🏠 to return to the default start page

The Back and Forward buttons allow you to review recently loaded Web pages without keying the URL or using the Favorites list. To reload the U.S. House of Representatives Home page from the Back button list:

Step 1	*Click*	the Back button list arrow ⬅▾ on the toolbar
Step 2	*Click*	United States House of Representatives

4.e Using Directories and Search Engines

Because the Web is so large, you often need to take advantage of special search tools, called search engines and directories, to find the information you need. To use some of the Web's numerous search engines and directories, you can click the Search button on the

QUICK TIP

Another way to load a favorite is to use the Favorites button to open the Favorites list in the **Explorer bar**, a pane that opens at the left side of your screen.

CAUTION TIP

Any Web page you load is stored in the Temporary Internet Files folder on your hard disk. Whenever you reload the Web page, Internet Explorer compares the stored page to the current Web page either each time you start the browser or each time you load the page. If the Web page on the server has been changed, a fresh Web page is downloaded. If not, the Web page is retrieved from the Temporary Internet File folder rather than downloaded. To view and change the Temporary Internet File folder options (and other Internet Explorer options), click the Internet Options command on the Tools menu.

chapter
four

Standard toolbar to open the Search list in the Explorer bar. To view the Search list:

Step 1	*Click*	the Search button 🔍 on the toolbar
Step 2	*Observe*	the search list options

Search engines maintain an index of keywords used in Web pages that you can search. Search engine indexes are updated automatically by software called **spiders** (or **robots**). Spiders follow links between pages throughout the entire Web, adding any new Web pages to the search engine's index. You should use a search engine when you want to find specific Web pages. Some of the most popular search engines include AltaVista, HotBot, and Northern Light.

Directories use a subject-type format similar to a library card catalog. A directory provides a list of links to broad general categories of Web sites such as "Entertainment" or "Business." When you click these links, a subcategory list of links appears. For example, if you click the "Entertainment" link you might then see "Movies," "Television," and "Video Games" links. To find links to Web sites containing information about movies, you would click the "Movies" link. Unlike search engines, whose indexes are updated automatically, directories add new Web sites only when an individual or a company asks that a particular Web site be included. Some directories also provide review comments and ratings for the Web sites in their index. Most directories also provide an internal search engine that can only be used to search the directory's index, not the entire Web. You use a directory when you are looking for information on broad general topics. Popular directories include Yahoo and Magellan Internet Guide.

To search for Web pages containing "movie guides:"

Step 1	*Key*	movie guides in the search list text box
Step 2	*Click*	the Search button or press the ENTER key
Step 3	*Observe*	the search results (a list of Web pages in the search list)

The search results list consists of Web page titles as hyperlinks. To load a page from the list, simply click the hyperlink. To close the Explorer bar and search list:

Step 1	*Click*	the Search button 🔍 on the toolbar

Guidelines for Searching the Web

Before you begin looking for information on the Web, it is a good idea to think about what you want to accomplish, establish a time frame in which to find the information, and then develop a search strategy. As you search, keep in mind the following guidelines:

1. To find broad, general information, start with a Web directory such as Galaxy or Yahoo.

2. To find a specific Web page, start with a search engine such as Alta Vista or HotBot.

3. Become familiar with a variety of search engines and their features. Review each search engine's online Help when you use it for the first time. Many search engine features are revised frequently so remember to review them regularly.

4. Search engines use spider programs to index all the pages on the Web. However, these programs work independently of each other, so not all search engines have the same index at any point in time. Use multiple search engines for each search.

5. **Boolean operators** allow you to combine or exclude keywords when using a search engine. **Proximal operators** allow you specify that search keywords be close together in a Web page. Boolean and proximal operators are words that allow you to specify relationships among search keywords or phrases using (brackets), OR, NOT, AND, NEAR, and FOLLOWED BY. Not all search engines support Boolean and proximal operators, but use them to reduce the scope of your search when they are available. For example, if you are looking for gold or silver and don't want Web pages devoted to music, try searching by the keywords *metals* not *heavy*. To make sure the keywords are in close proximity use the NEAR or FOLLOWED BY proximal operators.

6. Use very specific keywords. The more specific the phrase, the more efficient your search is. For example, use the phrase "online classes" plus the word genealogy (*"online classes" + genealogy)* rather than simply *genealogy* to find Web pages with information about classes in how to trace your family tree.

7. Watch your spelling. Be aware how the search engine you use handles capitalization. In one search engine "pear" may match "Pear", "pEaR", or "PEAR." In another search engine, "Pear" may match only "Pear."

8. Think of related words that might return the information you need. For example, if you search for information about oil, you might also use "petroleum" and "petrochemicals."

9. Search for common variations of word usage or spelling. For example, the keywords deep sea drilling, deepsea drilling, and deep-sea drilling may all provide useful information.

10. The search returns (or **hits**) are usually listed in order of relevance. You may find that only the first 10 or 12 hits are useful. To find more relevant Web pages, try searching with different keywords.

CAUTION TIP

You get varying results when using several search engines or directories to search for information on the same topic. Also, search tools operate according to varying rules. For example, some search engines allow only a simple search on one keyword. Others allow you to refine your search by finding words within quotation marks together, by indicating proper names, or by using special operators such as "and," "or," and "not" to include or exclude search words. To save time, always begin by reviewing the search tool's online Help directions, then proceed with your search.

After you find the desired information, "let the user beware!" Because the Web is largely unregulated, anyone can put anything on a Web page. Evaluate carefully the credibility of all the information you find. Try to find out something about the author and his or her credentials, or the about validity of the origin of the information.

chapter
four

Summary

► A network is a group of two or more computers linked by cable or telephone lines and the Internet is a worldwide "network of networks."

► The Internet began in the late 1960s as the military Internet ARPAnet. By the 1980s the National Science Foundation assumed responsibility for the non-military portions and the term Internet became widely used.

► The World Wide Web is a subset of the Internet that uses computers called Web servers to store documents called Web pages.

► To access the Internet, your computer must have some physical communication medium, such as a cable or dial-up modem and a special communication program.

► An Internet Service Provider (or ISP) maintains a host computer on the Internet. In order to connect to the Internet, you need to connect to the host computer.

► Each host computer has an Internet address or IP address consisting of a series of numbers and a descriptive name based on the computer name and domain of the host. In addition to the host computer IP address and descriptive name, each user has a name that identifies their account at the Internet Service Provider.

► Large commercial enterprises, colleges, and universities may have a computer network on the Internet and can provide Internet access to their employees or students.

► There are many challenges to using the Internet—including the amount of available information, communication speed, the dynamic environment, lack of presentation standards, and privacy/security issues.

► You should carefully evaluate the source and author of information you get from the Internet and confirm any business-critical information from another source.

► Other external networks related to the Internet are large commercial networks, such as America Online, the Microsoft Network, and USENET.

► You use Web browsers, such as Internet Explorer, to load Web pages.

► Web pages are connected by hyperlinks, which are text or pictures associated with the path to another page.

► Directories and search engines are tools to help you find files and Web sites on the Internet.

Commands Review

Action	Menu Bar	Shortcut Menu	Toolbar	Keyboard
Load a Web page	File, Open			ALT + F, O Key URL in the Address bar and press the ENTER key
Save a favorite	Favorites, Add to Favorites	Right-click hyperlink, click Add to Favorites	Drag URL icon to Links bar or Favorites command	ALT + A, A CTRL + D
Manage the Standard toolbar, Address bar, and Links bar	View, Toolbars	Right-click the Standard toolbar, click desired command	Drag the Standard toolbar, Address bar, or Links bar to the new location	ALT + V, T
Load the search, history, or favorites list in the Explorer bar	View, Explorer Bar			ALT + V, E

Concepts Review

Circle the correct answer.

1. To post messages of common interest to electronic bulletin boards, use:
[a] search tools.
[b] e-mail.
[c] file access.
[d] newsgroups.

2. A network is:
[a] the Internet.
[b] a group of two or more computers linked by cable or telephone wire.
[c] a group of two or more computer networks linked by cable or telephone lines.
[d] a computer that stores Web pages.

3. The Internet began as the:
[a] MILNET.
[b] NSFnet.
[c] SLIPnet.
[d] ARPAnet.

4. Which of the following is not a challenge to using the Internet?
[a] chat groups.
[b] dynamic environment and heavy usage.
[c] volume of information.
[d] security and privacy.

Circle **T** if the statement is true or **F** if the statement is false.

T   F   1. An IP address is a unique identifying number for each host computer on the Internet.

T   F   2. A host computer's descriptive name identifies it by name and organizational level on the Internet.

T   F   3. Commercial networks that provide specially formatted features are the same as the Internet.

T   F   4. USENET is the name of the military Internet.

Skills Review

Exercise 1

1. Open the Internet Explorer Web browser.

2. Open the Internet Options dialog box by clicking the Internet Options command on the View menu.

3. Review the options on the General tab in the dialog box.

4. Write down the steps to change the default start page to a blank page.

5. Close the dialog box and close the Web browser.

chapter four

Exercise 2

1. Connect to your ISP and open the Internet Explorer Web browser.

2. Open the search list in the Explorer bar. Search for Web pages about "dog shows."

3. Load one of the Web pages in the search results list. Close the Explorer bar.

4. Print the Web page by clicking the Print command on the File menu and close the Web browser.

Exercise 3

1. Connect to your ISP and open the Internet Explorer Web browser.

2. Load the National Public radio Web page by keying the URL, *www.npr.org*, in the Address bar.

3. Print the Web page by clicking the Print command on the File menu and close the Web browser.

Exercise 4

1. Connect to your ISP and open the Internet Explorer Web browser.

2. Load the AltaVista search engine by keying the URL, *www.altavista.digital.com*, in the Address bar.

3. Save the Web page as a favorite. Search for Web pages about your city.

4. Print at least two Web pages by clicking the Print command on the File menu and close your Web browser.

Case Projects

Project 1

Your supervisor asks you to prepare a fifteen-minute presentation describing the Internet Explorer toolbar buttons. Review the toolbar buttons and practice using them. Write an outline for your presentation that lists each button and describes how it is used.

Project 2

Your manager is concerned about Internet security and wants to know more about Internet Explorer security features. Click the Contents and Index command on the Internet Explorer Help menu to locate and review the topics about security. Write a note to your manager discussing two security topics.

Project 3

You are working for a book publisher who is creating a series of books about popular movie actors and actresses from the 1920s to the 1950s, including Humphrey Bogart and Lionel Barrymore. The research director asks you to locate a list of movies on the Web that the actors starred in. Use the Explorer bar search list and the Yahoo directory search tool to find links to "Entertainment." Close the Explorer bar and then, working from the Yahoo Web page, click "Movies" within the Entertainment category, scroll down and click the Actors and Actresses link. Search for Humphrey Bogart in the Actors and Actresses portion of the database. Link to the Web page that shows the filmography for Humphrey Bogart. Print the Web page that shows all the movies he acted in. Use the History list to return to the Actors and Actresses search page. Search for Lionel Barrymore, link to and print the filmography for him. Close the Internet Explorer Web browser.

Project 4

You are the new secretary for the Business Women's Forum. The association's president asked you to compile a list of Internet resources. Connect to your ISP, open Internet Explorer, and search for pages containing the keywords "women in business" (including the quotation marks). From the search results, click the Web page title link of your choice. Review the new Web page and its links. Create a favorite for that page. Use the Back button list to reload the search results and click a different Web page title from the list. Review the Web page and its links. Create a favorite for the Web page. Load and review at least five pages. Return to the default home page. Use the Go menu and the History bar to reload at least three of the pages. Print two of the pages. Delete the favorites you added, and then close Internet Explorer.

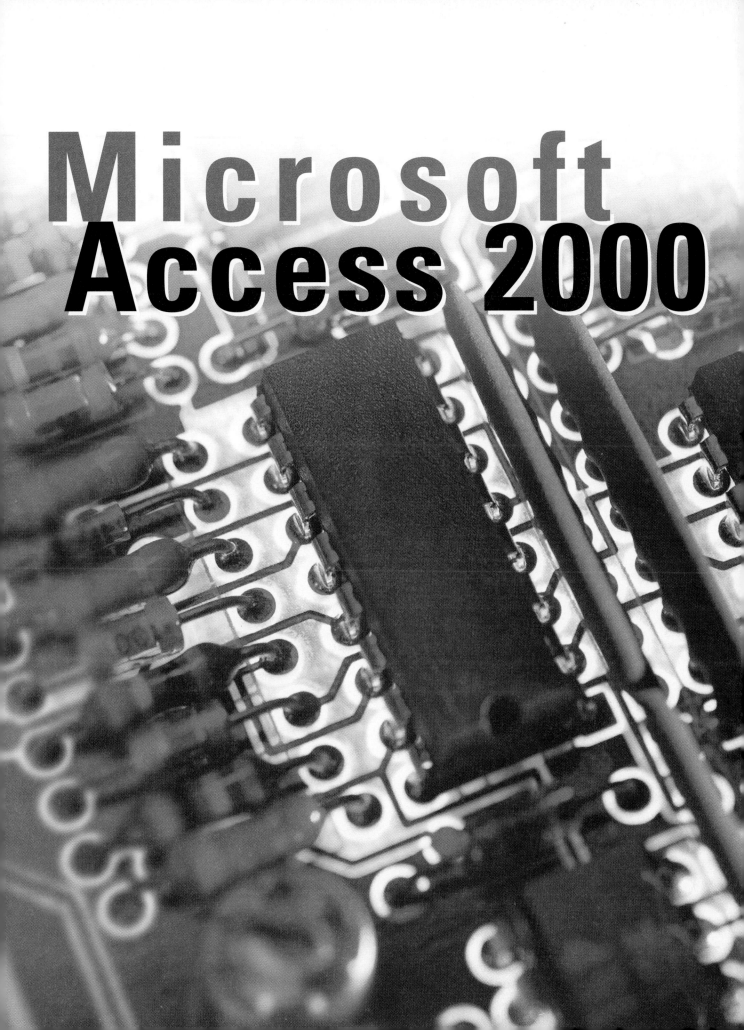

Microsoft
Access 2000

Introduction to Access

Chapter Overview

In this chapter, you explore the format and design of Access. You learn about the purpose of this database application, become familiar with its menus and toolbars, and view some of its objects, including a table, form, query, report, and data access page. You also learn how to use online Help.

LEARNING OBJECTIVES

- ▶ Define Access
- ▶ Open the Access application
- ▶ View the Access window
- ▶ Get help
- ▶ Identify Access objects
- ▶ Exit Access

Case profile

You work for Dynamic Inc., an import/export company that has been in business for the past three years. The company imports and exports household and personal items. As the Information Services Manager, you are responsible for creating and managing one of the company's databases, which needs to include accurate information about its products, customers, orders, and personnel. You use Microsoft Access 2000 to create and maintain this database. You decide to view one of Dynamic's existing Access databases, *mdbImporters*, so you can better understand how to use its powerful features.

chapter one

notes This text assumes that you have little or no knowledge of Access. It also assumes that you have read Office Chapters 1–4 of this book and that you are familiar with Windows 95 or Windows 98 concepts.

[handwritten note: Fields - vertical (columns) Records - horizontal (rows)]

1.a Defining Access

In its simplest form, Access is a database application. A **database** is a collection of records and files organized for a particular purpose. For example, you could use a database to store information about your friends and family, including their addresses and phone numbers. Access, however, is more powerful than a simple database because it uses a **relational database management model**, which means you can relate each piece of information to other pieces of information by joining them. For example, suppose you have a database table that lists customers and their addresses. In another table, you have information about the orders that these customers place with your company. You can join the two tables by using a relationship. This way you don't have to reenter customers' information every time they place an order. You will see how to take advantage of Access's power in the following pages.

You are now ready for your tour of Access.

1.b Opening the Access Application

Before you can work with Access, you must open the application. When you start Access, you see a dialog box asking if you want to create a new database or open an existing one. For your tour, open the existing database called *mdbImporters*.

To start Access and open an Access database:

Step 1	*Click*	the Start button [Start] on the taskbar
Step 2	*Point to*	<u>P</u>rograms
Step 3	*Click*	Microsoft Access

chapter
one

The Microsoft Access application and dialog box open and, as with other Office applications, the Office Assistant may appear. The Microsoft Access dialog box allows you to open an existing database, create a new blank database, or create a database by using a Database Wizard. See Figure 1-1.

FIGURE 1-1
Microsoft Access
Dialog Box

To become familiar with the Access window, open the sample database, *mdbImporters*. The Microsoft Access dialog box lists existing databases. If you want to open a database that is not on the list, click the More Files option. You can then locate a database on your hard drive, floppy drive, CD, or network.

Step 4	*Click*	More Files
Step 5	*Click*	OK
Step 6	*Change*	the Look in: list box to the drive and folder that contains your Data Disk
Step 7	*Click*	the *mdbImporters* database in the Open dialog box
Step 8	*Click*	Open

Your screen should look similar to Figure 1-2.

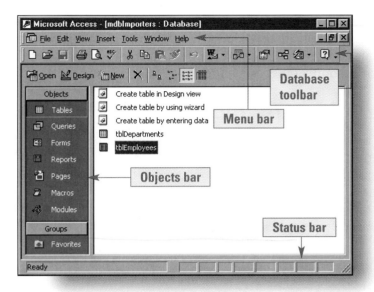

FIGURE 1-2
mdbImporters Database

> **QUICK TIP**
>
> Your screen may look differently if the database does not open in full-screen mode. If this is the case, maximize your mdbImporters Database window.

You are now ready to tour the Access window.

1.c Viewing the Access Window

 notes

Office 2000 features personalized menus and toolbars, which "learn" the commands you use most often. This means that when you first install Office 2000, only the most frequently used commands immediately appear on a short version of the menus and the remaining commands appear after a brief pause. Commands that you select move to the short menu, while those you don't use appear only on the full menu.

The Standard and Formatting toolbars appear on the same row when you first install Office 2000. When they appear in this position, you can see only the most commonly used buttons of each toolbar. All the other default buttons appear on the More Buttons drop-down lists. As you use buttons from the More Buttons drop-down list, they move to the visible buttons on the toolbar, while the buttons you don't use move into the More Buttons drop-down list. If you arrange the Formatting toolbar below the Standard toolbar, you can see all the buttons. Unless otherwise noted, the illustrations in this book show the full menus and the Formatting toolbar on its own line below the Standard toolbar.

When you look at Figure 1-2, some components of the Access window may seem familiar to you, because they are similar to other Office applications. However, other components are unique to Access, such as some of the toolbar buttons and menu options.

Database Toolbar

The default Access toolbar, the Database toolbar, appears below the menu bar. The Database toolbar changes according to the type of information you are showing on your screen. When you first start Access, you see the features that are common to all Office applications, such as the Save button. You also see many of the Access database tools, such as the Relationships button.

Status Bar

The **status bar** is an area of the Access screen that indicates the condition of the open database, such as READY. Other areas of the status bar indicate such features as NUM LOCK or CAPS LOCK.

Access Database Views

Access lets you view the information in your database from different perspectives. These **views** let you work with your database in different ways. **Datasheet view** displays records in a row-and-column format, similar to a table, and allows you to see many records at the same time. **Design view** lets you design and modify your database, such as its tables, queries, forms, reports, and macros. **Form view** displays records in a layout you design to make data entry easy. **SQL view** shows the SQL programming for the limiting factors of a query. **Print Preview** shows how your report looks when it is printed. **Layout Preview** shows a small portion of your data in a report before printing.

Menu Bar

The **menu bar** offers options that make using Access easier and more efficient. For example, the File menu includes the **Get External Data** command, which allows you to either import or link to an Excel spreadsheet or other database program. This feature expands the scope of the database by allowing you to access databases located on other computers in your network. Using the Edit menu, you can create a shortcut. A **shortcut** is a path to a resource on your network or local computer. This makes finding your work easier.

Many options on the Tools menu are unique to the Access application. **Relationships** shows the current relationships in the database and lets you create and edit them. **Analyze** allows you to run a diagnostic tool to locate potential problems in your database. **Security** helps you set a password and permissions for your database.

QUICK TIP

To customize your toolbars, click the View menu, point to Toolbars, and then click Customize. You can then choose the types of toolbars you want Access to display when you open the program.

The <u>W</u>indow menu allows you to change the way you view the items on your screen. It also lets you hide a database window without closing it.

Finally, the <u>H</u>elp menu provides ways to get help in Access. Getting help in Access is critical to learning how to use its powerful features. You can either use the <u>H</u>elp menu or the Office Assistant.

1.d Getting Help

You can use the extensive online Help in Access to find a wealth of help topics. Many topics guide you step-by-step through a procedure; others provide quick answers or definitions.

Using the Help Menu

To find a help topic, you click <u>H</u>elp on the menu bar and then click Microsoft Access <u>H</u>elp. You can then click the Contents tab, click a Help book icon, and then click a page icon to open the topic. You can also click the Index tab and then type the topic you want to find. Or, when you're working with a dialog box, you can get context-sensitive help by pressing the F1 key or by clicking the Help button. Finally, you can also get context-sensitive help on menu options. Highlight an option and then press the F1 key to see a related help topic.

Using the Office Assistant

The **Office Assistant**, an animated character you can use to search for online Help topics, may appear automatically when you work in Access unless you hide it or turn it off. In the illustrations in this book, the Office Assistant is hidden. To hide the Office Assistant, if necessary:

Step 1	*Right-click*	the Office Assistant
Step 2	*Click*	<u>H</u>ide

After you hide the Office Assistant multiple times, you may see a dialog box that asks if you want to turn off the Office Assistant. If you do turn off the Office Assistant, you can turn it back on by clicking the Show the <u>O</u>ffice Assistant command on the <u>H</u>elp menu.

Now that you are more familiar with the Access window, you are ready to view the database objects.

QUICK TIP

When you're working anywhere in Access, including a wizard, dialog box, or toolbar, press the Shift + F1 keys to switch to the Help pointer. You can then click on any item, such as a button or field, to see a quick explanation.

MOUSE TIP

You can change the Office Assistant by right-clicking the Office Assistant icon and then clicking <u>C</u>hoose Assistant. Under the Gallery tab, choose the Assistant that appeals to you.

chapter
one

1.e Identifying Access Objects

Access uses **objects**, which are the components of the database. They relate to the data stored in the database. The most frequently used objects are the table, form, query, report, and data access page. More advanced Access objects include macros and modules.

Tables

Tables are at the heart of every database; when you create a database, you most often start by creating tables. **Tables** store the information in records and fields. **Records** are database entries (such as information about a customer), which are stored in rows. **Fields** are categories of information (such as first name, last name, and phone number), which are stored in columns.

Each table contains information about a specific topic. For example, tblEmployees contains Importers' personnel information. When you open your database, the tables are shown by default.

To open the *mdbImporters'* tblEmployees table by using the Objects bar:

Step 1	*Click*	Tables on the Objects bar in the database window
Step 2	*Double-click*	tblEmployees to open it

Your screen should look similar to Figure 1-3.

FIGURE 1-3
tblEmployees Table

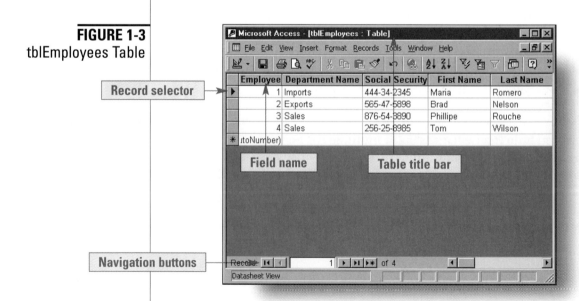

Figure 1-3 shows the parts of an Access table. Notice that the Database toolbar is now the **Table Datasheet toolbar**, which contains tools for working with the Access table. The status bar also shows that you are in Datasheet view. The **record selector** allows you to select or highlight an entire record in a table. Record selector symbols include a triangle, which points to the current record; an asterisk, which shows a new blank record; a drawing pen, which tells you that you are editing a record; and a null symbol, which indicates the record is locked and cannot be changed.

Tour **navigation buttons** allow you to move from one record to the next. The middle two buttons move one record at a time in the direction of each arrow. The first button on the left moves to the first record in the table. The fourth button on the right moves the insertion point to the last record. The **New Record button** adds a new, blank record to the table. The **Specific Record box** indicates the number value of the current record as related to the rest of the records in the table. Finally, the **horizontal scroll bar** allows you to view the rest of the fields. These navigational tools work the same for all database objects.

After you have examined the table, you should close it before viewing other Access objects.

To close the tblEmployees table:

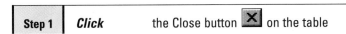

| Step 1 | *Click* | the Close button on the table |

Once you create a table, you often create a form next.

Forms

A **form** is a convenient way to enter or find information in tables. Although you can enter information directly into a table, it is easier to use a form. The form displays a blank template that you tab through as you enter data. Each box is labeled so that you know the type of information you are entering. You can also use forms to search or review your data.

One advantage of forms is that they are easily changed. You can add graphics or rearrange the fields to make them more helpful and appealing for the person entering the data. Further, Access links the form information to the tables you used when creating the form. Whenever you use the form to enter data, it places the data in the table to which it is linked.

QUICK TIP

When you open an object, you may also see part of the database window in the screen. Although Access does not allow you to open more than one database at a time, you can open more than one object (table, query, form, report, etc.). This is beneficial when you want to compare information in different Access objects.

QUICK TIP

You can use a single form to enter data into several tables at once.

chapter
one

To look at the parts of an Access form:

| Step 1 | *Click* | Forms   on the Objects bar in the database window |
| Step 2 | *Double-click* | frmEmployees |

The status bar tells you that you are in Form view, that is, that the active window contains a form. Your screen should look similar to Figure 1-4.

FIGURE 1-4
frmEmployees Form

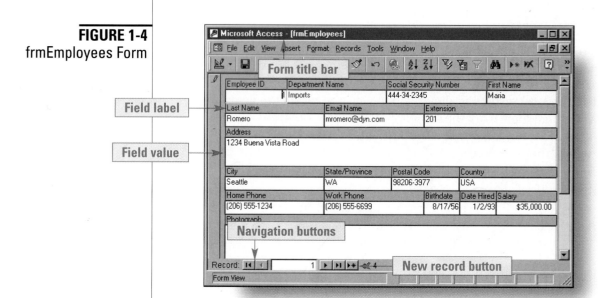

The field names on a form are called **labels**. These are the same fields found in the tables used to generate the form. A **value** is the data that is entered and contained in a single field in a single record. For example, an employee's last name, such as Romero, is a value.

After you finish looking at the layout of the form, you need to close it. To close the frmEmployees form:

| Step 1 | *Click* | the Close button on the frmEmployees title bar |

After creating a form, you use it to enter data into one or more Access tables. Once you enter the data, you can then locate specific data by using queries.

Queries

One of the most powerful features of Access is the **query**, which allows you to ask questions of your information. Access then uses your questions to generate a subset of the data in your database. The data may be drawn from multiple tables. Start by opening the query.

Opening a Query in Design View

If you double-click a query object to open it, you open the results of the query. Because you want to look first at the design of a query, you must click the <u>D</u>esign button in the database window.

To open an Access query:

Step 1	*Click*	Queries 🔳 on the Objects bar in the database window
Step 2	*Click*	qryEmployees
Step 3	*Click*	<u>D</u>esign 📐 on the Database toolbar

Your screen should look similar to Figure 1-5.

M O U S E   T I P

To open a query quickly in Design view, highlight the object name, right-click, and then click <u>D</u>esign view.

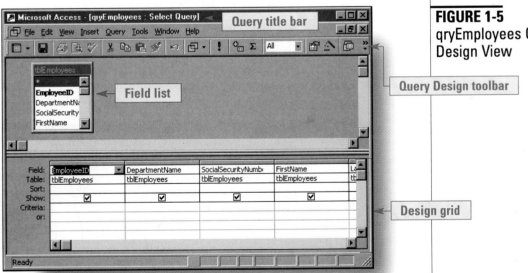

FIGURE 1-5
qryEmployees Query in Design View

Figure 1-5 shows the parts of a query. Notice that the current toolbar is now the Query Design toolbar, which contains tools that you use only for an Access query.

The query title bar indicates the name (here, qryEmployees) and type of query (here, Select Query). The default query type is the **select query**, which you use when you want to view a set of records for examination or modification. The **field list** contains all the fields from

chapter
one

MOUSE TIP

When the query is open in Design view, the option showing in the View button on the Query Design toolbar is the Datasheet View icon . Conversely, when the query is open in Datasheet view, the Design View icon shows on the View button.

the table or query being used in the query. In designing your query, you may choose fields from different tables and use as many fields in your query as you wish.

The **design grid** resembles a table and contains the criteria used in the query. The **Field: row** is the top row of the design grid and contains fields used in the query. The **Table: row** indicates the name of the tables that your query is based on. The **Sort:** row indicates the sort order of a particular field. The **Show:** check box indicates the field is shown in query results. If you remove the check mark from the Show check box for a field, that field does not appear in the query results. This is useful if you want to query on a certain field but do not want that field to be shown in the results. The **Criteria: row** is used to determine which records appear in the query results. This is a limiting feature such as "France" or "<25." Finally, the **or: row** is used in sorting the information similar to the Criteria: row.

You can see the results of a query by switching to Datasheet view.

Switching Between Object Views

You can easily switch views of any object by clicking the appropriate View button on the Query Design toolbar. You can also switch views by clicking <u>V</u>iew on the menu bar.

To see the query results by switching views:

| Step 1 | *Click* | the View button  on the Query Design toolbar |

The results of the query should look similar to Figure 1-6.

FIGURE 1-6
Results of qryEmployees

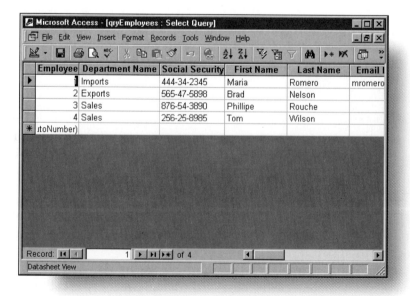

The employees are listed in numerical order according to their employee ID number. You can also re-sort the data by using any other field, such as the Last Name field. Sorting information allows you to view the same information from a different perspective.

To sort on the Last Name field:

| Step 1 | *Click* | the Last Name field to highlight the entire column |
| Step 2 | *Click* | the Sort Ascending button  on the Query Datasheet toolbar |

M O U S E   T I P

To sort on a field, click the field, right-click, and then click the sort option of your choice.

After looking at the sort, you need to close the query.

| Step 3 | *Click* | the Close button ⊠ on the query title bar |

You do not want to save changes.

| Step 4 | *Click* | <u>N</u>o |

After a query has been performed, you then typically print a report.

Reports

A **report** is an organized presentation, designed to be printed, of the information in your tables or queries. You can create a report from a single table or from a query of two or more tables. A report can also process data and can automatically calculate and show subtotals and totals. Finally, inserting graphic elements and using formatting techniques often improve the readability and attractiveness of reports.

To open the rptEmployees report:

| Step 1 | *Click* | Reports ▣ on the Objects bar in the database window |
| Step 2 | *Double-click* | rptEmployees |

Your screen should look similar to Figure 1-7.

**chapter
one**

FIGURE 1-7
rptEmployees Report

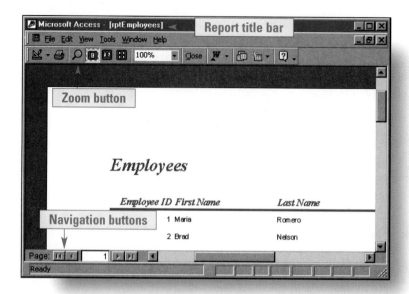

FIGURE 1-7
rptEmployees Report

Figure 1-7 identifies the parts of a report. The Database toolbar is now the Print Preview toolbar and contains tools used by Access reports. For example, the **Zoom** button allows you to magnify a particular area of the report. Notice the report is in Print Preview, which allows you to see what the report looks like when it is printed. This saves you time and paper, as you can determine what needs to be modified before you print.

After you look at the report, you need to close it.

To close the rptEmployees report:

Step 1	*Click*	the Close button ☒ on the report title bar

The final Access object you tour is the data access page.

internet

Data Access Pages

A **data access page (DAP)** allows you to extend the database by creating HyperText Markup Language (HTML) pages quickly and easily. HTML pages are written for use on an intranet or the Internet, and let you share information with others in any location.

Data access pages are stored as an HTML file, not a database file. This allows others who do not have Access installed on their computers to browse the information. A DAP can be mailed to your co-workers using **Outlook**, which is Microsoft's e-mail application. Access and Outlook are completely compatible, which is not always true with other e-mail applications.

DAPs are more than Internet packaging for Access; they are a new way to interact with Access data. People with whom you share your data can view, sort, and print the data, even if they do not have Access loaded on their computers.

You open the DAP created for *mdbImporters*.

To open a DAP:

Step 1	*Click*	Pages 🖼 on the Objects bar in the database window
Step 2	*Double-click*	dapEmployees
Step 3	*Switch*	to Design View

Note the Caution tip. If the DAP and database were still located in the same place they were originally stored, your screen would look similar to Figure 1-8. Because the DAP and database files were moved, you must click through a series of error messages until you can select the new file location. When you see a blank DAP, continue with Step 3 and direct Access to the new location for the database.

CAUTION TIP

Because of the way Access stores data access pages, you may see some error messages when you try to open a DAP. Click OK to respond to the message boxes until you see the Data Link Properties dialog box. In the select or enter a database name: text box, enter or select the location and name of the *mbdImporters* database.

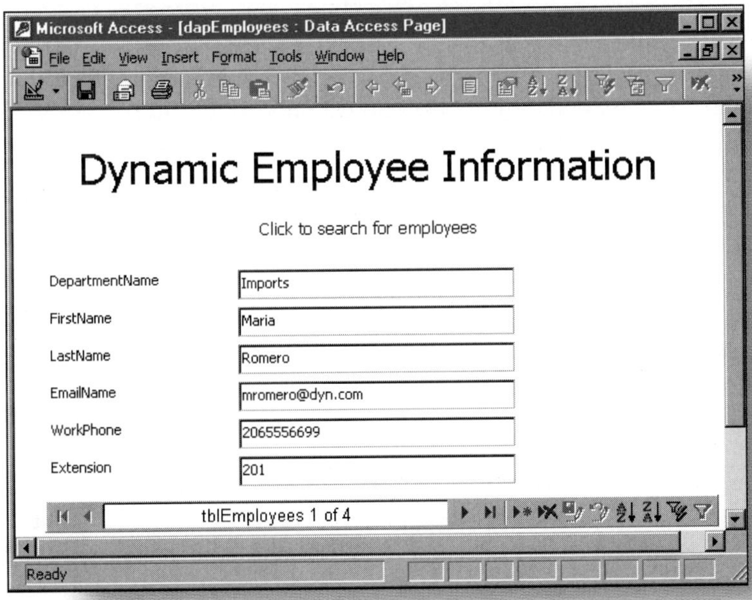

FIGURE 1-8
dapEmployees Data Access Page in Preview Mode

Figure 1-8 shows the components of a DAP. Notice that there are no tools available at this time. This is because you are in **Preview mode**, which lets you browse records but not enter information or make changes. The DAP's navigation bar allows you to view the records included in the DAP. To modify a DAP, first switch from Preview mode to Design view.

chapter
one

Your screen should look similar to Figure 1-9.

FIGURE 1-9
dapEmployees Data
Access Page in
Design View

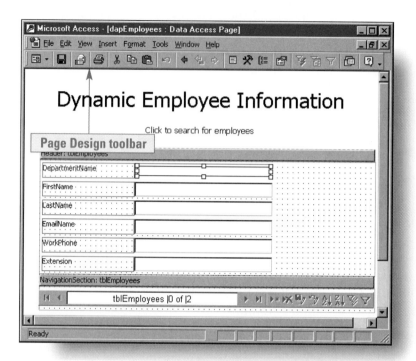

In Design view, you can create and edit a DAP using the Web Editing toolbar. The **Web Editing toolbar** includes tools for modifying the text, background, and placement of objects on the DAP. The **Page Design toolbar** allows you to add, delete, group, and sort the fields that you chose for your HTML file. Finally, the **Toolbox** has the tools you need to build the fields for the HTML page.

After you finish looking at the dapEmployees DAP, you should close it. To close the dapEmployees DAP:

Macros

An Access **macro** is a set of one or more actions that perform a particular operation, such as opening a form or printing a report. A **macro group** is a collection of related macros stored together under a single macro name.

Modules

Modules are programs written in the Visual Basic language. Office applications use Visual Basic (VB) 6. With Visual Basic you can program all aspects of your Access database, including your own tables, forms, reports, and queries. Although this is a challenge at first, modules can provide incredible functionality to your database. For example, you can use a module to check the accuracy of the typed information in your database, or to check for redundant data.

You are now familiar with the Access objects. Next, you exit the application.

1.f Exiting Access

Access automatically saves changes whenever you exit the application. However, if you made changes to the *design* of any database objects since you last saved them, Access asks if you want to save these changes before quitting. When saving your database, Access automatically compresses it, saving space on your hard drive and making it easier to transfer the file to other locations on your network.

To exit Access:

Step 1	*Click*	File
Step 2	*Click*	Exit

The Access application and the *mdbImporters* database close. Because you did not make any changes to the database, Access did not prompt you to save changes.

CAUTION TIP

If you turn off your computer without exiting Access, your database may become damaged. Always save your work and exit Access first.

chapter
one

Summary

▶ A database is a collection of related information. An example of a database is a list of customers and their contact information.

▶ Access includes many views. The most common are Design view and Datasheet view. Design view is where you create the look of the database. Datasheet view is where you view your data.

▶ The menus provide you with many useful tools and options in creating and viewing your database.

▶ Access uses objects such as tables, queries, forms, reports, and data access pages. These objects all relate to the data that is stored in the database.

▶ An Access table contains data in columns (fields) and rows (records) called a **datasheet**. A field in a database contains the same type of information, such as customers' phone numbers. A record in a database contains all of the fields for one item, such as for one customer.

▶ Use Access forms to enter, update, search, or review data in tables.

▶ An Access query allows you to ask questions about your data. A query shows you specific data with which you want to work.

▶ Create Access reports to share database information in printed form.

▶ A data access page (DAP) allows you to create an interactive HTML page using the information stored in your Access database. This tool allows you to share your database with others who may not have Access installed on their computers.

▶ Macros and modules are advanced Access features that allow you to customize the database and automate tasks that you perform on a regular basis.

▶ When you exit Access, your changes are automatically saved. You should always exit Access before turning off your computer.

Commands Review

Action	Menu Bar	Shortcut Menu	Toolbar	Keyboard
Open an existing database	File, Open			CTRL + O ALT + F, O
Open an object	View, Database Objects	Right-click object	Select object, click	ALT + V
Get help	Help, Microsoft Access Help			F1
Close an object	File, Close	Right-click object, click Close	on the object's title bar	ALT + F, C
Exit Access	File, Exit	Right-click the application button on the taskbar, click Close		ALT + F4 ALT + F, X

Concepts Review

Circle the correct answer.

1. A database is a:
 [a] tool for editing documents.
 [b] way to automate common tasks.
 [c] collection of related information.
 [d] link to the World Wide Web.

2. Access 2000 has special menus and toolbars that:
 [a] learn what you do.
 [b] are the same for all objects.
 [c] are exactly the same as the toolbars in other Office products.
 [d] never change.

3. In Datasheet view, you can:
 [a] design tables and forms.
 [b] view data in rows and columns.
 [c] preview your printed reports.
 [d] customize the Database toolbar.

4. Which of the following is not an Access database object?
 [a] table
 [b] form
 [c] query
 [d] datasheet

5. A category of information, such as last names or phone numbers, is called a:
 [a] field.
 [b] record.
 [c] form.
 [d] module.

6. Which record selector symbol points to the current record in a table?
 [a] drawing pen
 [b] asterisk
 [c] null symbol
 [d] triangle

chapter one

7. To enter, update, search, or review data quickly, use a:
[a] form.
[b] table.
[c] data access page.
[d] query.

8. You can switch between Design view and Datasheet view by clicking the:
[a] Queries object tab.
[b] Switch command on the <u>V</u>iew menu.
[c] View button, and then clicking a view option.
[d] select query title bar.

9. A data access page lets you:
[a] access a database.
[b] create a Web site using your database.
[c] write an HTML page.
[d] select a page to print.

10. Modules are:
[a] a selection of commands used to automate repetitive tasks.
[b] programs written in Visual Basic.
[c] object tabs.
[d] a group of records.

Circle **T** if the statement is true or **F** if the statement is false.

T   F   1. An example of a database is a list of customers and their addresses and phone numbers.

T   F   2. You can open more than one database file at a time in Access.

T   F   3. You cannot hide or change the Office Assistant.

T   F   4. Access automatically opens a blank database when you start the program.

T   F   5. Tables store information in rows of records and columns of fields.

T   F   6. Layout Preview shows a small portion of data in a report before printing.

T   F   7. You can use the magnifier to zoom a particular area in Design view.

T   F   8. You can use a query to ask for help from the Office Assistant.

T   F   9. A macro forces you to perform one task at a time.

T   F   10. If you create a data access page, you can share your database with others, even if they don't use Access 2000.

Skills Review

Exercise 1

1. Start Access and open the *mdbImporters* database.

2. Change the Office Assistant.

3. Save and close the database.

Exercise 2

1. If necessary, open the *mdbImporters* database.

2. Open the tblEmployees table.

3. Move to the last record in the table.

4. Scroll to see all the fields in the record, including the last field.

5. Close the table.

Exercise 3

1. If necessary, open the *mdbImporters* database.

2. Open the frmEmployees form.

3. Click the first field—EmployeeID—and then press the TAB key to move to the next field.

4. Press the TAB key until you select the Address field.

5. Close the form.

Exercise 4

1. If necessary, open the *mdbImporters* database.

2. Open qryEmployees in Design view.

3. In the design grid, review the criteria for this query: the fields and tables used, sort order, and whether to show the field in the query results.

4. Switch to Datasheet view to see the query results.

Exercise 5

1. If necessary, open the *mdbImporters* database.

2. If necessary, open qryEmployees and switch to Design view.

3. Sort the list in ascending order by the first name of the employee.

4. Switch to Datasheet view to see the query results.

5. Close the Query window and do not save changes.

chapter one

Exercise 6

1. If necessary, open the *mdbImporters* database.

2. Open the rptEmployees report.

3. Preview the report.

4. Click the Print button in the Print Preview toolbar to print the report.

5. Close the report.

Exercise 7

1. If necessary, open the *mdbImporters* database.

2. Open the dapEmployees data access page.

3. Scroll to see all the employee records.

4. Close the DAP window and open dapEmployees in Design view.

5. Close the data access page without saving changes.

Exercise 8

1. If necessary, open the *mdbImporters* database.

2. Open any database object, such as a table, form, or report.

3. Get help on any part or feature of Access.

4. Close the object, and then exit Access.

Case Projects

Project 1

Your supervisor at Dynamic, Inc., asks you to write an introduction to Access databases, using *mdbImporters* as an example. People recently hired by Dynamic plan to use your introduction to learn the basics about Access databases. In a Word document, write two to three paragraphs defining terms every Access user should know. Explain the purpose of and provide an example for each term. Save and print the document.

Project 2

Create a new document for the Dynamic Employee Handbook that contains one to two paragraphs about getting help while working in Access, including using the online Help, the F1 key, and the SHIFT + F1 context-sensitive Help pointer. Use Word to create, save, and print the document.

Project 3

To increase efficiency, your supervisor at Dynamic asks you to create a chart of Microsoft Office shortcuts. Working with a coworker, use the Office Assistant to review the shortcut keys every Office application uses. In Word, create a table showing each shortcut command and the action it performs. Save and print the document.

Project 4

Dynamic is organizing a meeting for people new to Access. Your supervisor asks you to present solutions to common questions people have about Access and its features. Connect to the Internet and, using the Microsoft on the Web command on the Access Help menu, link to the Frequently Asked Questions page and research questions about Access and its features. Print at least two Web pages.

Project 5

You decide to create a notebook for your department that outlines the features of Access. Create a new document for your notebook that identifies one Access toolbar and lists the name and purpose of each button on the toolbar. (*Hint:* Use the What's This? command on the Help menu to get online Help for the buttons.) Use Word to create, save, and print the document.

Project 6

You decide to include information about the Access views in your Access notebook. Write two paragraphs explaining the purpose and features of two views. Use Word to create, save, and print the document.

Project 7

Your supervisor at Dynamic asks you to show several new employees how to open a database. Using the tools on the Help menu, research how to do this. In Word, create a new document with one to two short paragraphs describing how to open an existing database in Access. Save and print the document. Then demonstrate to your coworkers how to open a database in Access.

Project 8

Connect to your ISP and load the home page for a search engine. Search for companies on the Web who are similar to Dynamic, Inc. Print at least three Web pages for similar companies. Close the browser and disconnect from your ISP.

chapter one

Designing and Creating a Database

Chapter Overview

In this chapter, you plan a database for Dynamic, Inc. by learning and applying principles of effective database design. You then create the database by adding tables. You also learn how to modify a database table by changing field layouts, deleting field names, and rearranging fields. Finally, you print a database table.

LEARNING OBJECTIVES

- ▶ Plan a new database
- ▶ Create a database
- ▶ Save a database
- ▶ Create a table by using the Table Wizard
- ▶ Create a table in Design view
- ▶ Modify tables using Design view
- ▶ Print a table

Case profile

The owner of Dynamic Inc., Maria Moreno, asks you to design and create an Access 2000 database that tracks products and orders for the company as well as maintains current employee information.

chapter
two

2.a   Planning a New Database

Before you create a database, take some time to plan it. A good database design is the most important step in creating a database that does what you want it to do. When planning a database, follow the general steps listed below.

Determining Appropriate Data Inputs and Outputs for your Database

Start by describing the inputs and outputs of your database, that is, the data that will be entered into it and the information that it will provide. Talk to the people who will use your database and find out what they expect from the database. What are the subjects your database covers? These subjects become tables. What facts do you store about each subject? These facts become fields in the tables.

To determine the purpose of the Dynamic database, you talk with department managers to determine the kind of information they want to include and how they and their staff want to work with the database.

Once you determine what your database will include and how it will be used, your next step is to list the tables you need.

Changing Table Structures

List the subjects or types of information your database will cover, such as customer, product, and employee information. You'll store each type of information in a table. Be sure each table is dedicated to only one subject and that you don't duplicate information within a table or between tables.

Deciding What Tables Are Necessary

If you store each type of information in a separate table, you only have to go to one place to add or update the information. You also avoid duplicating records and entering the same information more than once. For example, store customer information in one table and the customer orders in another table. This way, if a customer changes an order, you modify only the order information, not the customer information.

Maria asks you to include three types of information for the Dynamic database: product, order, and employee information. Though Dynamic has hundreds of products, ranging from clothing to gifts, they fit into only a few categories. It simplifies data entry and tracking to also maintain information about product categories. For the Dynamic database, you need four tables: one listing employee information (tblEmployees), one containing product categories (tblCategories), one tracking products in each category (tblProducts), and one tracking customer orders (tblOrders).

chapter
two

After you determine the tables you need, your next step is to decide which fields to include in each table.

Determining Essential Fields

Each table contains facts about the same subject; each field in a table contains specific facts about that subject. When determining the fields for each table, keep the following four principles in mind: (1) relate each field to the subject of the table, (2) omit any calculated data, (3) include all of the information you need, and (4) store information in small bits (e.g., "last name" and "first name").

For the tblEmployees table, Maria asks you to include the following information about each employee: their ID number, first and last name, address, including city and state, and home phone number.

After planning and consideration, you determine the necessary fields for the four tables, as shown in Table 2-1.

TABLE 2-1
Planned Dynamic Database
Tables and Fields

Required Tables	Necessary Fields
Employees	Employee ID, Department ID, Last Name, First Name, Address, City, State, Postal Code, Home Phone
Categories	Category ID, Category Name
Products	Product ID, Product Name, Product Description, Per Unit Cost
Customer Orders	Order ID, Customer ID, Order Date, Name, Address, City, State, Phone Number, Shipping Date

After you plan and review your database, you can begin to create it. You can create one by starting with a blank database or using a wizard.

2.b Creating a Database

The **Database Wizard** guides you step-by-step through the process of creating a database. Access includes a number of sample databases, such as those for contact, order, or personal information. If you create a database of similar information, you can use the wizard to choose a sample database. Access then creates all the necessary tables and fields (as well as forms and reports) for that type of database. You can change the information to suit your needs. The Database Wizard saves you time when creating common types of databases.

If the database you want to create is not similar to one of the sample databases, you can start with a blank database. You have more flexibility when you start with a blank database.

To learn all the steps of creating a database, you start with a blank one. You use a wizard later in this chapter when creating tables.

To open the Access application and the Access dialog box:

Step 1	*Click*	the Start button [Start] on the taskbar
Step 2	*Point*	to Programs
Step 3	*Click*	Microsoft Access
Step 4	*Click*	the Blank Access database option button

Your screen should look similar to Figure 2-1.

FIGURE 2-1
New Database Dialog Box

QUICK TIP

If you are already working in Access, you can create a new database by clicking the New button on the Standard toolbar, and then double-clicking the Blank Database icon from the General tab in the New dialog box.

Step 5	*Click*	OK

Now save the database you just created.

2.c Saving a Database

Whenever you create a new database file, Access requires you to name and save the file before continuing. Access gives your database a temporary name, such as "db1," which you see in the File name: text box. Accept or switch to the location where you want to store your file (a floppy disk or a folder on your hard disk or network server), and then type the filename you want to use. A filename can have up to 255 characters including the disk drive reference and path, and can contain letters, numbers, spaces, and some special characters in any combination.

chapter
two

CAUTION TIP

Filenames cannot include the following special characters: the forward slash (/), the backward slash (\), the colon (:), the semicolon (;), the pipe symbol (|), the question mark (?), the less than symbol (<), the greater than symbol (>), the asterisk (*), the quotation mark ("), and the period (.).

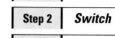

Be sure to check with your instructor if you do not know which disk drive and folder to use to save your documents.

To save the database:

Step 1	*Click*	the Save in: list arrow
Step 2	*Switch*	to the appropriate disk drive and folder
Step 3	*Key*	*mdbDynamicInc2* in the File name: text box
Step 4	*Click*	Create

The *mdbDynamicInc2* database window opens. Your screen should look similar to Figure 2-2.

FIGURE 2-2
mdbDynamicInc2
Database Window

You are ready to create the first table.

QUICK TIP

 Once you create and save a database, you should also take advantage of the Create Replica menu command, which you can use to quickly back up your database. Click the Tools menu, point to Replication, and then click Create Replica. You can then use the backup copy to restore data that may get lost, for example, due to a power surge.

2.d Creating a Table by Using the Table Wizard

Access provides three options for creating tables: You can open a blank empty table and then enter the data, use the Table Wizard, or create one in Design view. The **Table Wizard** allows you to create a table by choosing from a list of commonly used table templates. For your database, you create tables using both the Table Wizard and Design view.

You create your first table, the tblEmployees table, using the Table Wizard, because it is similar to one of the wizard's templates.

To create the tblEmployees table using the wizard:

Step 1	***Double-click*** the Create table by using wizard option

Your screen should look similar to Figure 2-3.

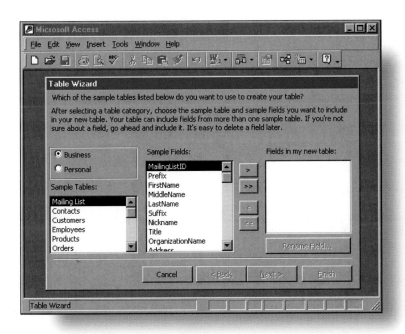

FIGURE 2-3
Table Wizard

Step 2	***Click***	Employees in the Sample Tables: list

Access displays the selected table templates fields in the Sample Fields: list.

Step 3	***Click***	LastName

QUICK TIP

The Table Wizard includes two separate lists of table templates; the default is the Business list. To view the Personal list, click the Personal option button above the Sample Tables: list.

chapter
two

> **QUICK TIP**
>
> To move the entire contents of the selected Sample Table to your table, click the >> button.
>
> If you see a field similar to one you want but it has a different name, add it to your list. Then select the field in your database field list, click the Rename Field button, type a new name in the Rename field: text box, and then click OK.

Step 4	***Click***	the > button to move the selected field to the Fields in my new table: list

Refer to Table 2-1 for the fields you need in your tblEmployees table.

Step 5	***Repeat***	Steps 3 and 4 until you choose all of the field names you need to include in the tblEmployees table (rename the State or Province field to State and any other field name as necessary)
Step 6	***Click***	Next >

Access asks you to name the table. The default name is Employees. You also want to use tblEmployees. Access also asks if you want a primary key. A **primary key** is the designated field that uniquely identifies the record (you learn more about the primary key later in this chapter). For now, choose Yes, which is already selected as the default. You are ready to continue.

Step 7	***Key***	tblEmployees in the What do you want to name your table? field
Step 8	***Click***	Next >

Access now asks if you want to enter data into the table. To keep it simple, have Access design a form for you.

Step 9	***Click***	the Enter data into the table using a form the wizard creates for me option button
Step 10	***Click***	Finish

Your screen should look similar to Figure 2-4.

FIGURE 2-4
tblEmployees Form

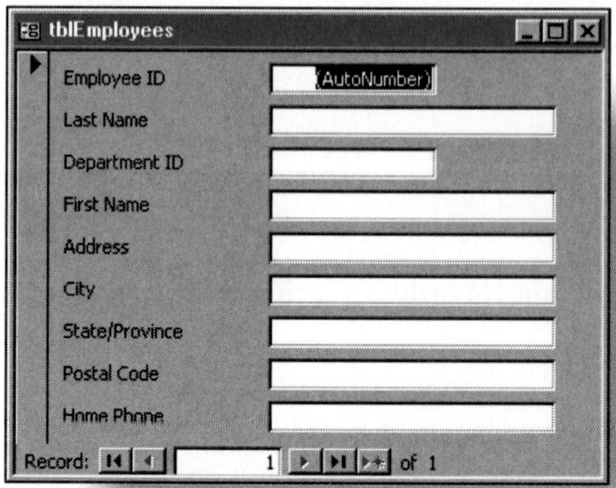

Access displays the form it created for the tblEmployees table. Because you want to create the other database tables before entering records, close the form now.

| Step 11 | *Click* | the Close button  on the tblEmployees form title bar |

A dialog box opens and asks if you would like to save the changes to the form.

Step 12	*Click*	Yes
Step 13	*Key*	frmEmployees in the Form Name: text box in the Save As dialog box
Step 14	*Click*	OK

If you click Forms on the Objects bar, you now see that the frmEmployees form is included in the list of forms for this database.

Using the Table Wizard allows you to quickly create tables of common information. For unique or very simple tables, however, such as the tblProduct Categories table in the *mdbDynamicInc2* database, use Design view.

2.e Creating a Table in Design View

Design view gives you complete control over the contents of your tables. You add fields and assign a data type to each. A **data type** determines what kind of information each field can contain, such as a number or a date, and helps guide you when entering data. You can then set properties for each field—the characteristics of a field, such as the number of characters it can contain or whether the field is required. You can also set a primary key to use when sorting records. For example, if you make the Last Name field the primary key, Access sorts the table alphabetically according to last name. Finally, you can customize the design of your table, such as changing the column widths so you can see necessary information.

Using Multiple Data Types

As mentioned above, you select a data type for each field to determine the kind of information the field contains. For example, if

C

chapter
two

you select Currency as the data type, Access formats that field to include a dollar sign and a decimal point. Most databases contain multiple data types; the more specific you are when selecting a data type for a field, the more likely your database will include the correct inputs. You can select the following data types.

Text

Use the **Text data type,** the default in Access, to enter the following in a field: text; numbers that do not require any calculations, such as phone numbers or zip codes; or a combination of text, numbers, and symbols. A text field can contain up to 255 characters per record.

Memo

Use the **Memo data type** to enter lengthy text or combinations of text and numbers or symbols. Memo fields can contain up to 65,535 characters per record. You can also use returns or tabs within a memo data type.

Number

Use the **Number data type** to include simple numbers, such as those that identify a record, and numeric data in mathematical calculations. By entering a simple formula, the calculations become part of the data. Do not use this data type for phone numbers, Social Security numbers, and so forth that are not used in calculations; instead, use the text data type.

Date/Time

Use the **Date/Time data type** to include the date and time values for the year 100 through the year 9999. The date and time data type is useful for calendar or clock data. It also lets you calculate seconds, minutes, hours, days, months, and years. For example, use a date/time field to find the difference between two dates.

Currency

Use the **Currency data type** to insert the currency symbol and calculate numeric data with one to four decimal places. This data is accurate to 15 digits on the left of the decimal point and up to 4 digits on the right of the decimal point. Currency has the accuracy of integers, but with a fixed number of decimal places.

AutoNumber

The **AutoNumber data type** is a unique number Access automatically inserts each time you add a new record to a table. These numbers follow a consecutive number sequence, such as 1, 2, 3, and so on. You cannot change or update an AutoNumber field. Access uses the AutoNumber

---

QUICK TIP

C You can further optimize data type usage by specifying what type of number should be entered. For example, for the Category ID field, enter an integer (int).

data type to generate the primary key value. You can only include one field using the AutoNumber data type in a table.

Yes/No

The **Yes/No data type** can contain only information that uses one of three values: Yes/No, True/False, On/Off. Use a yes/no data type, for example, to flag accounts paid or unpaid, active or inactive, or orders filled or not filled.

OLE Object

The **OLE Object data type** contains an object (Excel spreadsheet, Word document, or graphic image) that is linked or embedded into an Access table. A linked object is one where the source is not a part of the Access database. An embedded object is placed in the database as part of the data.

Hyperlink

The **Hyperlink data type** stores a path and filename to a Web page URL on your computer, another computer, or a Web address. This provides a link to a customer's home page, or to a file on the Intranet that will provide additional information about a product or service. When you enter or select the hyperlink, you "jump" to the associated location.

Lookup Wizard

Use the **Lookup Wizard data type** to choose a value from another table or from a list of values by using a list box or combo box. This is a useful tool for an order form—you can then select a product from a list, or type the first few letters of the product and insert the complete name in the field. When you select the Lookup Wizard data type, you start the Lookup Wizard, which guides you through the steps of creating the list or combo box.

Now that you are familiar with the data types, you can begin to create your second table.

To create tblCategories in the *mdbDynamicInc2* database:

Step 1	*Click*	Tables 🔲 on the Objects bar in the database window
Step 2	*Double-click*	Create table in Design view

Your screen should look similar to Figure 2-5.

QUICK TIP

 To create a Lookup Field, choose Lookup Wizard from the Data Type drop-down list. Use the Lookup Wizard to create a lookup column which displays a list of values you can choose from. Once you create Lookup Fields, you can also modify them in Design view by changing their properties.

C

chapter
two

FIGURE 2-5
New Table in Design View

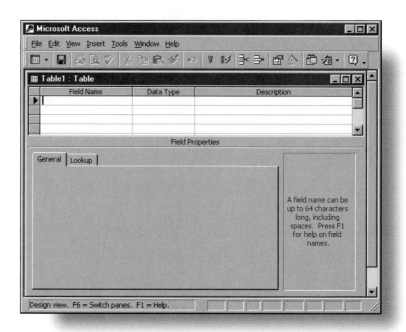

You are now ready to add fields to your table.

Using Design View to Add Fields

The Design View window contains two panes, field name at the top and field properties at the bottom. You add field names and data type information in the top pane and then set individual field properties in the bottom pane (you learn about field properties later in this chapter). The Help box in the lower-right corner of the window displays help text for the column where your insertion point is located.

You are now ready to add fields to your new table. You can move the insertion point from column to column in the top pane using the TAB key or arrow keys.

To begin adding fields to the table:

Step 1	*Verify*	the insertion point is in the top field name box in the Field Name column
Step 2	*Key*	Category ID
Step 3	*Press*	the TAB key to move the insertion point to the Data Type column

The Text data type (the default) appears in the Data Type column. You can select a different data type from a list box by clicking the Data Type list arrow. Because the Category ID field will contain simple numbers to identify each record, change the data type to Number.

| Step 4 | *Click* | the list arrow |

The contents of the Help box now define the term "data type."

| Step 5 | *Click* | Number |
| Step 6 | *Repeat* | Steps 1–3 to key in the second field name of Category Name with data type Text |

This completes the field names for the tblCategories table; your screen should look similar to Figure 2-6.

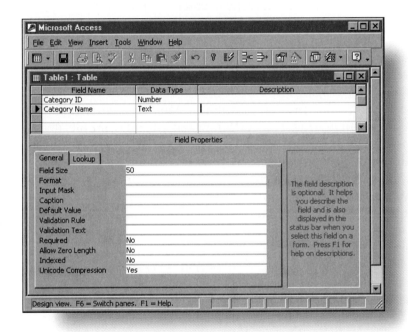

FIGURE 2-6
Table in Design View

You created a simple table in Design view using the field name pane to enter fields. If you need to change the information, you can also do so in Design view. For example, you can change the properties of the Category ID field so it only contains certain kinds of information.

Modifying Field Properties

Field properties are characteristics of a field, such as their length or format. Selecting properties for your fields ensures the information in your records is consistent—every state field, for example, contains two uppercase characters. The General tab in Design view groups the

QUICK TIP

C Setting validation rules helps to ensure that your database contains correct information. You can set, for example, validation text for a field containing state names, so that users can only enter (and edit) accepted two-letter abbreviations, such as GA for Georgia.

QUICK TIP

C Define data validation criteria when creating a database table. For example, you can set the criteria for seven digits to be entered for the Phone Number field. You can then set validation text that indicates how to correct the mistake. For example, if someone entered only six digits for a phone number, you could display an error message that reads "A phone number must contain seven digits."

field properties you can modify when you enter a new field in a table, as follows:

The **Field Size property** indicates the maximum number of characters someone can enter in this field. Although the default size is 50 characters, a Text field can have a maximum number of 255 characters.

The **Format property** indicates how you want the information to appear. For example, if a field should contain all uppercase text, as in a state abbreviation, choose All Uppercase for this field property.

The **Decimal Places** property indicates the number of digits to the right of the decimal separator.

The **Input Mask property** defines a standard pattern for the appearance of all data entered in this field. For example, if the field is a Social Security number, you can have Access insert the hyphens in the correct places (e.g., 123-45-6789), which makes it easier to enter accurate data.

The **Caption property** appears as the column header in the table and overrides the field name you entered in the field name pane. For example, if you enter the caption "Category Number," the caption appears on the table, form, or report instead of the field name Category ID.

The **Default Value property** is information Access automatically enters in the field when you add a new record. For example, if you almost always enter "50" in the Price field, you could enter "50" as the Default Value property. Access then inserts 50 in the Price field of every new record. You can enter a value other than 50 if necessary.

A **Validation Rule** is an expression that limits what information you can enter into a field. An **expression** is a set of specific instructions. Access only accepts information that fulfills the expression requirements. For example, if a salary cannot be greater than $50.00 per hour, Access will not allow you to key $60.00. The **Validation Text property** is the error message you display when an entry breaks the validation rule.

The **Required property** indicates whether you must complete the field for all records. If the field is required, change this property to Yes; Access does not save the record until information is entered in this field.

In contrast to the Required property, the **Allow Zero Length property**, when set to Yes, tells Access that it is acceptable if no value is entered in this field. You can use this option in only Text, Memo, or Hyperlink data types.

The **Indexed property** creates an index for the primary key. For example, if you search for a specific product category in the table you are creating, you can create an index to speed up sorting and searching. Keep in mind, however, if a table contains several indexes, it may slow data entry.

The **Unicode Compression property** tells Access to compress the Unicode file format, which lets you code data so it can be used in the world's major languages. A Unicode file format makes it easier for multinational organizations to share documents, because it prevents font compatibility issues.

Review the current properties of the Category ID field: the default size is Long Integer, the Required property box indicates that the field can remain blank, and the Indexed property box indicates duplicate Category ID numbers can exist in the table.

You can modify these properties to prevent data entry errors and to maintain consistency among records. Change the field size to two characters, make it a required field so all records have a Category ID, and make sure no other records have the same ID. These changes create **data integrity**, which is a set of rules to ensure the information in your database is accurate.

To change the field properties, move the insertion point into the field properties pane by clicking in the pane. You can also move from one pane to another by pressing the F6 key. To move from one property box to another, press the UP ARROW, DOWN ARROW, TAB, or SHIFT + TAB keys. As you move the insertion point to a different property box, the Help box displays text for the property.

To modify the Category ID field properties:

| Step 1 | *Click* | in the Category ID field |
| Step 2 | *Press* | the F6 key to move the insertion point to the field properties pane |

The Field Size property box is selected. Notice the new help text in the Help box.

Step 3	*Click*	the Field Size list arrow
Step 4	*Select*	Double from the drop-down list
Step 5	*Move*	the insertion point to the Required property box
Step 6	*Click*	the Required list arrow
Step 7	*Click*	Yes
Step 8	*Move*	the insertion point to the Indexed property box
Step 9	*Click*	the Indexed property box list arrow
Step 10	*Click*	Yes (No Duplicates)

You changed the field properties for the Category ID field. You can also include a description for this field.

To add a description:

| Step 1 | *Move* | the insertion point to the Description box |

chapter
two

The text in the Help box now defines a field description. The **field description** is optional information for a text field. Field descriptions appear on the status bar when you select the field to enter data in a form or table.

Step 2	*Key*	Enter the number of the product category
Step 3	*Repeat*	Steps 1 and 2 to include the field description "Enter the name of the product category" in the Description box for the Category Name field

Once you enter all the fields in a table, you can set a primary key.

Setting Primary Keys

Recall that a primary key is a field you designate to uniquely identify a record. Primary keys prevent the duplication of an entry in that field. When you open a table that has a primary key field, records are sorted by that field in ascending order. **Ascending order** lists the data from A–Z or from 1–100. **Descending order** lists the data from Z–A or from 100–1.

Every table must have at least one field that is used as the primary key. Select the field you want to use as the primary key—it should be one with no duplicates, such as the Category ID field.

To select a field as a primary key:

Step 1	*Click*	in the Category ID field
Step 2	*Right-click*	to open the shortcut menu
Step 3	*Click*	Primary Key

Your screen should look similar to Figure 2-7.

FIGURE 2-7
Table1 Primary Key

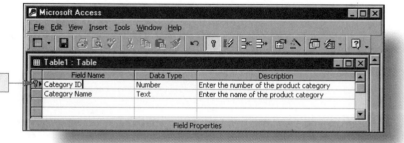

After you complete the table, you should close it.

Step 4	*Click*	the Close button ☒ on the table title bar

Access asks if you want to save the table.

Step 5	*Click*	<u>Y</u>es
Step 6	*Key*	tblCategories
Step 7	*Click*	OK

Your table is now closed and saved.

You create the tblProducts table and the tblOrders table in the Skills Review exercises at the end of the chapter.

To open tblCategories in Datasheet view:

Step 1	*Double-click*	tblCategories

Looking at the table, you notice you need to add more space for the fields. You can allow for more space by increasing the column width.

Changing Column Widths

Access uses the same column width for every field you enter in a table. But often, as in the tblCategories table, one or more columns are too narrow to display the entire field name. This text is not lost, just hidden. If you widen the column, you can see the full field name.

To change column width:

Step 1	*Point to*	the right edge of the Category Name in the field labels row, so that the mouse pointer changes to a double-headed arrow

This allows you to adjust the width of the column in the table.

Step 2	*Drag*	the mouse pointer to the right until you can see the entire field label, Category Name
Step 3	*Repeat*	Steps 1 and 2 to increase the width of the other column if necessary so that you can read all the field labels

chapter
two

Your screen should now look similar to Figure 2-8.

FIGURE 2-8
tblCategories with
Adjusted Column Widths

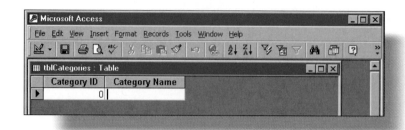

| Step 4 | *Click* | the Close button ⊠ on the table title bar |

You are now prompted to save your changes.

| Step 5 | *Click* | Yes |

You have created two tables for your database. You should review your work to see if you need to make any modifications.

2.f Modifying Tables Using Design View

Once you create a table, you should carefully review it to ensure you designed it accurately. If you need to make changes, modifying a table (using Design view) is easy as long as you haven't entered any data yet. Once you start entering data, modifying a table design becomes increasingly more difficult.

When you review your tables and fields for *mdbDynamicInc2's* database, you notice you need a field for employees' Social Security numbers. This is important data as employees cannot be paid without it. You add this field to the tblEmployees table now.

Adding Fields

Even after you save a table, you can still enter new fields anywhere in the table by inserting a row where you want the field.

QUICK TIP

C After you enter data and use a database, you may need to use the Compact and Repair tool. This tool makes the most efficient use of disk space by compacting the data in your database and reducing the file size. You can also use this tool to repair errors in your database, such as data appearing in the wrong field.

To add the Social Security field:

Step 1	*Open*	the tblEmployees table

When you open the table, you see it in Datasheet view. Switch to Design view to modify the table.

Step 2	*Switch*	to Design view
Step 3	*Click*	in the first blank row in the Field Name column
Step 4	*Key*	SS Number
Step 5	*Press*	the TAB key to move to the Data Type column

You do not need to change the default Text data type, but because all Social Security numbers follow the same pattern (000-00-0000), you choose the Input Mask property for this field. To set the Input Mask property, you use the Input Mask Wizard.

Using the Input Mask Wizard

Recall that the Input Mask field property sets the display format and limits the type of data that can be entered, making data entry faster and more precise. The **Input Mask Wizard** guides you through the tasks of creating an input mask.
To use the Input Mask Wizard:

Step 1	*Click*	in the Input Mask field property box

You should now see an ellipsis icon at the right side of the box.

Step 2	*Click*	the ellipsis icon

Access reminds you to save your table and then starts the Input Mask Wizard. Your screen should look similar to Figure 2-9.

chapter
two

FIGURE 2-9

Input Mask Wizard

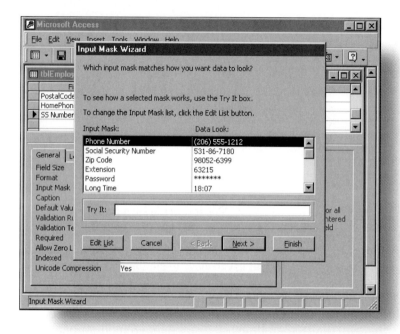

Step 3	*Click*	Social Security Number
Step 4	*Click*	Next >

Access shows you the input mask for Social Security numbers and asks what placeholder you want to use. For a Social Security number, you want to use a hyphen (-) to separate the numbers.

Step 5	*Click*	in the Placeholder character: field and select the _ placeholder option from the menu
Step 6	*Click*	in the Try It: box to make sure this is the option you want
Step 7	*Click*	Next >

Access asks how you want to store the data. You can store the data with or without the hyphens.

Step 8	*Click*	the With the symbols in the mask, like this: option
Step 9	*Click*	Finish
Step 10	*Switch*	to Datasheet view to review your changes (Access lets you save your changes before switching)

Reviewing the table, you realize you don't need the Department ID field. You delete it from the tblEmployees table.

Deleting Fields

Though it's easy to delete a field, be careful before you do so. If you delete the field and any information stored in it, you cannot reverse your action with the Undo command.

To delete the Department ID field:

| Step 1 | *Switch* | to Design view |
| Step 2 | *Click* | the box to the left of the Department ID row |

This highlights the entire row. Your screen should look similar to Figure 2-10.

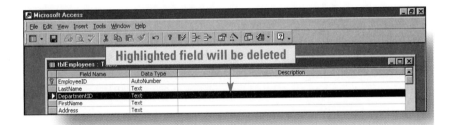

| Step 3 | *Click* | Edit |
| Step 4 | *Click* | Delete |

You see a warning explaining that you are about to delete the field and all of its indexes and a question asking if you want to proceed.

| Step 5 | *Click* | Yes |

The field is deleted.

Looking at the tblEmployees table, you notice that the fields are not in a user-friendly order. You can rearrange the fields to make data entry more efficient.

FIGURE 2-10
Deleting a Field

chapter
two

Rearranging Fields

After you add fields, you can rearrange them so they appear in a logical order. For the tblEmployees table, it might make sense to move the LastName field after the FirstName field.

To rearrange a field:

Step 1	*Verify*	that tblEmployees is open in Design view
Step 2	*Click*	in the box to the left of the row that contains the LastName field information
Step 3	*Click*	and drag the LastName field after the FirstName field

After you finish modifying the tblEmployees table, you can print it.

2.g Printing a Table

A printed copy of a table, with or without data, can be useful. For example, you can print a copy of a table to check its structure and field order before entering data, or you can verify data in a table.

Maria wants to see the fields you created for the tblEmployees table. You print a copy for her.

To print the tblEmployees table:

Step 1	*Switch*	to Datasheet view

Access reminds you to save the table first.

Step 2	*Click*	Yes

Step 3	*Click*	the Print Preview button  on the Table Datasheet toolbar

You see a preview of the datasheet on your screen. The mouse pointer appears as a magnifying glass. You can use the magnifying glass to zoom in to see the data.

| Step 4 | *Move* | the zoom pointer over the data and click to enlarge your view |

You are satisfied with how the table appears. You are ready to print.

| Step 5 | *Click* | the Print button 🖨 on the Print Preview toolbar |

After the table prints, close the table.

| Step 6 | *Close* | the tblEmployees table |

Save your changes.

| Step 7 | *Exit* | Access |

The *mdbDynamicInc2* database now contains two tables: the tblEmployees table and the tblCategories table. It also contains one form: frmEmployees form.

MENU TIP

You can print by selecting the Print command from the File menu. You then see the Print dialog box, which offers a variety of print options, such as number of copies.

chapter
two

Summary

▶ When designing a database, determine the fields you need to include in a table, what type of information appears in each field, and how to arrange the fields in each record.

▶ Access offers field data types to help make tables unique and descriptive.

▶ Each field in a table has properties such as the field size or format. You can control data entry by choosing appropriate properties for each field. For example, you can require that fields contain data, and that the data is unique to that record.

▶ You create table fields and modify properties in Design view. Enter data in a table in Datasheet view.

▶ Set a primary key in a table that Access can use to identify each unique record.

▶ Select and size columns in Datasheet view to view all of your data without wasting screen space.

▶ After you create a table and enter data, you can still modify the table by adding new fields or changing the name of existing fields.

Commands Review

Action	Menu Bar	Shortcut Menu	Toolbar	Keyboard
Create a new table	File, New		or	ALT + F, N CTRL + N
Open a table	File, Open	Right-click table name, click Open		ALT + F, O
Switch between panes in Design view			Click in the pane	F6
Select a field property			Click in the field properties pane	UP or DOWN ARROW, TAB or SHIFT + TAB
Set a primary key	Edit, Primary Key	Right-click field, click Primary Key		ALT + E, K
Resize columns in a table	Format, Column Width	Right-click column	Drag column boundary	ALT + O ALT + F, M
Delete a field	Edit, Delete	Right-click a field, click Delete Rows		DELETE
Close and save a table				
Print a table	File, Print	Right-click a table, click Print		ALT + F, P CTRL + P

Concepts Review

Circle the correct answer.

1. Which of the following is not a data type?
[a] text
[b] currency
[c] date/time
[d] HTML

2. To move the insertion point in Design view, you can press the:
[a] TAB key.
[b] F1 key.
[c] BACKSPACE key.
[d] SHIFT + ESCAPE keys.

3. You can change a field's properties in:
[a] Datasheet View.
[b] the table pane.
[c] the query pane.
[d] Design View.

4. Which key can you press in Design view to get online Help for a field property?
[a] F6
[b] SHIFT + F6
[c] F1
[d] ENTER

5. The Input Mask field property controls the:
[a] number of characters in a field.
[b] default value of a field.
[c] label for a field that you see on a report.
[d] pattern for how data appears in a field.

6. You can delete a field:
[a] in Design view.
[b] by dragging it out of Datasheet view.
[c] by highlighting the field text and pressing the DELETE key.
[d] only after creating a new table.

7. Printed tables allow you to:
[a] check your responses to the Table Wizard.
[b] see the fields and the information they contain.
[c] preview how a report will look.
[d] list the field data types.

8. The first step in designing your database is determining the:
[a] data type for each field.
[b] purpose of the database.
[c] field properties you will use.
[d] fields you need.

9. A database wizard is a:
[a] magician who does your work for you.
[b] tool that guides you through the steps of creating a database.
[c] way to modify the tables in a database after you have entered data.
[d] shortcut for saving data.

10. A primary key:
[a] defines a special table in the database.
[b] is the default value of a field.
[c] is always chosen for you.
[d] uniquely defines a record.

Circle **T** if the statement is true or **F** if the statement is false.

T F   1. An employee identification number must be a Number field.

T F   2. After entering field names and modifying properties, you should set a primary key for a table.

T F   3. The default size for a Text field is 30 characters.

T F   4. You cannot change the position of a field in a table once you have saved the table.

T F   5. If a field's Required property is set to "Yes," you can skip that field when entering data.

T F   6. The Counter data type automatically displays a unique identifying number for a record.

T F   7. You must use a Number field for integers or decimal numbers that can be values in calculations.

T F   8. You cannot add a new field to a table once it has been saved.

T F   9. You can change the appearance of a table after you create one.

T F   10. A table is the framework for storing data in a database.

Skills Review

Exercise 1

1. Open the *mdbDynamicInc2* database created in this chapter.

2. Use the Table Wizard to create a new table based on the Orders sample table.

3. Add the following nine fields to the new table: OrderID, CustomerID, OrderDate, ShipName, ShipAddress, ShipCity, ShipState Or Province, Phone Number, Shipping Date, renaming fields as necessary.

4. Name the new table *tblOrders* and let Access set the primary key.

5. When the Table Wizard asks which other tables in the database are related to the one you are creating, simply click Next to allow the automatic relationships to be created.

6. Let Access design a form for entering data into the tblOrders table.

7. Close and save the form as frmOrders for the tblOrders table.

Exercise 2 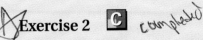 completed

1. If necessary, open the *mdbDynamicInc2* database.

2. Create a new table in Design view.

3. Add the following fields to the table: Product ID, Product Name, Product Description, and Per Unit Cost.

4. Assign the appropriate data type to each field: Product ID (number), Product Name (text), Product Description (text), and Per Unit Cost (number).

5. Set the Product ID field as the primary key.

6. Close the table and save it with the name tblProducts.

Exercise 3 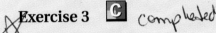 completed

1. If necessary, open the *mdbDynamicInc2* database.

2. Use the Table Wizard to create a new table based on the Contacts sample table.

3. From the list of Contacts sample fields, use only those for Contact ID, First and Last Name, Address, and City. Rename the ContactID field to ClientID.

4. Save the table as tblClients.

5. Set ClientID as the primary key. Choose the option of allowing Access to automatically assign consecutive numbers to new records for the type of data you want the primary key field to contain.

6. Allow the relationships to be automatically created by the wizard.

7. Enter the data directly into the table.

8. In Datasheet view, enter the following information in the appropriate fields:
   Antonio Fuentes, Mataderos 2312, Mexico D.F.
   Thomas Tolliver, 120 Hanover Square, London
   Rene Phillipe, 2743 Toulouse Street, Montreal

9. Print the new tblClients table.

10. Save and close the tblClients table.

Exercise 4 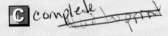 complete

1. If necessary, open the *mdbDynamicInc2* database.

2. Open the tblClients table in Design view.

3. Add a new 15-character Text field named Sales Rep.

4. Position the Sales Rep field after the ClientID field.

5. In Datasheet view, add the following sales representatives for each record:
Record 1	*Wilson*
Record 2	*Howard*
Record 3	*Nguyen*

chapter two

6. Resize all the column widths to accommodate the longest entry in each column.

7. Print the tblClients table.

8. Save and close the tblClients table.

Exercise 5

1. If necessary, open the *mdbDynamicInc2* database.

2. Open the tblEmployees table in Design view.

3. Change the caption of the Postal Code field to Zip Code.

4. Save the tblEmployees table.

5. Change to Datasheet view.

6. Resize the State field.

7. Print the tblEmployees table.

8. Save and close the tblEmployees table.

Exercise 6

1. If necessary, open the *mdbDynamicInc2* database.

2. Open the tblOrders table in Design view.

3. Assign the Text data type to the OrderID field.

4. Save and close the tblOrders table.

Exercise 7

1. If necessary, open the *mdbDynamicInc2* database.

2. Open the tblOrders table in Design view.

3. Change the CustomerID field properties so that the data type is text, it can contain only two characters, must be completed for all records, and that duplicates are not allowed.

4. Save and close the tblOrders table.

Exercise 8

1. If necessary, open the *mdbDynamicInc2* database.

2. Open the tblEmployees table in Design view.

3. Delete the Home Phone field.

4. Add a new field named Primary Phone as the last field.

5. Use the Input Mask Wizard to set the standard pattern for this field as (xxx) xxx-xxxx where x is a number. Store the data without symbols.

6. Save and close the tblEmployees table.

Case Projects

Project 1

Using the Microsoft on the <u>W</u>eb command on the <u>H</u>elp menu, open the Microsoft home page and then link to pages that provide basic information about Access databases. Print at least two of the Web pages.

Project 2

Connect to your ISP and load the home page for a search engine. Search for companies on the Web who export products from the United States to other countries. Research the types of products they export, who their customers are, and how they ship and deliver the products. Print the relevant Web pages. Use this information for Projects 3–8.

Project 3

Maria asks you to create a database called *mdbExporters* for Dynamic Inc. This database includes information about the Dynamic's export customers and the types of products they export. You need to design four new tables for this database. You create these tables in Projects 4–7.

Project 4

Use the Table Wizard to create the first table that contains Customer information. Dynamic exports products to companies, not individuals. Include fields for the customer ID, company name, billing address, phone number, and postal code information of the Dynamic customers. Add two other appropriate fields, such as Country and E-mail address.

Project 5

Create the second table that contains Export Product information. Include any fields for identifying the products Dynamic exports, such as product ID, description, and price.

Project 6

Create the third table that contains Subcontractor information. Dynamic works with other companies around the United States to provide packaging, shipping, and customs services. The company gives preference to long-term suppliers who provide discounted rates or special terms for large orders. Include a field to identify these special suppliers.

Project 7

Create the fourth table by using the Lookup Wizard to create a list of possible choices for the Region Description field. Then modify the Lookup field to add other regions that Dynamic may use in the future: Australia and Eastern Europe.

Project 8

Maria wants to make it easy for users to enter valid data. Define data validation criteria for at least one field in a table in mdbExporters. Open the table in Design view and click the field. Click the Validation Rule box, and then key the rule. For example, to validate a field containing a state abbreviation, key =2 to make sure users enter two characters. Click the Validation Text box, and then key a message, such as "You must key two characters."

chapter two

Entering and Editing Data into Tables

Chapter Overview

I n this chapter you enter, modify, and edit data into tables. You also insert pictures into data fields.

LEARNING OBJECTIVES

► **Enter records using a datasheet**
► **Navigate through records**
► **Modify data in a table**
► **Add pictures to records**

Case profile

Maria Moreno, the owner of Dynamic Inc., approves the design of the tables in the database you created for her. She gives you the go-ahead to begin the next phase: entering the data into the database.

chapter three

3.a Entering Records Using a Datasheet

Once you design your database, create its tables, and define the tables' fields, you're ready to enter records. Recall that a record is a row in your table and contains specific information about the table's subject. You can enter values for each record directly in the table datasheet, that is, in the columns of your table. A **value** is the data in each field of the record. For example, Moreno would be the value of the Last Name field for Maria Moreno. A **cell** is where the column and row meet, similar to a cell in a spreadsheet.

Start by entering data in the tblCategories table. To enter data into the table:

Step 1	*Start*	Microsoft Access
Step 2	*Open*	*mdbDynamicInc3* located on the DataDisk
Step 3	*Click*	Tables 🔲 on the Objects bar in the database window
Step 4	*Double-click*	tblCategories

Notice this table contains only two fields, and one contains an AutoNumber data type. You will enter data only in the Category Name field. The six categories of Dynamic's import and export products are: Machinery, Clothing, Housewares, Automotive, Toys, and Electronics. You enter these categories now.

Step 5	*Click*	in the first row of the Category Name field
Step 6	*Key*	Machinery

Your screen should look similar to Figure 3-1.

Entering records directly into a table is a good choice when you only have to enter one or two records. If you have several records to enter, use a form instead. Remember that if you use the Table Wizard, you can also let Access automatically create a form for you.

If you set up a field automatically listing the record number, such as a Customer ID field, make sure you start entering data in the second field.

FIGURE 3-1
tblCategories Table with One Record Entered

chapter three

QUICK TIP

You can insert the current date by pressing the CTRL + ; (semicolon) keys and insert the current time by pressing the CTRL + : (colon) keys. If you have a default value set for the field, you can enter it by pressing the CTRL + ALT + SPACEBAR keys. To repeat the same value from the same field in the previous record, press the CTRL + ' (apostrophe) keys.

Step 7	**Press**	the TAB key twice to move to the second row of the Category Name field
Step 8	**Key**	Clothing
Step 9	**Repeat**	Steps 7 and 8 to enter the remaining four categories
Step 10	**Close**	the tblCategories table

You now enter data into the tblDepartment table. Dynamic has six departments: Administration, Accounting, Sales, Imports, Exports, and Customer Service. To enter information in the tblDepartment table:

Step 1	**Double-click**	tblDepartment to open it
Step 2	**Click**	in the first row of the Department Name field
Step 3	**Key**	Administration
Step 4	**Press**	the TAB key twice
Step 5	**Repeat**	Steps 3 and 4 to enter the remaining five departments

Your screen should look similar to Figure 3-2.

FIGURE 3-2
tblDepartment Table

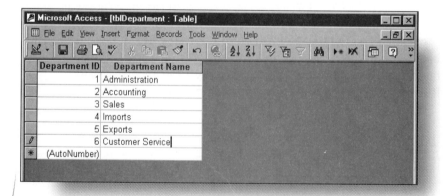

| Step 6 | **Close** | the tblDepartment table |

After you entered several records, you want to know how to navigate through the datasheet more easily. You learn some shortcuts next.

3.b Navigating Through Records

Using the TAB key to move around in an Access table as you enter records is often the most efficient method. That way you do not have to move your hand from the keyboard to use the mouse. Table 3-1 lists the keys you can use to move around a table.

To Move to the	Press
Next field	TAB
Previous field	SHIFT + TAB
Last field of a record	END
First field in a record	HOME
Same field in the next record	DOWN ARROW
Same field in the previous record	UP ARROW
Same field in the last record	CTRL + DOWN ARROW
Same field in the first record	CTRL + UP ARROW
Last field in the last record	CTRL + END
First field in the first record	CTRL + HOME

TABLE 3-1
Shortcut
Navigational Keys

MOUSE TIP

After you enter data, you might find using the mouse more effective for navigating a table. You can click directly in any cell at any time to move the insertion point.

Your assistant Chang entered additional records into the *mdbDynamicInc3* database. You decide to review his work. If you need to make corrections, you can easily modify the data.

3.c Modifying Data in a Table

Access allows you to edit table data easily. You can correct text, add and copy data, and delete information as necessary. Your first modification is to correct text.

Correcting Data in a Table

When you review the tblEmployees table in *mdbDynamicInc3*, you notice that Jan Sinclair's last name is incorrectly listed as Bouchard, her maiden name. Because this data is completely wrong, the most efficient method of correcting it is to reenter the entire field.

chapter
three

To replace data by reentering it:

Step 1	**Open**	the tblEmployees table
Step 2	**Click**	in the cell with the last name Bouchard
Step 3	**Point**	to the left edge of the field so that the mouse pointer becomes a cross
Step 4	**Click**	to select the entire contents of the cell
Step 5	**Key**	Sinclair

The new data then replaces the old data that was in the cell. Your screen should look similar to Figure 3-3.

FIGURE 3-3
Modified
tblEmployees Table

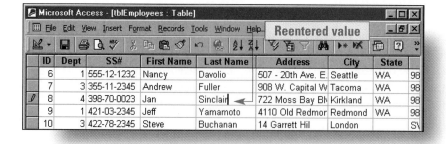

If the modification you need to make involves minor editing changes, you don't have to retype completely the information in a field. For example, Steve Buchanan's e-mail address changed to sBuchanan@dyn.com. You can edit the text of his current e-mail address.

To edit a cell's contents:

Step 1	**Click**	in the cell containing Steve Buchanan's e-mail address
Step 2	**Move**	the insertion point to where you want to make the change
Step 3	**Press**	the BACKSPACE key to remove the word "rio"

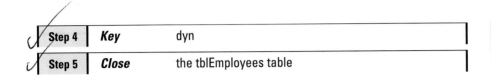

Step 4	*Key*	dyn
Step 5	*Close*	the tblEmployees table

You can use the mouse to click in the appropriate place within a cell, or you can use the keyboard commands shown in Table 3-2.

To Move	Press
One character to the right	RIGHT ARROW
One character to the left	LEFT ARROW
One word to the right	CTRL + RIGHT ARROW
One word to the left	CTRL + LEFT ARROW
To the end of the line	END
To the end of the field	CTRL + END
To the beginning of the line	HOME
To the beginning of the field	CTRL + HOME

TABLE 3-2
Shortcut Keys for
Editing Data

If you have data in one field that you want to use in another, you can copy the data.

Copying Data into a Table

Cut, Copy, and Paste are commands that you can use with all Windows programs. In Access, you can use these commands to move data within records.

The tblCustomers table includes an Address field. As your assistant Chang begins to enter data, he discovers he needs a second field to enter complete address information. You can save time by copying a field and all of its attributes instead of creating a new field from scratch. To add a second address field, copy the Address field and rename it Address 2.

To copy and paste a field within a table:

Step 1	*Open*	the tblCustomers table
Step 2	*Switch*	to Design view

Your next step is to determine where to locate the new field. It makes sense to place the Address 2 field immediately after the Address field. To do this, you need to insert a new row. By default, the Insert Rows command inserts a blank row before the selected field, so you need to select the City field.

chapter
three

To insert a new row:

Step 1	*Click*	in the City field
Step 2	*Click*	Insert
Step 3	*Click*	Rows

This inserts a new row after the Address field. Your screen should now look like Figure 3-4.

FIGURE 3-4
New Row in tblCustomers

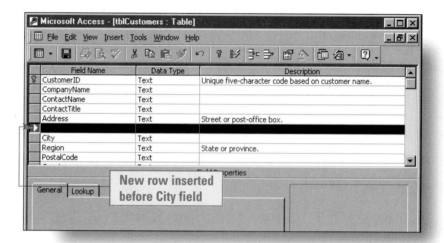

You are ready to copy and paste the duplicate billing address field into the blank row.

Step 4	*Click*	to select the Address field

Your screen should look like Figure 3-5.

FIGURE 3-5
Address Field Selected
for Copying

M O U S E   T I P

To copy and paste an object, right-click and then use the commands on the shortcut menu.

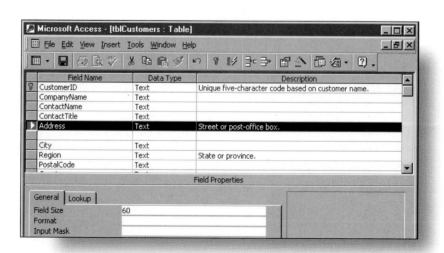

Step 5	**Click**	the Copy button on the Table Design toolbar
Step 6	**Select**	the blank row
Step 7	**Click**	the Paste button on the Table Design toolbar

You must now rename the field.

| Step 8 | **Click** | the new field |
| Step 9 | **Key** | 2 at the end of the field name |

It should now read Address2.

| Step 10 | **Close** | the tblCustomers table, saving your changes |

You can use the same copy-and-paste process when copying records, cells, or text. You can also move and copy entire objects between databases.

In addition to using cut-and-paste or copy-and-paste to modify a database, you can use the Clipboard toolbar. The **Clipboard toolbar**, which is available in all Office applications, stores up to 12 text or other selections that you cut or copy. You can then choose the item you want to paste into an object. If you try to store more than 12 items on the Clipboard, you can either delete the first item or keep the original 12 without adding the new 13th item. The contents of the Clipboard are available to all Office applications until you close them.

To view the Clipboard toolbar, you simply click the View menu, point to Toolbars, and then click Clipboard. The Clipboard toolbar appears on your screen, as shown in Figure 3-6.

MENU TIP

You can also use the Cut, Copy, and Paste commands on the Edit menu.

QUICK TIP

If the Clipboard toolbar is floating in the middle of your screen, remember you can dock it, as you would any other toolbar.

C

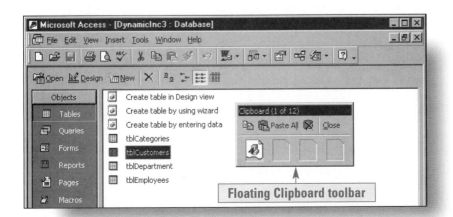

FIGURE 3-6
Clipboard Toolbar

chapter
three

If you make a mistake entering or editing data, you can reverse or undo a change that you made to a record in Datasheet or Form view.

Undoing a Change

To undo changes, you click the Undo button on the Table Datasheet toolbar. This restores your most recent change. If you already saved changes to the current record, or moved to another record, you can still undo the last change.

Deleting Records from a Table

When you want to delete data, consider whether you need to remove only part of a record or the entire record. To delete selected parts of the record, use the Delete command on the Edit menu. To delete the entire record, use the Delete Record command.

In the tblEmployees table, delete the record of Andrew Fuller, who left the company last week.

To delete a record from a table:

Step 1	*Open*	tblEmployees
Step 2	*Click*	in the record selection area of Andrew Fuller's record
Step 3	*Click*	Edit
Step 4	*Click*	Delete Record

A dialog box asks if you want to delete this record, and reminds you that if you delete this record you will not be able to retrieve it.

| Step 5 | *Click* | Yes |

Your last task in modifying your database is adding photographs of Dynamic's employees.

QUICK TIP

You can undo changes by pressing the ESCAPE key.
Press the CTRL + Z keys to undo the last change.
You can also undo changes by clicking Undo Saved Record on the Edit menu.

CAUTION TIP

If you delete information using the DELETE key, the deleted data is not stored on the Clipboard.
You can undo a field deletion but not a record deletion, so be careful what you choose to delete.

3.d Adding Pictures to Records

Access lets you add pictures and clip art to records. Each image is saved as an **OLE object**, which means it was created in another program but appears as a separate object in Access. There are two types of OLE objects, linked and embedded. A **linked object** is not saved as part of the Access database, but includes a reference to the location of the file so Access can find it. An **embedded object**, however, is stored as part of your Access database.

Link an object if you want to keep the database small, the object being linked is still under construction, you are sure that a server containing the file is stable, or you will not be sending the file via e-mail. (A linked file expects the server to be in a specific location, and if you e-mail the file, that location is not available to the end user.)

Embed an object if you have enough room for a large database, you do not need to keep the file as a separate document, or you will be sending the document via e-mail or disk.

To add photographs to a record, they must first be saved as bitmap images. You can do this by using **Microsoft's Photo Editor**. This is a simple image program that ships with Office 2000, and is fully integrated into the Office suite. You do not need additional hardware or software.

You already received the bitmap image containing the photograph of Catherine Moore, the Executive Vice President of Dynamic. You are ready to add it to the tblEmployees table.

To add (embed) a picture to a table record:

Step 1	*Open*	the tblEmployees table, if necessary
Step 2	*Click*	in the Photograph cell of Catherine Moore's record
Step 3	*Click*	Insert
Step 4	*Click*	Object

The Insert Object dialog box opens, as shown in Figure 3-7.

chapter
three

FIGURE 3-7
Insert Object Dialog Box

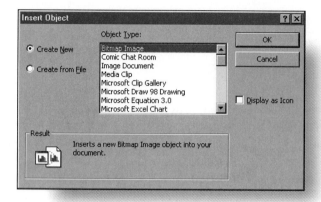

Step 5	*Click*	Bitmap Image, if necessary
Step 6	*Click*	the Create from File option button
Step 7	*Click*	Browse to see the images available on the Data Disk
Step 8	*Click*	*Moore.bmp* located on the Data Disk
Step 9	*Click*	OK

If you wanted this image to be linked instead of embedded, you would click the Link box in the Insert Object dialog box.

Step 10	*Click*	OK in the Insert Object dialog box

The image is now embedded in the Access database. When you look at the Datasheet view of the table, the Photograph cell lets you know you have a bitmap image for this record, as shown in Figure 3-8.

FIGURE 3-8
Datasheet View of
Photograph Cell

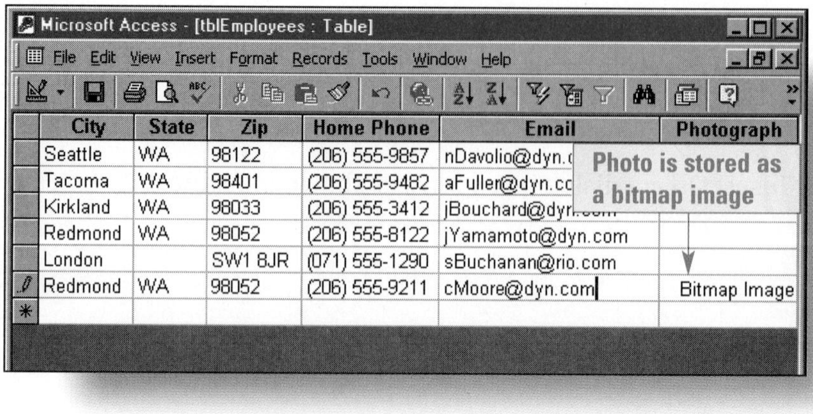

Microsoft Access - [tblEmployees : Table]

File   Edit   View   Insert   Format   Records   Tools   Window   Help

	City	State	Zip	Home Phone	Email	Photograph
	Seattle	WA	98122	(206) 555-9857	nDavolio@dyn.c	Photo is stored as
	Tacoma	WA	98401	(206) 555-9482	aFuller@dyn.cc	a bitmap image
	Kirkland	WA	98033	(206) 555-3412	jBouchard@dyn.com	
	Redmond	WA	98052	(206) 555-8122	jYamamoto@dyn.com	
	London		SW1 8JR	(071) 555-1290	sBuchanan@rio.com	
	Redmond	WA	98052	(206) 555-9211	cMoore@dyn.com	Bitmap Image
*						

You can view the photograph only in Form view of the tblEmployees table. To do so, you first need to close the table.

Step 11	*Close*	the tblEmployees table

The tblEmployees table has an associated frmEmployees form. You need to open that form to view the photograph.
To view the image in the frmEmployees form:

Step 1	*Click*	Forms 🔳 on the Objects bar in the database window
Step 2	*Double-click*	frmEmployees
Step 3	*Select*	Catherine Moore's record by pressing the PAGE DOWN key until you see the appropriate record

After you view the record and see the photo, close the form and exit Access.

Step 4	*Close*	the frmEmployees form
Step 5	*Exit*	Access

As you can see, you can enter photographs in a database table just as easily as you enter text.

chapter
three

Summary

▶ A cell is the intersection between a row and a column.

▶ To navigate through records, you can use the mouse, the TAB key, and a variety of other keys.

▶ To replace text in a cell, click in the cell and re-key the information.

▶ You can copy a field and its attributes and then paste it to save time when creating new fields.

▶ The Office Clipboard stores up to 12 items you cut or copied and can paste into your current file.

▶ You can undo many mistakes made when entering data.

▶ The Delete command deletes the item you are working with; the Delete Record command deletes the entire record.

▶ To insert a picture in a table, use the Object command on the Insert menu. You can only view the picture on the screen, however, in Form view.

Commands Review

Action	Menu Bar	Shortcut Menu	Toolbar	Keyboard
Enter the current date				CTRL + ;
Enter the current time				CTRL + :
Repeat the same value				CTRL + '
Enter the default values set for the field				CTRL + ALT + SPACEBAR
Go to the next field				TAB
Go to the previous field				SHIFT + TAB
Go to the last field of a record				END
Go to the first field in a record				HOME
Go to the same field in the next record				DOWN ARROW
Go to the same field in the previous record				UP ARROW
Go to the same field in the last record				CTRL + DOWN ARROW
Go to the same field in the first record				CTRL + UP ARROW
Go to the last field in the last record				CTRL + END
Go to the first field in the first record				CTRL + HOME
Move one character to the right				RIGHT ARROW
Move one character to the left				LEFT ARROW
Move one word to the right				CTRL + RIGHT ARROW
Move one word to the left				CTRL + LEFT ARROW
To the end of the line				END
Go to the end of the field				CTRL + END
Go to the beginning of the line				HOME
Go to the beginning of the field				CTRL + HOME
Undo a change	Edit, Undo		↺	ESC CTRL + Z ALT + E, U
Delete a record	Edit, Delete Record	Delete	✗	DELETE ALT + E, R

Concepts Review

SCANS

Circle the correct answer.

1. When you enter records, you enter data in the form of:
[a] cells.
[b] values.
[c] pictures.
[d] linked objects.

2. To enter the current date, press the:
[a] CTRL + D keys.
[b] CTRL + ' keys.
[c] CTRL + ; keys.
[d] CTRL + : keys.

3. To enter the current time, press the:
[a] CTRL + T keys.
[b] CTRL + ' keys.
[c] CTRL + ; keys.
[d] CTRL + : keys.

4. Besides using a table to enter data, you can use a(n):
[a] datasheet.
[b] Clipboard.
[c] embedded object.
[d] form.

5. To enter data into the table:
[a] press the TAB key.
[b] press the INSERT key.
[c] click in the cell and type.
[d] press the ENTER key.

6. One way to create a new field is to:
[a] insert a blank row and then copy information from another field.
[b] press the CTRL + HOME keys.
[c] undo a deleted field.
[d] press the SHIFT key to select more than one record.

7. You can use the Clipboard to:
[a] take notes while entering data.
[b] store and paste multiple items.
[c] delete data from a table.
[d] undo a change you made to a record.

8. To work with an entire record, click or press the:
[a] DELETE key.
[b] gray box to the left of the record.
[c] CTRL + END keys.
[d] LEFT ARROW key.

9. If you select several records in a table, a triangle marks:
[a] all the selected records.
[b] the first and last records.
[c] the first record.
[d] the last record.

10. When you add a picture to a record, Access saves the image as a:
[a] photograph.
[b] form or table.
[c] linked or embedded object.
[d] hypertext link.

Circle **T** if the statement is true or **F** if the statement is false.

T   F   1. You can only enter data in a table.

T   F   2. You can enter data by keying text.

T   F   3. Once you enter data in a field and save a table, you cannot edit the data.

T   F   4. To delete a record, you must delete each field one at a time.

T   F   5. You can use the Cut, Copy, and Paste commands to move data within records.

T   F   6. You can select a record by clicking in the record selection area.

T   F   7. To add a picture to table, you must link the picture.

T   F   8. An OLE object can be either embedded or linked.

T   F   9. To view a picture that is placed in a table, you must be in Datasheet view.

T   F   10. You can reverse your last change by using the Redo option.

Skills Review

Exercise 1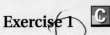

1. If necessary, open the *mdbDynamicInc3* database.

2. Open the tblRegions table.

3. Enter the following region names: *Mexico, Canada, Northern Europe, Southern Europe, Asia.*

4. Resize the Region Name column.

5. Save and close the table.

Exercise 2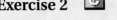

1. If necessary, open the *mdbDynamicInc3* database.

2. Open the frmOrders form.

3. Enter two new records of information based on the ones already in the frmOrders form.

4. Save and close the form.

Exercise 3

1. If necessary, open the *mdbDynamicInc3* database.

2. Open the tblRegions table.

3. Edit the region names to match the following: *Mexico, Canada, N. Europe, S. Europe, Asia.*

4. Save and close the table.

Exercise 4

1. If necessary, open the *mdbDynamicInc3* database.

2. Open the tblOrders table.

3. Insert a blank row after the Ship Address field. Copy and paste the information from the Ship Address field to the new row. Edit the field name to be BillAddress. Edit caption to be Billing Address.

4. Save and close the tblOrders table.

Exercise 5

1. If necessary, open the *mdbDynamicInc3* database.

2. Open the tblCategories table.

3. Copy the text in the Category Name field for Housewares and Electronics, and then close the tblCategories table.

chapter three

4. Open the tblProducts table.

5. Add the following two new records:
29-0085   Portable radio $19.99
39-5875   Swiss cheese cutter $29.99
Paste the appropriate Category Name field text from the Clipboard toolbar to the two new records.

6. Clear the Clipboard toolbar and close it.

7. Save and close the tblProducts table.

Exercise 6

1. If necessary, open the *mdbDynamicInc3* database.

2. Open the tblProducts table.

3. Change Housewares in the Category Name field to *Kitchen Supplies*.

4. Undo the change.

5. Delete the record for the Swedish building set.

6. Save and close the tblProducts table.

Exercise 7

1. If necessary, open the *mdbDynamicInc3* database.

2. Open the tblProducts table.

3. In the Sample field for the Electronic pocket watch, insert the *Sample* clip art image from the Data Disk. Add it as an embedded object.

4. Save and close the tblProducts table.

Exercise 8

1. If necessary, open the *mdbDynamicInc3* database.

2. Use the Table Wizard to create a new table based on the Contacts sample. Use the following fields: ContactID, FirstName, LastName, Address, City, StateorProvince, and PostalCode.

3. Name the new table tblContacts.

4. Let Access create a form based on the new table.

5. Enter three records using the form and the following data:
a) Pedro Morales, 233 E. Union Street, Tacoma, WA 98322-0233
b) Gary Gleason, 56 Wildwood Trail, Tacoma, WA 98322-0056
c) Madeleine Schwartz, 9002 S. Loveland, Tacoma, WA 98322-9002

6. Save the form as frmContacts and close it.

Case Projects

Project 1

Using the *mdbDynamicInc3* database, enter information for two new customers in the tblCustomers table. Use a keyboard shortcut to enter some data. For example, press the CTRL + ' (apostrophe) keys to insert the same city for both customers.

Project 2

Using the *mdbDynamicInc3* database, enter information for two new employees in the frmEmployees form. Use keyboard shortcuts to navigate the form.

Project 3

Using the *mdbDynamicInc3* database, edit all of the department names in the tblDepartment table. Use keyboard shortcuts to navigate the table.

Project 4

Using the *mdbDynamicInc3* database, open the tblOrders table and add two new fields for phone numbers. Create the first and enter data for two or three records. Then create a field for a second phone number, such as for a fax machine or mobile phone. Copy data from the first Phone Number field and modify it.

Project 5

Using the *mdbDynamicInc3* database, create a new table called tblInvoices. Add fields for Invoice ID, Invoice Date, Customer ID, and Shipping Cost. Use the Clipboard to copy data from the tblCustomers table and paste it where appropriate in the new table.

Project 6

Using the *mdbDynamicInc3* database, open the frmEmployees form. Edit some of the data, but undo all of your changes. Delete one record.

Project 7

Connect to your ISP and load the home page for a search engine. Search for an online computer dictionary or encyclopedia and look up information on at least three terms defined in this chapter, such as value, OLE, Clipboard, and embedded object. Print the explanations.

Project 8

Connect to your ISP and load the home page for a search engine. Search for a site offering copyright-free clip art. Download one small bitmap file. Add it to an appropriate table in *mdbDynamicInc3*.

chapter three

Designing and Using Basic Forms

Chapter Overview

In this chapter, you explore how to design and create forms using the Form Wizard. You learn why forms are useful, what they look like, and how to use them. You also modify your form designs.

- ▶ **Understand forms**
- ▶ **Create a form with the Form Wizard**
- ▶ **Create a custom form**
- ▶ **Modify a form design**
- ▶ **Use the Control toolbox to add and modify controls**
- ▶ **Modify format properties**
- ▶ **Print a form**

Case profile

You designed and created an Access database for Dynamic Inc. Now, Kang Leing, the warehouse manager, and Natasha Diggins, the personnel manager, ask you to make it easy for their department personnel to use the database. Because forms simplify data entry and viewing, you can create several Access forms to meet their needs. Create a form Natasha's staff can use to efficiently enter new employee information. Then create a form Kang's warehouse staff can use to enter and track the company products.

chapter four

4.a Understanding Forms

Most people prefer to use forms when they enter or view information in a database. Like paper-based forms, electronic Access forms can be visually appealing and can guide users through the process of entering data. Use Access forms to accomplish the following tasks.

Enter and view data. The most common use of forms is to enter and view data in records. Well-designed forms make it easy to enter data by using clear field labels and including only the necessary fields. They also make it easy to view data by arranging fields in appealing, logical ways.

Automate your tasks. Forms can work with Access programming features, such as macros or Visual Basic, to automate certain actions. With macros and Visual Basic, you can open other forms, run queries, and restrict the data you display. You can also use macros or modules in forms to provide data values, which let you perform calculations quickly and accurately.

Provide instructions. You can include instructions, tips, notes, and other information on your forms to provide information about how to use Access or special features of your database.

Print information. You can use forms to increase your flexibility when printing information. For example, you can design an order form that has two sets of headers and footers: one for entering data and the other for printing a customer invoice based on the order information.

You are ready to create your first form. Start with the form for Natasha's Personnel department.

4.b Creating a Form with the Form Wizard

From your discussions with Natasha, you understand she wants a form so her staff can efficiently enter, update, and maintain information for new employees. With that in mind, you list the fields you want to include in the form, such as name, address, home phone, and Social Security number.

Now that you know the purpose and content of the form, you are ready to create it. You create the form using the Form Wizard. Like other Access wizards, the **Form Wizard** guides you through the steps of creating a form. You can use it to create a simple form that includes all the fields from a related table, or you can select the fields to include in a form. Although the Form Wizard saves you time, it limits your design decisions.

chapter
four

Using the Form Wizard

As you step through a Form Wizard, you locate and select the information to include in the form, and then Access creates the form for you. Your first step is to start the Form Wizard.

To start the Form Wizard:

Step 1	**Open**	the *mdbDynamicInc4* database
Step 2	**Click**	Forms 📇 on the Objects bar in the database window
Step 3	**Double-click**	Create form by using wizard

The dialog box on your screen should look similar to Figure 4-1.

FIGURE 4-1
Form Wizard

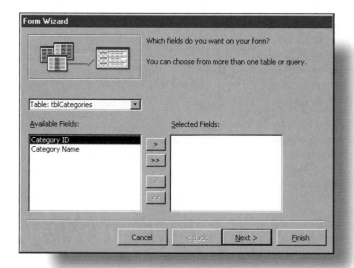

The Form Wizard can create a simple columnar form that contains all of the fields in the tblEmployees table. You can also select only some fields from the tblEmployees table. For your form, you use all the fields, except for the Photograph field. Natasha's department is not sure they want to include photographs at this time.

Step 4	**Click**	Table: tblEmployees in the Table/Queries list box

In the Available Fields: list box, you see the fields you can use, as shown in Figure 4-2.

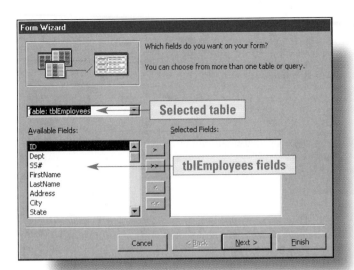

FIGURE 4-2
Available Fields from the
tblEmployees Table

The most efficient way to choose all the fields except the Photograph field is to select all the fields at once, and then move the Photograph field back to the Available Fields: list box.

Step 5	*Click*	>>
Step 6	*Click*	Photograph in the Selected Fields: list box
Step 7	*Click*	<
Step 8	*Click*	Next >

The dialog box on your screen should look similar to Figure 4-3.

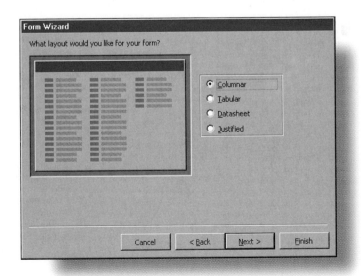

FIGURE 4-3
Form Layout Options

chapter
four

Use this dialog box to choose a layout for the form. Choose a columnar, tabular, datasheet, or justified layout. Click an option to see a sketch of that layout. For Natasha's form, use the columnar layout, which is the default.

To continue using the Form Wizard:

| Step 1 | *Click* | the Columnar option button, if necessary |
| Step 2 | *Click* | Next > |

Use the next dialog box to select the background design of your form. Click an option to see a sample of the background. For example, selecting the International style inserts a background graphic of a globe in your form. Because you want to keep Natasha's form as simple as possible, choose the Standard style, which is the default.

| Step 3 | *Click* | Standard, if necessary |
| Step 4 | *Click* | Next > |

The last Form Wizard dialog box asks you for a form title, and whether you want to open the form at this time or modify it.

| Step 5 | *Key* | frmEmployees as the name of the form |

The dialog box on your screen should look similar to Figure 4-4.

FIGURE 4-4
Completing the
Form Wizard

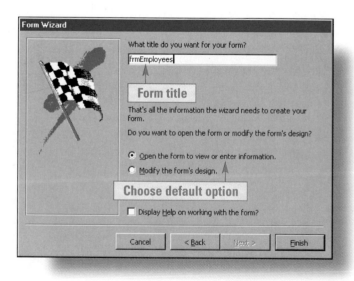

Step 6	*Click*	<u>F</u>inish

Your screen should look similar to Figure 4-5.

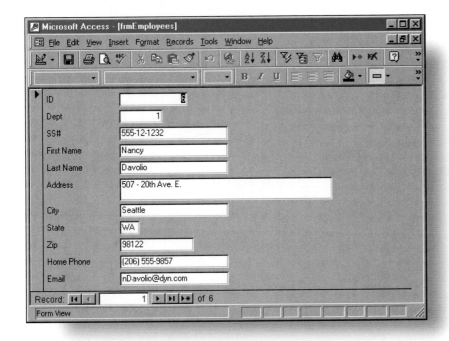

FIGURE 4-5
frmEmployees Form

You used the Form Wizard to create the frmEmployees form. To make sure that it serves Natasha's purposes, use the form to enter data.

Entering Records Using a Form

One purpose of creating forms is to make data entry more efficient. A form is often created to "mask" the datasheet. Some datasheets are overwhelming, especially to novice users, and the mask provides a user-friendly interface for data entry.

To enter data into a form:

Step 1	*Click*	the New Record button on the Form View toolbar
Step 2	*Press*	the TAB key to accept the ID field (AutoNumber)
Step 3	*Key*	2 in the Dept field
Step 4	*Press*	the TAB key
Step 5	*Key*	the information shown in Table 4-1 to complete the record

chapter
four

TABLE 4-1
Information to Enter in
frmEmployees

Field	Data	Field	Data
Social Security Number	546-58-2139	State	WA
First Name	Marcia	Zip Code	98056
Last Name	Wilson	Home Phone	(425) 555-6897
Address	315 Garden Ave N	Email Name	mwilson@dyn.com
City	Bellevue		

Access automatically saves the data after you enter it.

Step 6	*Click*	the First Record navigation button to go to the first record

Now make sure that Natasha's department can easily modify records using the form.

Modifying an Existing Record Using a Form

To modify a record in a form, first locate the record. You can do so using the Find command, or you can scroll through the records using the navigation buttons. Then edit the record as you would edit any other item: Click in the field containing the value you want to change, and then use standard editing commands to modify the value. As a test, find and modify Marcia Wilson's record.

To find and modify a record in the Form window:

Step 1	*Click*	Edit
Step 2	*Click*	Find

The dialog box on your screen should look similar to Figure 4-6.

FIGURE 4-6
Find and Replace
Dialog Box

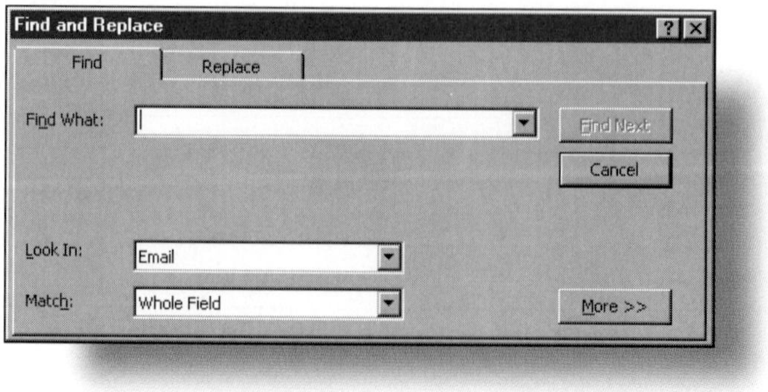

Step 3	*Key*	Marcia in the Fi<u>n</u>d What: text box
Step 4	*Click*	frmEmployees in the <u>L</u>ook In: text box
Step 5	*Click*	<u>F</u>ind Next
Step 6	*Close*	the Find and Replace dialog box

You now see Marcia's record. Change her address to 351 Garden Ave. S.

| Step 7 | *Click* | in the Address field |
| Step 8 | *Change* | the field to 351 Garden Ave S. |

You completed the frmEmployees form for Natasha's department. You can now close the form.

| Step 9 | *Close* | frmEmployees |

You are ready to create another form, this one for Kang's department. To fit his needs, you create a custom form.

4.c Creating a Custom Form

You can use the Form Wizard to create more complex and custom forms, such as those that allow you to enter information from several tables at once. For Kang's department, this is useful because his staff needs to enter information about both products and suppliers, as shown in Table 4-2.

tblProducts Fields	tblSuppliers Fields
Product ID, Category Name, ProductDescription, and SupplierID	SupplierName, Address, City, State, Zip Code

TABLE 4-2
Fields Needed for Kang's Custom Form

Create a custom form that includes parts of the tblProducts and tblSuppliers tables.
To create a custom form:

| Step 1 | *Click* | Forms  on the Objects bar in the database window |

chapter
four

Step 2	**Double-click**	Create form by using wizard
Step 3	**Click**	Table: tblProducts in the Tables/Queries list box
Step 4	**Move**	ProductID, Category Name, ProductDescription, and SupplierID to the Selected Fields: list box
Step 5	**Click**	Table: tblSuppliers table in the Tables/Queries list box
Step 6	**Move**	SupplierName, Address, City, State, and Zip Code to the Selected Fields: list box
Step 7	**Click**	Next >

This dialog box asks how you want to view your data. Because Kang's department works primarily with suppliers, tblSuppliers is the "parent" category for this form.

Step 8	**Click**	by tblSuppliers

The dialog box on your screen should look similar to Figure 4-7.

FIGURE 4-7
Creating a Custom Form

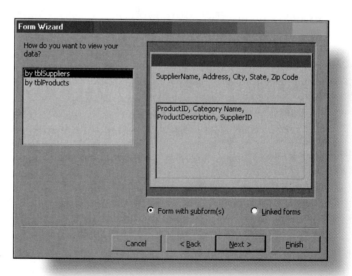

The dialog box indicates you are creating a form with a subform, which occurs when you use more than one table to create a form.

Step 9	**Click**	Next >

The rest of the Form Wizard dialog boxes are similar to those you used when creating the frmEmployees form.

To complete your custom form using the Form Wizard:

| Step 1 | *Click* | Datasheet if necessary to accept the default layout for the form |
| Step 2 | *Click* | Next > |

The next dialog box concerns the style of the form. You can choose a more decorative background for this form.

Step 3	*Click*	Sumi Painting
Step 4	*Click*	Next >
Step 5	*Key*	frmSuppliers and frmProducts Subform as the title

Accept the defaults in the dialog box, because you want frmSuppliers to be the form with the product information as a subform. You also want to open the form after Access creates it.

| Step 6 | *Click* | Finish |

When the form opens, your screen should look similar to Figure 4-8.

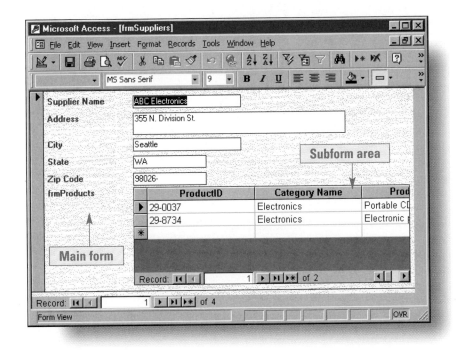

FIGURE 4-8
frmSuppliers Form with
frmProducts Subform

chapter
four

Now that you created the form using the Form Wizard, you can modify it as necessary using Design view.

4.d Modifying a Form Design

After you create a form, you can modify its design without affecting its data. For the frmSuppliers form, you decide to rearrange the fields on the form, as well as move and enlarge the frmProducts subform.

Rearranging Fields and Moving the Subform

After you use the Form Wizard to create a form, you may often find that you want to modify the appearance of the form on the screen. In this case, you want to move some of fields as well as the subform. To redesign frmSuppliers and move fields:

| Step 1 | *Switch* | to Design view |

Your screen should look similar to Figure 4-9.

FIGURE 4-9
frmSuppliers in
Design View

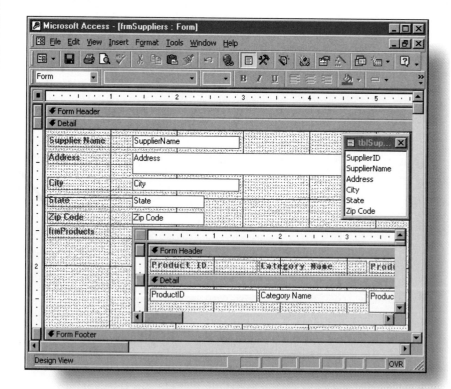

Step 2	Click	anywhere in the Zip Code field to select it

You see **selection handles** around the field. They indicate you can move the field around the form.

Step 3	Point to	the Zip Code field's outline until the pointer becomes a hand
Step 4	Drag	the Zip Code field about .25" lower than its current position (it will overlap the frmProducts label temporarily)

Your next task is to move the frmProducts subform below the frmProducts field label and then enlarge it, so that users can see the fields more clearly.

To move the frmProducts subform and enlarge it:

Step 1	Click	the frmProducts subform to select it (note the selection handles on the label and the subform)
Step 2	Point to	the upper-left corner selection handle of the frmProduct label until the mouse pointer becomes a pointing hand
Step 3	Drag	the label downward approximate .25"
Step 4	Point to	the upper-left corner selection handle on the subform
Step 5	Drag	the subform so that it is positioned directly below the frmProducts field label
Step 6	Deselect	the subform

Your screen should now look similar to Figure 4-10.

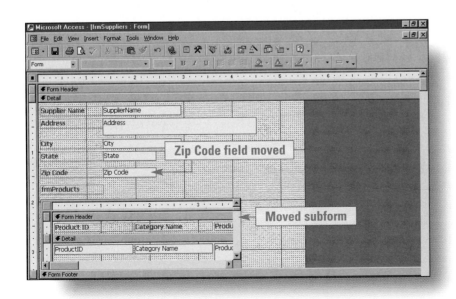

FIGURE 4-10
Modified frmSuppliers/Products Form

chapter
four

| Step 7 | **Select** | the subform |

| Step 8 | **Point to** | the right center selection handle on the subform |

The mouse pointer becomes a double arrow.

| Step 9 | **Drag** | the selection handle to the right so that the width fills the form page |

| Step 10 | **Deselect** | the subform |

Your screen should look similar to Figure 4-11.

FIGURE 4-11
Enlarged Subform Area

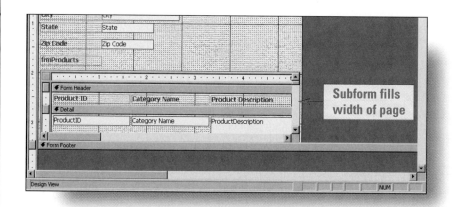

| Step 11 | **Close** | frmSuppliers, saving your changes |

Now that you modified Kang's form, you decide to modify Natasha's form by adding a field.

Adding Fields

You can also use Design view to add (and delete) fields in your form. Natasha's Personnel department is ready to add a photograph of each employee to their record. You now need to add the field to the form.
To add a field to the frmEmployees form:

| Step 1 | **Open** | frmEmployees in Design view |

| Step 2 | **Click** | <u>V</u>iew |

Step 3	*Click*	Field List
Step 4	*Drag*	the Photograph item in the Field List dialog box to the right of the City label and field in the Detail area of the form

Your screen should look similar to Figure 4-12.

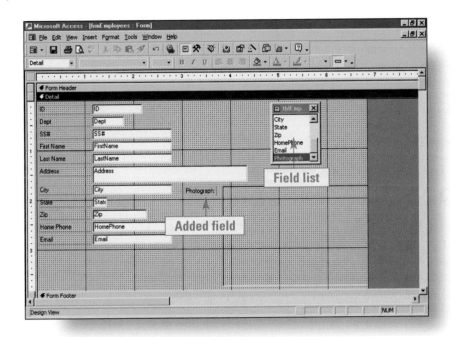

FIGURE 4-12
Adding a Field

Step 5	*Close*	the form, saving your changes

Now that you added the fields, you can add form controls.

4.e Using the Control Toolbox to Add and Modify Controls

The data in a form is contained in **controls**, such as a text box. Other controls include option buttons, check boxes, toggle buttons, and option groups, which are similar to the controls you find on standard Office dialog boxes.

Use option buttons, check boxes, toggle buttons, and option groups when you display information that can have two or three valid choices. For example, if you have a Yes or No choice, use a check box. If the user

chapter
four

checks the box, the answer is yes; an unchecked box means no. Option groups provide controls for more than two choices. If options are grouped, then users can select only one option.

Use a **list box** when you want to list values from which users can select. A **combo box** is a list box with drop-down options. Use a combo box when you are trying to conserve space on the form.

You decide to create a combo box for the frmEmployees form, which will allow a valid department to be entered by selecting the department name or typing the first few letters of the department. This speeds up data entry. To create a combo box, use the **Combo Box Wizard**, which guides you through the steps of creating a combo box.

To create a combo box entry:

MENU TIP

To display the toolbox, click <u>V</u>iew on the menu bar, and then click <u>T</u>oolbox.

Step 1	*Open*	the frmEmployees form
Step 2	*Switch*	to Design view
Step 3	*Click*	the Dept field
Step 4	*Press*	the DELETE key
Step 5	*Display*	the Toolbox, if necessary
Step 6	*Click*	the Combo Box button 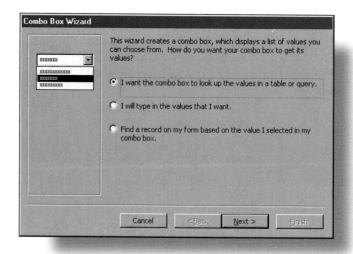 on the toolbox
Step 7	*Move*	the mouse pointer to the blank space in the Detail area created by deleting the Dept field
Step 8	*Click*	the blank space to start the Combo Box Wizard

The Combo Box Wizard dialog box on your screen should look similar to Figure 4-13.

FIGURE 4-13
Combo Box Wizard

You are now ready to use the Combo Box Wizard to complete your combo box.

To use the Combo Box Wizard:

Step 1	*Click*	the I want the combo box to look up values in a table or a query option button, if necessary
Step 2	*Click*	Next >
Step 3	*Click*	the Tables option button, if necessary, to select it
Step 4	*Click*	tblDepartment from the list box
Step 5	*Click*	Next >
Step 6	*Double-click*	the Department Name field to add it to the Selected Fields: list

The dialog box on your screen should look similar to Figure 4-14.

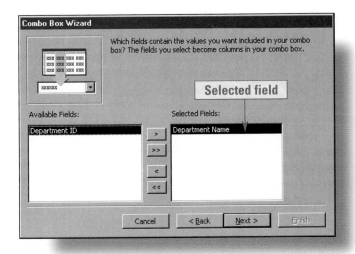

FIGURE 4-14
Selected Field for
Combo Box

Step 7	*Click*	Next >

As you complete the Combo Box Wizard, you can have the combo box adjust its width to accommodate the text it contains. You decide to do this, as it gives you more flexibility when displaying records.

chapter
four

To complete the Combo Box Wizard:

Step 1	**Double-click**	the right border of the Department Name column header
Step 2	**Click**	Next >
Step 3	**Click**	the Store that value in this field option button
Step 4	**Select**	Dept from the list in the combo box
Step 5	**Click**	Next >
Step 6	**Key**	Department as the label for the combo box
Step 7	**Click**	Finish

Now reposition the combo box and combo box label on the form.

Step 8	**Drag**	the new combo box and label to the position shown in Figure 4-15 and resize them as necessary

FIGURE 4-15
Combo Box Position

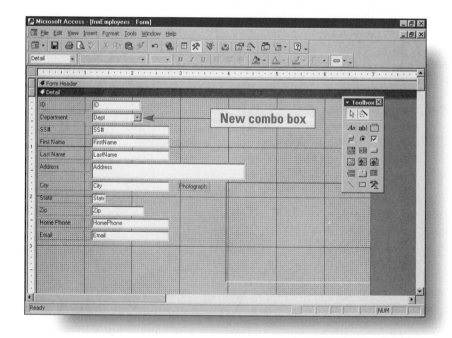

When you show the form to Natasha, she tests it by entering data. She notices that she skips around the form instead of moving from one field to another in logical order. You can change the **tab order** of the form to define which field becomes active when the user presses the TAB key.

To change the tab order of a form:

Step 1	*Click*	View
Step 2	*Click*	Tab Order
Step 3	*Select*	the FirstName field in the Customer Order: list
Step 4	*Press & Hold*	the SHIFT key
Step 5	*Select*	the LastName field and release the SHIFT key
Step 6	*Drag*	the First Name and Last Name fields before the Social Security field in the Customer Order: list
Step 7	*Click*	OK

QUICK TIP

Move the fields that are not often used to the end of the tab order list to make data entry easier.

You decide to enhance frmEmployees further by modifying some of its format properties.

4.f Modifying Format Properties

You can enhance a form's design by modifying format properties, such as the form's font, style, font size, and color. You decide to enhance Natasha's form by setting a theme, modifying the form's header, and inserting a picture.

To select a theme for the frmEmployees form:

Step 1	*Verify*	frmEmployees is open in Design view
Step 2	*Click*	Format
Step 3	*Click*	AutoFormat

MOUSE TIP

You can also select the AutoFormat button on the Design View toolbar.

One principle of good design is to be consistent. Use the same format for each record and for each form in a database. Because you used Sumi Painting as a background for the frmSuppliers form, you should use it as the format for the frmEmployees form.

Step 4	*Click*	Sumi Painting
Step 5	*Click*	OK

Now that you applied a theme to the form, you are ready to create a header and add a picture to it.

Using Form Sections

Recall that a form consists of three sections: Form Header, Detail, and Form Footer. The **Form Header** appears at the top of the form page, whereas the **Form Footer** appears at the bottom of the form page. You are already familiar with working with the Detail area. For the frmEmployees form, you decide to add a header with the form's title, to let the Personnel staff know they are entering data into the correct form.

To add a header to a form:

Step 1	*Verify*	that frmEmployees is open in Design view
Step 2	*Point to*	the boundary line between the Form Header and Detail sections of the form

The mouse pointer becomes a double-headed arrow.

Step 3	*Drag*	the boundary line downward about .5"
Step 4	*Click*	the Label button on the Toolbox
Step 5	*Click*	in the Form Header section
Step 6	*Key*	Dynamic Inc. Employees in the label
Step 7	*Select*	the label
Step 8	*Change*	the font size to 18, in the font of your choice
Step 9	*Size*	the label to view the larger text

You decide to insert a graphic in the Form Header section as well.

Inserting a Graphic on a Form

Inserting a graphic in a form often improves its appearance and makes it look more user-friendly. To insert a graphic, you use the Image tool in the toolbox.

To insert a graphic using the Control toolbox:

Step 1	*Click*	the Image button on the Toolbox
Step 2	*Click*	in the Header section to the left of the title
Step 3	*Locate*	*Employee.bmp* on your Data Disk
Step 4	*Click*	OK

The image now appears on the form.

Step 5	*Resize*	the image as necessary to fit within the header
Step 6	*Rearrange*	the image and label attractively in the header

Your screen should now look similar to Figure 4-16.

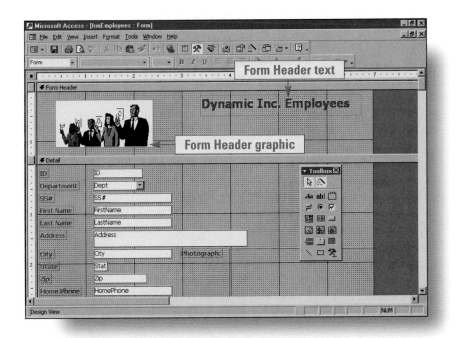

FIGURE 4-16
frmEmployees with
Form Header

You completed the form for Natasha's group.

4.g Printing a Form

Natasha wants a copy of the frmEmployees form to show to her department when she explains how to use it for data entry. You print the form for her.

To print the frmEmployees form:

Step 1	*Verify*	the frmEmployees form is open in Design view
Step 2	*Click*	File
Step 3	*Click*	Print Preview

You can now review the form. When you are satisfied, you can print from the Print Preview window.

Step 4	*Click*	the Print button on the Print Preview toolbar
Step 5	*Close*	frmEmployees, saving your changes
Step 6	*Exit*	Access

You may also want to print other forms. An order form, for example, may contain all the information that you want to send when you ship the order to your customer. Therefore, you can also print the form to use as a shipping invoice.

Summary

▶ Create an Access form to enter and view data in records, control application flow, automate your application, provide instructions, and print a version of the record and its data.

▶ Use the Form Wizard to create a simple form that contains all the fields in the related table or only selected fields. You can also use Design view to create a custom form to modify an existing form.

▶ Create a custom form when you need a form different from those offered by the Form Wizard or when you want to use information from more than one table.

▶ After you create a form, test it by using it to enter data and create records. Press the TAB key to move from one field to another. Click in a field and key in the data. To modify an existing record, first click the navigation buttons or the Find button to locate it. Then click in a field and key the modified data.

▶ Use Design view to modify a form's design without changing your data. You can add, delete, rearrange fields, add controls, insert pictures, change the background color, and choose a theme to improve the appearance and usefulness of your form.

▶ Form controls let you select options, as you do on a standard Windows dialog box. You can include text boxes, option buttons, check boxes, toggle buttons, option groups, list boxes, and combo boxes. Use a list box when you want to list all the valid values for a field. Use a combo box, which is like a list box with drop-down options, when you want to conserve space. Access includes a Combo Box Wizard to guide you through the steps of creating a combo box.

▶ One principle of good design is to be consistent. You can keep the design of all the forms in your database consistent by setting a theme.

▶ Add a header to a form to let users know the topic of the form. You can include text and graphics in the form's header.

▶ If a form contains information you want to print, as with an order form, you can print the form and specify its printed layout.

Commands Review

Action	Menu Bar	Shortcut Menu	Toolbar	Keyboard
When entering or editing form data:				
Open a combo box or a drop-down list		Right-click the box or list and select <u>O</u>pen	Click the list or drop-down arrow	F4 or ALT + DOWN ARROW
Move up or down one line			Click the line	UP or DOWN ARROW
Move to the previous or next page			Click the scroll arrows	PAGEUP or PAGEDOWN
Move to the next field			Click the next field	TAB
Find a record	<u>E</u>dit, <u>F</u>ind <u>E</u>dit, <u>G</u>o To	Right-click a record and select <u>F</u>ind		CTRL + F ALT + E, F ALT + E, E
When designing a form:				
Select a field			Click to see selection handles	TAB
Select more than one field			SHIFT + click to select adjacent fields; CTRL + click to select non-adjacent fields; double-click field list title bar to select all fields	SHIFT + ARROW or CTRL + ARROW

Concepts Review

SCANS

Circle the correct answer.

1. A form should:
[a] be visually appealing and guide users through the process of entering data.
[b] automate queries.
[c] help to create a paperless office.
[d] use macros to display images.

2. One of the purposes of a form is to:
[a] print the complete contents of a database.
[b] enter and view data.
[c] create special wizards.
[d] design a layout for your tables.

3. The form acts like a _____ to hide the database from the user.
[a] tool
[b] mask
[c] creator
[d] wizard

4. Editing records in a form is the _____ editing records in a table.
[a] same as
[b] opposite of
[c] result of
[d] only way of

5. To modify a form:
- [a] you must be in Datasheet view.
- [b] you must be in Design view.
- [c] use the Form Wizard.
- [d] you need to know advanced Access techniques.

6. When you want to create a simple form using all the fields in the related table use:
- [a] Design view.
- [b] the Form Wizard.
- [c] the Table Wizard.
- [d] Datasheet view.

7. Create a custom form when you want to:
- [a] add a visually appealing background.
- [b] use information from more than one table.
- [c] add a photograph to a record.
- [d] detach a form from a table.

8. Adding a title to a form:
- [a] lets you use information from more than one table.
- [b] lets you list valid options for a field.
- [c] tells the user the subject of the form.
- [d] is part of data entry.

9. Creating controls:
- [a] helps users know the purpose of a form.
- [b] lets users select a valid option from a list.
- [c] restricts field length.
- [d] provides instructions for printing the form.

10. You can enhance the design of a form by:
- [a] modifying it in Datasheet view.
- [b] choosing a theme.
- [c] entering all the required data.
- [d] creating a custom form.

Circle **T** if the statement is true or **F** if the statement is false.

T F 1. A control determines the format of a form.

T **F** 2. You can print a form, but not the data included in it.

T F 3. You can change the tab order of a form so users can move logically from one field to another.

T **F** 4. You can only create a form using the Form Wizard.

T F 5. You can create forms that will allow you to enter information from several different tables.

T F 6. Forms simplify data entry.

T **F** 7. To find a record you want to edit, you can use the Locate command.   *Find*

T **F** 8. You cannot delete or move fields once you finish designing a form.

T **F** 9. The Combo Box Wizard guides you through the steps of including a dialog box in your form.   *Combo box*

T **F** 10. One principle in good design is to use a lot of formatting features.

chapter four

Skills Review

Exercise 1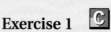

1. If necessary, open the *mdbDynamicInc4* database.

2. Use the Form Wizard to create a new form based on both fields in the tblRegions table. Use the Columnar layout and the Standard style.

3. Name the new form frmRegions.

4. Close and save the frmRegions form.

Exercise 2 C   *Completed*

1. If necessary, open the *mdbDynamicInc4* database.

2. Use the Form Wizard to create a new form based on the tblCustomers table. Use only the following fields in the form: Customer ID, Company Name, Billing Address, City, Country, and Phone.

3. Choose the justified layout and Standard style for the form.

4. Name the new form frmCustomers.

5. Save and close the frmCustomers form.

Exercise 3 C   *Completed*

1. If necessary, open the *mdbDynamicInc4* database.

2. Open the frmCustomers form you created in Exercise 2.

3. Enter the following information in new records in the form:

CANAD, Canadian Products, 12 N. Ontario, Ontario, Canada

MEXIC, Mexican Goods, Pampas 900, Mexico City, Mexico

JAPAN, Japanese Gifts, 67 Kyoto, Tokyo, Japan

4. Print the frmCustomers form with the data.

5. Save and close the frmCustomers form.

Exercise 4 C   *Completed – reprint Wednesday*

1. If necessary, open the *mdbDynamicInc4* database.

2. Open the frmCustomers form you created in Exercise 2 and added records to in Exercise 3.

3. In Design view, rearrange the labels and fields in the form. For example, move the City, Country, and Phone fields down and move the Address field below the Customer ID and Company Name.

4. Print the frmCustomers form.

5. Save and close the frmCustomers form.

Exercise 5

1. If necessary, open the *mdbDynamicInc4* database.

2. Open the frmCustomers form you revised in Exercise 4.

3. In Design view, add a combo box to the form to help you search for records by company name.
   a) Use the Find a record... option
   b) Select the CompanyName field and widen the field to view the entire company name
   c) Use "Select Company" as the label
   d) Size the combo box label as necessary and position the label and combo box as needed

4. Test the form by switching to Form view and selecting a company name from the list.

5. Close and save the frmCustomers form.

Exercise 6

1. If necessary, open the *mdbDynamicInc4* database.

2. Open the frmCustomers form you revised in Exercise 5.

3. Change the tab order of the form by repositioning the Phone field directly below the CompanyName field.

4. Test the tab order in the form.

5. Save and close the frmCustomers form.

Exercise 7

1. If necessary, open the *mdbDynamicInc4* database.

2. Open the frmCustomers form you revised in Exercise 6.

3. Choose a theme for the form's design.

4. Save and close the frmCustomers form.

Exercise 8

1. If necessary, open the *mdbDynamicInc4* database.

2. Open the frmCustomers form you revised in Exercise 7.

3. Add a header containing the "Dynamic Inc. Customers" label to the form. Size and format the label with an 18-point font of your choice.

4. Save and close the frmCustomers form.

chapter four

Case Projects

Project 1

Using the Microsoft on the Web command on the Help menu, open the Microsoft home page and then link to pages that provide basic information about Access forms. Print at least two of the Web pages.

Project 2

Connect to your ISP and load the home page for a search engine. Search for sites that provide principles for good design of paper-based publications, such as a newsletter, or electronic publications, such as a Web page. Print at least two of the Web pages. Use this information for Projects 3–8.

Project 3

Maria Moreno, the owner of Dynamic, Inc., asks you to create four forms for the other tables in *mdbDynamic4Inc*. Start by creating a simple form for the tblDepartment table. Choose a theme for the form. Modify and enhance the form to conform to the principles of good design.

Project 4

Use the Form Wizard to create the second form based on the tblProducts table. Use the same theme for the frmProducts form as you did for the frmDepartment form. Add a control that lists the values from the tblSuppliers table.

Project 5

Create the third form based on the tblOrders table. Use the same design as you did for the other forms. Rearrange the fields on the form. Check the tab order so users can complete the fields in logical order. Add a calculated control to calculate the total price of the orders. See online Help for instructions on adding a calculated control to a form.

Project 6

In Design view, create the fourth form based on the tblSuppliers table. Use the same design as you did for the other forms. Add other fields, such as phone and fax number. If necessary, use online Help for instructions on creating a form in Design view.

Project 7

Open one of the forms you created in Projects 3–6. Test the form design by entering data. Modify the design to make data entry easier.

Project 8

Open one of the forms you created in Projects 3–6. Test the form design by entering data. Enhance the design by adding a graphic (search the Office Clip Art folder, if necessary), adding a header, or changing the font styles of the field labels.

Integrating Access with Other Office Applications and the Internet

Chapter Overview

I n this chapter, you learn to use an Access database with other Office 2000 applications. You export an Access table to a Word document, import an Excel spreadsheet, and link an Excel spreadsheet. You also create hyperlinks to connect to the Internet and visit Web sites or send e-mail messages.

Case profile

Managers at Dynamic Inc., realize it is more efficient if they use information they create in other Office applications, such as Word and Excel, with the Access database information. For example, Kay Wong, the marketing manager, wants to create a product catalog listing the information from an Access table. Maria Moreno, the owner of Dynamic, wants to use information from Excel spreadsheets to create new Access tables. Maria also wants you to make it easy to send e-mail messages from Access.

integration

AX.a Exporting Database Objects

You may find it helpful to use information from your Access database in other Office 2000 applications. Using Office 2000, you do not need to re-enter the information. Instead, you can simply export the database object(s) to the appropriate Office application.

For example, Kay began creating a catalog of Dynamic's products and prices using Microsoft Word, but asks you to complete it by supplying the most current information. You realize that this information is already contained in the Access database, so you decide to export the data from an Access table to the Word document.

Exporting an Access Table to a Word Document

Word's **Mail Merge Helper** dialog box guides you through the steps of merging Access data into a Word document. First, you specify the main document—the Word document that will contain the Access data. Next, you identify the data source—the Access table containing the data you want to include in the Word document. You can merge selected fields and records, or all of them. If necessary, you can return to the main document and enter or edit text and fields. The main document can include text that doesn't change when you merge, as well as merge fields for information that comes from Access. For example, Kay's document includes text identifying the document as the Dynamic Product Catalog, and fields for the product information and prices.

When you're ready to merge, Word finds the table, records, and fields you specified, and merges that information into the main document. Figure AX-1 shows how the Access table, Word main document, and merged document relate.

FIGURE AX-1
Merging Access Data with
a Word Document

Access table   Main document   Merged document

Now that you understand the process, you are ready to start the Mail Merge Helper.

Starting the Mail Merge Helper

To start the Mail Merge Helper, you first open the Word document with which you merge the Access data.

To start the Mail Merge Helper:

Step 1	*Start*	Microsoft Word 2000
Step 2	*Open*	the *Catalog* Word document located on your Data Disk
Step 3	*Click*	Tools
Step 4	*Click*	Mail Merge

The Mail Merge Helper dialog box on your screen should look similar to Figure AX-2.

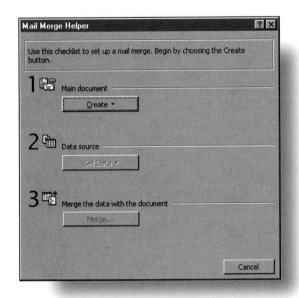

FIGURE AX-2
Mail Merge Helper
Dialog Box

The Mail Merge Helper dialog box includes three sections where you need to provide information: Main document, Data source, and Merge the data with the document. You first need to complete the Main document section.

Selecting the Main Document

The **main document** is the document you edit or create that stays the same each time you merge. In this case, the *Catalog* document you opened is the main document.

To select the main document:

Step 1	*Click*	Create in the Main document section

Step 2	*Click*	Catalog as the type of main document you are creating

A dialog box opens and asks if you want to use the open document or create a new one. Use the active document.

Step 3	*Click*	Active Window

The next step is to specify a data source by choosing the Get Data button.

Selecting the Data Source

The **data source** is the document or object containing the information you merge into the Word document. For the product catalog, this is the Access table containing product information.

To select the data source:

Step 1	*Click*	Get Data in the Data source section

Step 2	*Click*	Open Data Source

The Open Data Source dialog box on your screen should look similar to Figure AX-3.

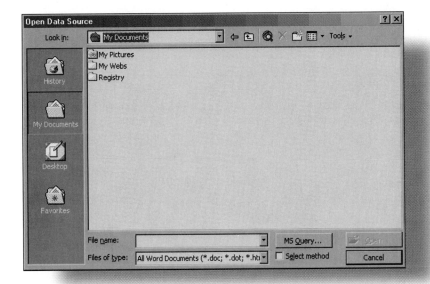

FIGURE AX-3
Open Data Source
Dialog Box

You need to locate the Dynamic database. To do that, change the file type in the Files of type: list box to MS Access Databases and change the Look in: list box as necessary to locate your Data Disk.

Step 3	*Locate*	mdbDynamicInt database on your Data Disk
Step 4	*Double-click*	mdbDynamicInt database to open it
Step 5	*Double-click*	tblProducts in the Tables tab of the Microsoft Access dialog box

You are now ready to set up the main document for merging.

Setting Up the Main Document for Merging

After you select the data source, a dialog box asks if you want to edit the main document. You can do so to enter and edit text and merge fields. In Kay's document, you include four fields for merging: ProductID, Category_Name, ProductDescription, and Unit_Price.

To set up the main document:

Step 1	*Click*	Edit Main Document

Your screen should look similar to Figure AX-4.

FIGURE AX-4
Word Main Document

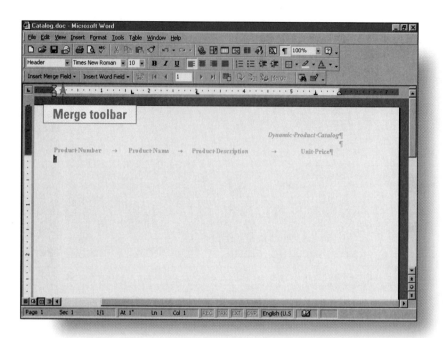

Notice the **Merge toolbar** at the top of the screen, which lets you perform your merging tasks.

CAUTION TIP

If you do not add a blank line following the merge field line, the catalog document will not merge properly.

Step 2	*Verify*	the insertion point is at the top of the document
Step 3	*Click*	the Insert Merge Field button on the Merge toolbar
Step 4	*Click*	ProductID in the field name list
Step 5	*Press*	the TAB key
Step 6	*Repeat*	Steps 3–5 to insert the Category_Name, ProductDescription, and Unit_Price fields
Step 7	*Press*	the ENTER key after inserting the Unit_Price merge field

Your screen should look similar to Figure AX-5.

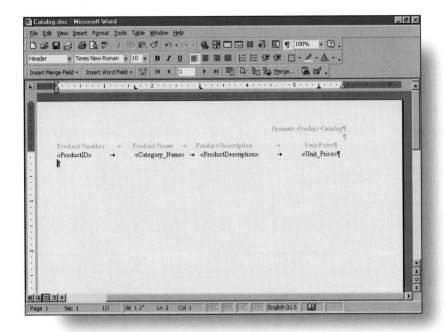

FIGURE AX-5
Main Document with
Access Fields

All the fields you selected for merging are shown within << >> characters, which means the data source supplies the information. Now you're ready to insert the data into these fields.

Merging the Data

After you select and set up the main document, you're ready to merge information from the data source, such as an Access table, into the document. When you merge, you replace the fields (the <<*text*>> items) with the corresponding data from each record you select in the data source. For the product catalog, merge the ProductID, Category_Name, ProductDescription, and Unit_Price records from the tblProducts table into the appropriate fields in the *Catalog* document.

To merge the data:

Step 1	*Click*	Tools
Step 2	*Click*	Mail Merge

integration

The Merge button is now available in the Merge the data with the document section of the Mail Merge Helper dialog box.

| Step 3 | *Click* | <u>M</u>erge |

The Merge dialog box on your screen should look similar to Figure AX-6.

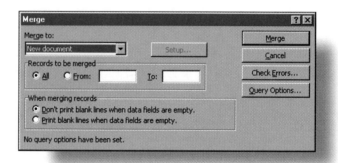

Use this dialog box to select the document you want to merge into, and to select the records you want. If you want to create address labels or envelopes, click the <u>P</u>rint blank lines when data fields are empty option button. For the Dynamic product catalog, you accept the default choices: new document, all records, and do not print blank lines. You are ready to merge.

| Step 4 | *Click* | <u>M</u>erge |

The Mail Merge Helper inserts the data from the fields in the tblProducts table into the *Catalog* document. Your screen should look similar to Figure AX-7.

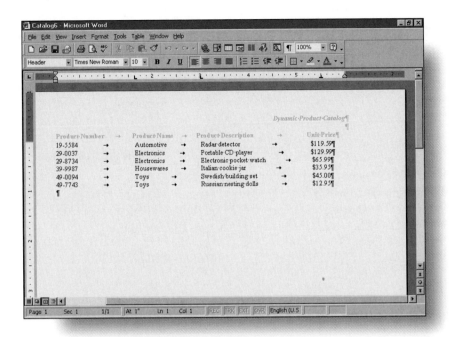

> **QUICK TIP**
>
> You can also use the Merge toolbar to perform other merging tasks. Use the Merge tools to check for errors, merge to a new document, merge to a printer, or merge with the current settings.

You need to save your work.

Saving the Merged Document

After you merge, you want to save the new document you created that contains the actual data, not the fields. In this case, you want to save the merged *Catalog* document, which lists Dynamic's products and prices.

To save a merged document:

Step 1	*Click*	File
Step 2	*Click*	Save As
Step 3	*Save*	the document as *Dynamic Catalog*
Step 4	*Exit*	Word without saving the Catalog.doc document

You can also merge Access information into other Office applications, such as Excel.

C **AX.b** Exporting Database Records to Excel

If you want to use your Access data in Excel or another spreadsheet program, you can export your Access records. You can export a datasheet with or without formatting, such as fonts and colors. Exporting data without formatting speeds up the export process. You can also save the formatted output of a datasheet, form, or report as an Excel file. If you want to immediately work with the exported information, you can export records by loading them directly into Excel.

Maria wants to export tblProducts so she can work with unit price information in Excel. You can export all the records in the table to an Excel file.

To export records to an Excel file:

Step 1	*Open*	mdbDynamicInt
Step 2	*Click*	Tables on the Objects bar in the Database window
Step 3	*Click*	tblProducts
Step 4	*Click*	File
Step 5	*Click*	Export

You see the Export Table To dialog box, where you can select the name, location, and type of file you want to export. You can save the exported file in the default location, which should be your Data Disk.

Step 6	*Click*	the File name: text box, if necessary
Step 7	*Key*	Products
Step 8	*Click*	the Save as type: list arrow
Step 9	*Click*	Microsoft Excel 97-2000 (*.xls)
Step 10	*Click*	the Save formatted check box

This saves the field widths in tblProducts. If tblProducts also contained fonts, colors, or data from Lookup fields, checking the Save formatted check box would also save that formatting. The Export Table To dialog box on your screen should look similar to Figure AX-8.

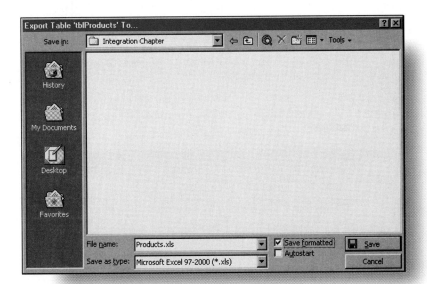

FIGURE AX-8
Export Table To Dialog Box

| Step 11 | *Click* | Save |

Access creates the spreadsheet file containing the records from tblProducts, and puts the field names in the first row of the spreadsheet.

Now Maria wants to select only a few records from tblProducts and load them directly into an Excel spreadsheet. You can do this by using an Office Links command.

To export selected records and open an Excel file:

| Step 1 | *Double-click* | tblProducts in the Database window |
| Step 2 | *Drag* | down in the record selection column to select the first three records |

Your screen should look similar to Figure AX-9.

integration

FIGURE AX-9
Records Selected in
tblProducts

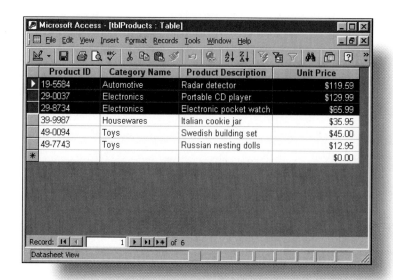

Step 3	*Click*	<u>T</u>ools
Step 4	*Point to*	Office <u>L</u>inks
Step 5	*Click*	<u>A</u>nalyze It With MS Excel

Access saves the records as an Excel file in the default database folder, and then Excel automatically starts and opens the file.

| Step 6 | *Exit* | Excel |
| Step 7 | *Close* | the tblProducts table |

You can also share other Office application data with Access by importing or linking.

AX.c Using Excel Data with Access

If you work with Microsoft Excel, you can easily include spreadsheets in your Access database by importing or linking the Excel data. When you import, you take information from an Excel spreadsheet and copy it into an Access table. The Excel data becomes part of your Access database—you can change the imported data without affecting the original file. When you link, you insert an object in your database that names an Excel spreadsheet and its location. You insert a reference to the Excel file so Access can display the information in the spreadsheet. The major advantage of linking is that if you change the original Excel file, the Access database reflects those changes, and vice versa—if you change the linked data, you change the original file.

In general, link Excel data when you expect that data to change. Import when you simply want to insert a copy of Excel data in your database without changing it. The Table AX-1 lists considerations for deciding when to import and when to link Excel data.

	When Importing Excel Data	**When Linking Excel Data**
Disk storage required	You copy information from an Excel spreadsheet into your database, which requires extra disk storage space.	You insert an object in your database that references an Excel spreadsheet. Because you are inserting a link, and not the data itself, you do not need extra disk space.
Original file status	You do not need an up-to-date copy of the original Excel file.	Access must be able to find the file so it can display up-to-date information.
Data format	You convert the Excel data to Access format.	The Excel data remains in its original format, but acts like an Access database.
Properties and structure	You can change all properties and structure.	You can change some properties, but not the structure.
Performance Deletions	Access performs at normal speed. You delete the data when you delete the object, such as a table, containing it.	Access performs more slowly. You delete the data, but not the data from the original file.
Data type translations	You translate some data types from Excel to Access.	Access does not translate linked data types.

TABLE AX-1
Importing or Linking Excel Data

CAUTION TIP

Before you link or import an Excel spreadsheet, make sure that the data in the spreadsheet is arranged in a tabular format, and that the spreadsheet has the same type of data in each field (column) and the same fields in every row.

integration

Importing Data to a New Table

Dynamic recently purchased a small candy factory. Ben Mayer, the sales manager for the Sweet Tooth Candy Company, created an Excel spreadsheet listing their product types. Maria, Dynamic's owner, asked you to add the product type information to your database. To do this, you decide to import the information into your Access database because the product types do not frequently change.

To begin importing Excel data into Access:

Step 1	*Verify*	mdbDynamicInt is open
Step 2	*Click*	File
Step 3	*Point to*	Get External Data
Step 4	*Click*	Import

The Import dialog box on your screen should look similar to Figure AX-10.

FIGURE AX-10
Import Dialog Box

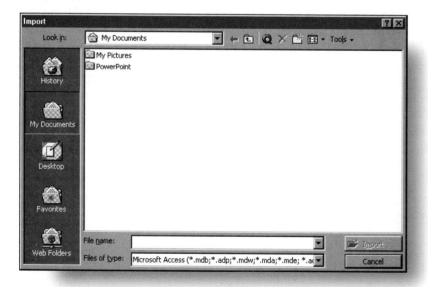

You do not see any Excel files listed in the dialog box because you need to change the Files of type: list box to read Microsoft Excel.

Step 5	*Switch*	to the Data Disk
Step 6	*Click*	Microsoft Excel in the Files of type: list
Step 7	*Double-click*	*Sweet_Tooth_Products* to open the Excel file

The Import Spreadsheet Wizard dialog box on your screen should look similar to Figure AX-11.

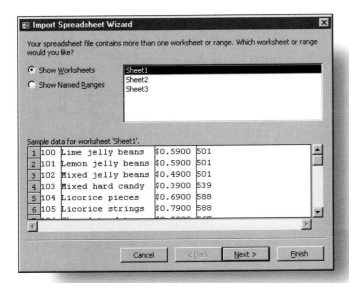

The **Import Spreadsheet Wizard** guides you in both selecting the information to import from the Excel file and determining how you want it to appear in your Access database.

The first dialog box in the wizard asks which worksheet or ranges you want to use and previews the data.

integration

To begin the Import Spreadsheet Wizard:

Step 1	*Click*	<u>N</u>ext >

This dialog box asks you if the first row contains the column headings. In the preview, you see that there are no headings, so do not click the box.

Step 2	*Click*	<u>N</u>ext >

You can now import the information into a new table.

Step 3	*Click*	<u>N</u>ext >

Your screen should look similar to Figure AX-12.

FIGURE AX-12
Selecting Fields with
the Import Spreadsheet
Wizard

Field column label

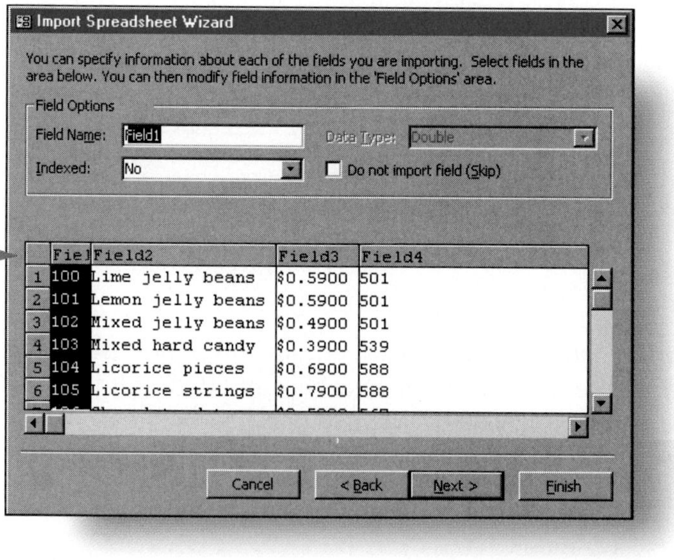

You can now select the fields you want to import. (When you import an Excel spreadsheet where the column headings are in the first row, Access automatically selects the appropriate fields.) Select the first three fields for Product ID, Product Name, and Unit Price fields to import, but skip the last field for Supplier ID.

Step 4	*Click*	the Field1 column label, if necessary
Step 5	*Key*	Product ID in the Field Na<u>m</u>e: box
Step 6	*Repeat*	Steps 4 and 5 to name Fields2 and 3 Product Name and Unit Price, respectively

Now indicate that you don't want to import the Supplier ID field.

Step 7	*Click*	the Field4 column label
Step 8	*Click*	the Do not import field (<u>S</u>kip) check box

Your screen should look similar to Figure AX-13.

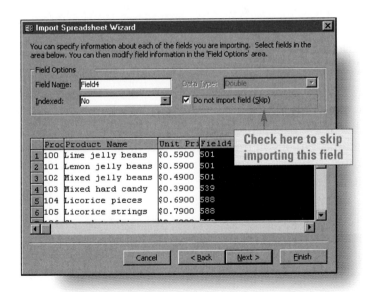

FIGURE AX-13
Fields to Import

integration

Step 9	*Click*	Next >

Access asks if you want to select the primary key. Choose Product ID as the primary key, otherwise Access will add an ID field to use as the primary key.

Step 10	*Click*	Choose my own primary key

Access shows the first field, Product ID, as the primary key. You can now complete the Import Spreadsheet Wizard.

To complete the Import Spreadsheet Wizard:

Step 1	*Click*	Next >

Although Access usually gives the table the same name as the original table, you can change the name if necessary.

Step 2	*Key*	tblSweetProducts
Step 3	*Click*	Finish
Step 4	*Click*	OK

Access imports the data, which may take some time depending on the size of the Excel spreadsheet and the processing speed of your machine. Once you import the table, it becomes an Access object. You can then use Access commands to change the table. Open the table to check it.

Step 5	*Double-click*	tblSweetProducts

You can now modify the data or the table design as you would any Access table. For example, you could resize the Product Name field to see all the complete entries.

When you finish working with the table, you are ready to close it.

Step 6	*Close*	tblSweetProducts

When you import data, any changes you make to the table do not affect the original Excel spreadsheet. When you link data, however, any changes you make are also reflected in the original file.

Linking to Existing Data

Ben Mayer's Excel spreadsheet lists the sales representatives and their commission rates. Maria asks you to also add this information to your database. Because this information periodically changes, link the data. That way, any changes in the original Excel spreadsheet are reflected in your database. You use the Link Spreadsheet Wizard, which is similar to the Import Spreadsheet Wizard.

To link an Excel table to an Access database:

Step 1	*Click*	<u>F</u>ile
Step 2	*Point to*	<u>G</u>et External Data
Step 3	*Click*	<u>L</u>ink Tables

The Link dialog box opens. You need to change the file type.

Step 4	*Click*	Microsoft Excel from the Files of <u>t</u>ype: list
Step 5	*Double-click*	*Sweet_Tooth_Sales*

Access now starts the Link Spreadsheet Wizard.
To use the Link Spreadsheet Wizard:

Step 1	*Click*	<u>N</u>ext >

integration

This dialog box asks if the first row contains the column headings. In this spreadsheet, the first row does contain the column headings.

Step 2	*Click*	the First Row Contains Column Headings check box, if necessary
Step 3	*Click*	<u>N</u>ext >
Step 4	*Key*	tblSweetSales in the linked Table Name: text box
Step 5	*Click*	<u>F</u>inish
Step 6	*Click*	OK

Now you can open the new table.

Step 7	*Double-click*	tblSweetSales

Your screen should look similar to Figure AX-14.

FIGURE AX-14
Table with Linked Data

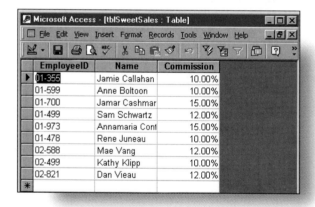

The Link Spreadsheet Wizard creates the tblSweetSales table with a link to the *Sweet_Tooth_Sales* Excel spreadsheet. When you work with the linked table, you change the data in both the Access tblSweetSales table and the original *Sweet_Tooth_Sales* spreadsheet.

You are ready to close the table.

| Step 8 | *Close* | the table |

Your final task is to enable Dynamic's database users to connect easily to the Internet.

AX.d Integrating Access with the Internet

You can integrate your Access database with the Internet to connect to sites on the World Wide Web as well as to send e-mail messages. Maria Moreno wants you to add a field to the new tblSweetProducts table so she can instantly connect to the Sweet Tooth Web site and other related Web sites. She also wants you to add a button to the frmEmployees form to include the employee's e-mail address. You can create a command button Maria can click to create an e-mail message.

Creating and Adding Hyperlinks

If your users have access to the Internet, they can visit Web sites from within an Access database. To do this, you simply add a **hyperlink field**, a field containing a Web address, to a table. You can insert a hyperlink to connect to the Sweet Tooth Web site so Maria can visit the site while she's working with the tblSweetProducts table.

To add a field with a hyperlink:

Step 1	*Click*	Tables on the Objects bar
Step 2	*Double-click*	tblSweetProducts
Step 3	*Switch*	to Design view
Step 4	*Key*	Web Site in the first blank field
Step 5	*Click*	the Data Type column list arrow
Step 6	*Click*	Hyperlink

C

Your screen should look similar to Figure AX-15.

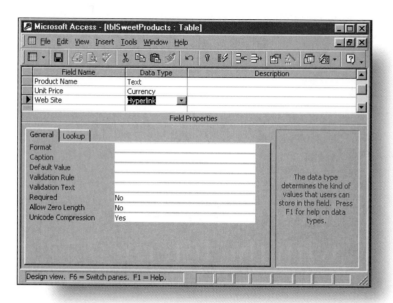

| Step 7 | **Click** | the Save button 🖬 on the Database toolbar |

You can now enter Web addresses in the tblSweetProducts table. To enter a Web address:

Step 1	**Switch**	to Datasheet view
Step 2	**Key**	www.sweettooth.com in the first Web Site field
Step 3	**Widen**	the Web Site column to view the entire hyperlink

Your screen should look similar to Figure AX-16.

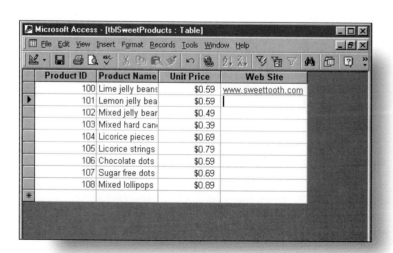

Step 4	*Close*	the table, saving your changes

Now that you created a hyperlink, you are ready to create a command button.

Creating E-Mail Messages from Within Access

If your users have access to the Internet, they can send e-mail messages from an Access object, such as a form. You can create a command button on the frmEmployees form. When Maria clicks the button, Access opens her e-mail application and creates a new message, with the address already filled in.

To create a command button to send e-mail messages:

Step 1	*Click*	Forms 🗔 on the Objects bar
Step 2	*Double-click*	frmEmployees
Step 3	*Switch*	to Design view

Deselect the Control Wizards tool on the toolbox, if necessary.

Step 4	*Verify*	the Control Wizards button 🗔 is not selected
Step 5	*Click*	the Command Button 🗔 on the Toolbox
Step 6	*Click*	the form where you want to place the command button; in the frmEmployees form, click next to the Employee ID field

Your screen should look similar to Figure AX-17.

FIGURE AX-17
Adding a Command
Button to a Form

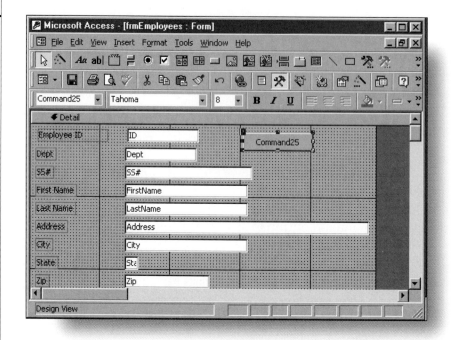

Now you're ready to set up the button so you can click it to send e-mail messages.

To set up the command button to send e-mail messages:

Step 1	*Right-click*	the Command button
Step 2	*Click*	<u>P</u>roperties
Step 3	*Click*	in the Hyperlink Address field on the Format tab in the Command Button dialog box
Step 4	*Click*	the Hyperlink Address ellipses button to open the Insert Hyperlink dialog box

The Insert Hyperlink dialog box opens, allowing you to specify the type of hyperlink you want to create. Your screen should look similar to Figure AX-18.

FIGURE AX-18
Insert Hyperlink
Dialog Box

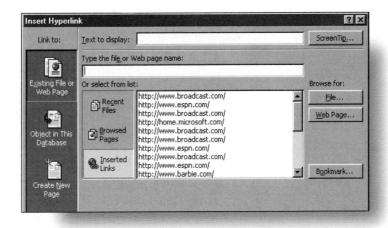

Step 5	*Click*	E-mail Address in the Link to: column on the left of the dialog box, if necessary
Step 6	*Key*	E-mail in the Text to display: box
Step 7	*Key*	kWong@dyn.com in the E-mail address: box
Step 8	*Click*	OK
Step 9	*Close*	the Command Button Properties box

If necessary, you can reposition the command button on the form. You can now send e-mail messages from the frmEmployees form automatically addressed to kWong.

To test the hyperlink:

Step 1	*Switch*	to Form View
Step 2	*Click*	the E-mail hyperlink to open the e-mail message window
Step 3	*Close*	the e-mail message window without saving changes if asked
Step 4	*Close*	the form, saving your changes
Step 5	*Exit*	Access

Hyperlinks in Access make it easy for Dynamic managers to connect to the Internet and visit Web sites or send e-mail messages.

Summary

▶ You can merge data from an Access table to a Word document using Word's Mail Merge Helper. Specify the Word document to use as the main document and the Access table to use as the data source. Then enter or edit the text and merge fields in the main document, and merge the records and fields you selected from the Access table into the Word document.

▶ You can include Excel data in an Access table by importing or linking an Excel spreadsheet to a new or existing Access table.

▶ When you import an Excel spreadsheet, you copy the Excel data into an Access table. The Excel data becomes part of your Access database—you can change the imported data without affecting the original file.

▶ When you link an Excel spreadsheet to an Access table, you insert a reference to the Excel file so Access can display the information in the spreadsheet. If you click anywhere in the linked table, you can use Excel commands to enter and edit information.

▶ In general, link Excel data when you expect that data to change. If you change the original spreadsheet, the Access database reflects those changes. If you change the linked table, the Excel spreadsheet reflects those changes.

▶ You can connect to the Internet and the World Wide Web from Access. Add a hyperlink to a table or form so you can click it and use your e-mail application to send e-mail messages, or go to a specified site on the Web.

Commands Review

Action	Menu Bar	Shortcut Menu	Toolbar	Keyboard
Import a table	File, Get External Data, Import	Import		ALT + F, G, I
Link to a table	File, Get External Data, Link to a table	Link Tables		ALT + F, G, L
Export records	File, Export	Export		ALT + F, E
Export records and open Excel	Tools, Office Links		🖳▾	ALT + T, L
Insert a hyperlink	Insert, Hyperlink	Hyperlink	🌐	CTRL + K ALT + I, i

Concepts Review

Circle the correct answer.

1. Which option do you use to merge data between Word and Access?
[a] Merge
[b] Mail Merge
[c] Import Data
[d] Get External Data

2. When merging Access data into a Word document, the data source is:
[a] the Word document that will contain the Access data.
[b] the Access object containing the data you want to merge.
[c] the document containing the text that doesn't change when you merge.
[d] a list of fields you can merge.

3. In a Word document, all the fields you select for merging are shown as:
[a] {Field}
[b] <Field>
[c] [[Field]]
[d] <<Field>>

4. Which one is *not* a wizard used to integrate Access with other Office products?
[a] Mail Merge Wizard
[b] Import Spreadsheet Wizard
[c] Form Wizard
[d] Link Spreadsheet Wizard

5. Merge Access data into Word when you want to:
[a] insert a reference to Access within a Word document.
[b] create Word documents customized with Access information.
[c] copy an entire Access table into a Word document.
[d] change fields frequently.

integration

6. Link an Excel spreadsheet to an Access table when you:
[a] expect the Excel spreadsheet data to change.
[b] do not need up-to-date information.
[c] want to convert the spreadsheet to an Access table.
[d] want to merge the Excel data into Access.

7. Import Excel data to Access when you:
[a] expect the Excel spreadsheet data to change.
[b] want a copy of the data in an Access object.
[c] want to use Excel commands to edit the data later.
[d] want to merge the Excel data into Access.

8. Imported data does *not*:
[a] reference an external source.
[b] convert to Access format.
[c] work faster with Access.
[d] allow data type translation.

9. Linked data does *not*:
[a] require extra storage space.
[b] allow you to update information.
[c] work slower with Access.
[d] allow you to change any properties.

10. You can add a hyperlink to an Access object to:
[a] use an Excel spreadsheet in an Access table.
[b] simplify mail merging.
[c] visit a Web site or send an e-mail message.
[d] change the properties of a linked table.

Circle **T** if the statement is true or **F** if the statement is false.

T F 1. Merging data requires the help of a database expert.

T F 2. When you prepare to merge, you can create a main Word document and identify an Access table as a data source.

T F 3. The merge fields you insert in a Word document don't have to match any fields in the Access data source to merge successfully.

T F 4. When you import Excel data, you do not convert it into Access format.

T F 5. Access works fastest with a linked table.

T F 6. You must close Access before visiting sites on the World Wide Web.

T F 7. You can change all the properties of the Excel data you import.

T   F   8. Any changes made to linked data affect the original source.

T   F   9. Importing a table lets you make a copy of the data and turn it into an Access object.

T   F   10. If you need to include up-to-date data that changes frequently, you should import the data.

Skills Review

Exercise 1

1. Open the *PhoneList* Word document on your Data Disk.

2. Merge the tblEmployees table from *mdbDynamicInt* into the Phonelist document in Word using the Mail Merge Helper. Create a catalog main document. Merge the ID, Dept, FirstName, LastName, and HomePhone fields.

3. Edit the phone numbers with an appropriate format.

4. Print the merged document and save it as *PhoneList1*.

5. Close the *PhoneList* document without saving it.

Exercise 2

1. In Word, open the AddressList document.

2. Use the Mail Merge Helper to merge the tblEmployees table from *mdbDynamicInt* to create a merged catalog document.

3. In the AddressList main document, insert fields for each column heading.

4. Merge the data, and then save the document as *AddressList1*.

5. Print and close *AddressList1*.

Exercise 3

1. If necessary, open the *mdbDynamicInt* database.

2. Import the *Sweet_Tooth_Salary* Excel spreadsheet from the Data Disk. Use Employee ID as the primary key.

3. Save the imported table as tblSalary and then close it.

Exercise 4

1. If necessary, open the *mdbDynamicInt* database.

2. Import the *Sweet_Tooth_Staff* Excel spreadsheet. Select only the Employee ID, Name, and Total Salary fields to import. Retain their names. Let Access set the Primary key.

3. Save the imported table as tblStaff, and then open it.

4. Save and close the tblStaff table.

Exercise 5

1. If necessary, open the *mdbDynamicInt* database.

2. Link the *Sweet_Tooth_Staff* Excel spreadsheet from the Data Disk. Use all the fields.

3. Save the linked table as tblSweetTooth.

Exercise 6

1. If necessary, open the *mdbDynamicInt* database.

2. Open the tblProducts table form in Design view.

3. Add a field called Links with a Hyperlink data type. Save the table.

4. In Datasheet view, enter *www.mobilizenow*.com in the first hyperlink field.

5. Use it to connect to the MobilizeNow.com Web site.

6. Save and close the table.

Exercise 7

1. If necessary, open the *mdbDynamicInt* database.

2. Open the frmOrders form in Design view.

3. Add a command button to send an e-mail message to *mMoreno@dyn.com*.

4. Save and close the form.

Case Projects

Project 1

Maria Moreno, the owner of Dynamic Inc., asks you to find out if you can convert an Access 2000 database so someone with a previous version of Access can use it. Search the Access online Help for information on converting an Access 2000 database to a previous version. Use Word to create a document that provides the information. Print and save the document.

Project 2

Maria wants you to find a quick way to use *mdbDynamicInt* tables and queries in an Excel spreadsheet. Open Microsoft Excel and resize Excel and Access so you can see both windows on your desktop. In the Access Database window, click tblProducts and drag it from Access to a blank worksheet in Excel. Save and print the new spreadsheet.

Project 3

Maria thinks some information in your database is appropriate for the Dynamic Web site. You can publish HTML pages on the World Wide Web. Search the Access online Help for instructions on exporting an Access object as HTML. Then follow those instructions to export the tblProducts table in *mdbDynamicInt* as HTML. (Hint: Search Online Help using the keywords "save as html".)

Project 4

Maria asks you to create a supplement to the product catalog that lists the newest products—those offered in the last month. She created a query called qryNewProducts in *mdbDynamicInt* that finds all the new Dynamic products. Search the Word online Help for instructions on using an Access query as a data source for mail merge. Then follow the instructions to merge the records in qryNewProducts to a new Word document that you save as *Catalog Supplement*.

Project 5

Before you created the database for Dynamic, Maria stored important customer information in a text file. Now she wants you to import this text file—*Best_Customers*—into the tblCustomers table. Search the Word online Help for instructions on importing a Word text file to Access. Then follow these instructions to import the text in to the tblCustomers table.

Project 6

Using the Office on the Web command on the Help menu, open the Microsoft home page and then link to pages that provide information about data integration topics, such as mail merge, importing and exporting, and linking. Print at least two of the Web pages.

Project 7

Open the *mdbDynamicInt* database and create a new form based on the tblSweetProducts table. Name the form frmSweetProducts. Add a control to the new form that creates an e-mail message using a hyperlink and a command button. Save the form. Open the form in Form view and send an e-mail message to someone whose e-mail address you know.

Establishing Relationships Between Tables

Chapter Overview

I f you relate tables, Access links their information when you use the data in forms, queries, and reports. In this chapter, you learn how to plan relationships and then join or relate the tables.

► Establish table relationships
► Establish one-to-many relationships
► Enforce referential integrity
► Add additional tables to a relationship
► Specify join properties for relationships

Case profile

Dynamic Inc., stores its company information in several Access tables. Juanita Chavez, the customer service manager, maintains the customer data in one table. Kang Leing, the warehouse manager, tracks the product inventory data in a second table. Alan Golden, the sales manager, keeps the order data in a third table. They ask you to create an efficient way for them to use one another's information. To do this, you create relationships among the three tables.

chapter
five

5.a **Establishing Table Relationships**

Once you determine that you want to relate tables in your database, you start by defining the kind of relationship(s) you want to establish. Three table relationships are possible. A **one-to-one relationship** means each table has only one related field. A **one-to-many relationship** means the primary table can have more than one related record in the secondary table. A **many-to-many relationship** means each table can have many related records.

To determine which relationship you want to establish in your database tables, first look at the fields of your tables and how you use the data in the tables. For the Dynamic database, Juanita, Kang, and Alan maintain the data for their departments. At times, they want to access information in another manager's table, especially when they want to avoid entering information already contained in another table. To meet their goals, start by determining the relationships for the tables. You begin by opening all the tables and examining their fields.

To view the fields for each table:

Step 1	*Open*	mdbDynamicInc5
Step 2	*Open*	tblOrders, tblProducts, tblCustomers, and tblSuppliers in Design view
Step 3	*Click*	Window
Step 4	*Click*	Cascade
Step 5	*Move*	the four tables on your screen as necessary so you can see each table's field names

Your screen should look similar to Figure 5-1.

Some of the tables include identical fields. For example, both tblCustomers and tblOrders include a CustomerID field—that means you can relate the two tables based on the CustomerID field. You can also relate tblProducts with tblSuppliers and tblOrders with tblProducts based on the ProductID field. You can therefore establish three different relationships for these tables.

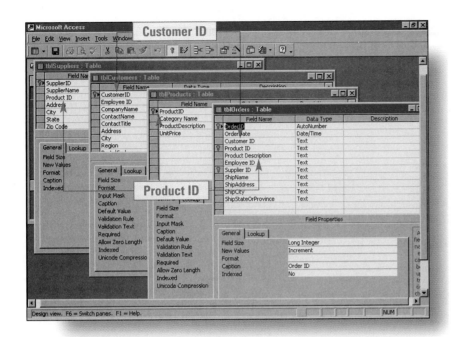

FIGURE 5-1
Viewing Tables for
Relationships

Because you no longer need to display the tables to establish the relationships, close the table windows.

Step 6	*Close*	the tables

You are ready to begin establishing relationships.

5.b Establishing One-to-Many Relationships

You establish relationships by creating a link between fields in different tables. The most common relationship is one-to-many. For example, one customer could have many orders. Set this relationship for tblCustomers with tblOrders based on the Customer ID field.

To set a one-to-many relationship between two tables:

Step 1	*Click*	the Relationships button on the Database toolbar
Step 2	*Click*	the Show Table button on the Relationship toolbar

The Show Table dialog box opens. If it doesn't, click the Show Table button on the Relationships toolbar.

chapter
five

Step 3	**_Double-click_**	tblCustomers and tblOrders

Step 4	**_Click_**	Close

The Relationships window on your screen should look similar to Figure 5-2.

FIGURE 5-2
Relationships Window

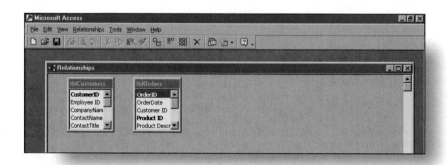

Step 5	**_Click & Hold_**	the CustomerID field in tblCustomers

Step 6	**_Drag_**	the mouse pointer to the Customer ID field in tblOrders

Step 7	**_Release_**	the mouse pointer when it changes to a small box

The Edit Relationships dialog box on your screen should look similar to Figure 5-3.

FIGURE 5-3
Edit Relationships
Dialog Box

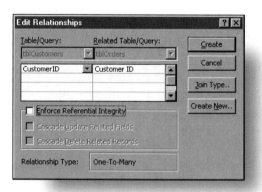

Step 8	**_Click_**	Create

Your screen should now look similar to Figure 5-4.

FIGURE 5-4
Creating a Relationship
Join Line

A **join line** indicates that the two fields in separate tables now have a relationship. You can now create the relationships between the other tables.

Step 9	*Click*	the Show Table button  on the Relationship toolbar
Step 10	*Double-click*	tblProducts and tblSuppliers
Step 11	*Click*	Close
Step 12	*Repeat*	Steps 4–6 to create two more relationships by joining the Product ID fields between tblProducts and tblSuppliers, and tblOrders and tblProducts

Your screen should look similar to Figure 5-5.

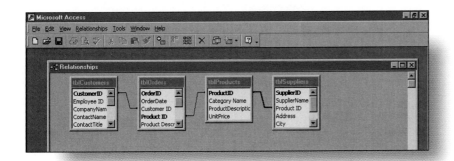

FIGURE 5-5
Completed Relationships

Now that you have established table relationships, you need to enforce referential integrity.

chapter
five

5.c # Enforcing Referential Integrity

Databases that contain related tables need to guarantee the integrity of the relationships. That is, the related tables need to stay connected to one another, even if you change the data. For example, suppose Juanita deletes the customer Ana Trujillo from tblCustomers. Remember that tblCustomers is related to tblOrders. What would happen to the orders that Ana had placed with the company? These order records in tblOrders would no longer be related to tblCustomers and would instead be considered **orphans**—they wouldn't belong to any table. The orders Ana placed would be orphaned because her customer ID number would no longer be valid.

Access helps to avoid orphans by letting you set **referential integrity**, which means you cannot delete a record that has an existing relationship unless you first delete the relationship. Referential integrity is a system of rules Access uses to ensure that relationships between records in related tables are valid, and that you don't accidentally delete or change related data.

To set the referential integrity on the relationships that you have created:

| Step 1 | **Double-click** the join line between tblCustomers and tblOrders |

The Edit Relationships dialog box opens.

| Step 2 | **Click** the Enforce Referential Integrity check box to select it |

The dialog box on your screen should look similar to Figure 5-6.

FIGURE 5-6
Enforcing Referential
Integrity

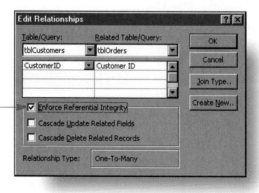

Check this box to enforce referential integrity

| Step 3 | *Click* | OK |
| Step 4 | *Repeat* | Steps 1–3 to enforce referential integrity between the other table relationships you have just established |

After establishing these three relationships, you decide to add the tblEmployees table to the relationship between tblCustomers and tblOrders.

5.d Adding Additional Tables to a Relationship

You can add any table to an existing relationship as long as the table includes a field that matches one in the other tables.

You decide to create a relationship between tblCustomers, tblOrders, and tblEmployees as each employee writes orders, and each employee is also responsible for a customer. Because you have already defined a relationship between tblCustomers and tblOrders, you will add tblEmployees to the relationship. To do this, add one join line between tblCustomers and tblEmployees and another between tblOrders and tblEmployees.

To add an additional table to a relationship:

Step 1	*Click*	View
Step 2	*Click*	Show Table
Step 3	*Click*	tblEmployees in the Show Table dialog box
Step 4	*Click*	Add
Step 5	*Click*	Close
Step 6	*Drag*	the tblEmployees table below the tblOrders and tblProducts tables

Access adds tblEmployees to the Relationships window. You are ready to set a relationship between tblEmployees and tblOrders using the Employee ID field.

| Step 7 | *Repeat* | the method you learned earlier to establish the relationship |
| Step 8 | *Repeat* | the method you learned earlier to enforce referential integrity |

chapter
five

Your screen should now look similar to Figure 5-7.

FIGURE 5-7
tblEmployees
Relationships

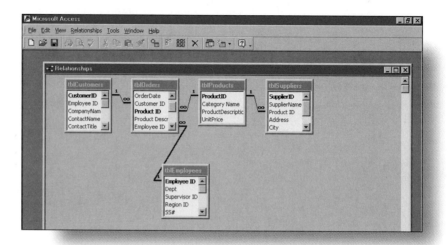

Reviewing the relationships you have established for your database tables, you decide you need to modify a join, to establish a different relationship. You want to modify the join to change the relationship between tblProducts and tblSuppliers.

5.e Specifying Join Properties for Relationships

A **join** is a relationship between a field in one table and a field with the same value in another table. A join is the actual link that defines the relationship between two tables. Access lets you set up three types of joins: inner join, outer join, and self-join. The type of join that you use in your table relationships depends on the information that you want from your data.

Inner Join

An **inner join,** the most common type, includes only the fields of those records that match exactly. For example, because the Customer ID field in tblProducts exactly matches the Customer ID field in tblSuppliers, you want an inner join. Because this is the default join type, you do not need to make any changes here.

Outer Join

An **outer join** includes every record from one table and only those records from the other table that match exactly. For example, you've joined tblCustomers and tblOrders. Suppose you add a new customer who has yet to place an order. This customer name would therefore not yet appear in tblOrders. If you set up an outer join, you can show all of the records in tblCustomers, even those who have not placed an order. This would also allow you to find out which customers have no orders.

You decide to change the join type for the tblCustomers/tblOrders relationship to an outer join.

To set join properties:

| Step 1 | **_Double-click_** | the join line between tblCustomers and tblOrders |
| Step 2 | **_Click_** | Join Type in the Edit Relationships dialog box |

The Join Properties dialog box opens, offering you three join type options, as shown in Figure 5-8.

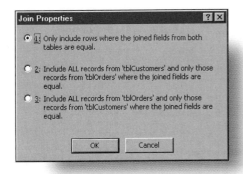

FIGURE 5-8
Join Properties
Dialog Box

Step 3	**_Click_**	the 2: option as the join type
Step 4	**_Click_**	OK
Step 5	**_Click_**	OK to close the Edit Relationships dialog box

You have changed the join type for the tblCustomers/tblOrders relationship. You can now examine the last join type, the self-join.

Self-Join

A **self-join** joins a second copy of the same table. Use a self-join to link tables that have different fields that contain the same type of information. For example, the tblEmployees table includes the Employee ID and Supervisor ID fields. Each employee reports to a

chapter
five

supervisor. However, supervisors are also considered employees and are listed in the same table. You can copy tblEmployees to join the Employee ID and Supervisor ID fields.

To create a self-join for the tblEmployees table:

Step 1	*Click*	V̲iew
Step 2	*Click*	S̲how Table
Step 3	*Click*	tblEmployees in the Show Table dialog box
Step 4	*Click*	A̲dd
Step 5	*Click*	C̲lose

You have now added a copy of the tblEmployees table, called tblEmployees_1:

Step 6	*Drag*	the tblEmployees_1 table below the tblSuppliers and tblProducts tables

Your screen should look similar to Figure 5-9.

FIGURE 5-9
Copy of tblEmployees

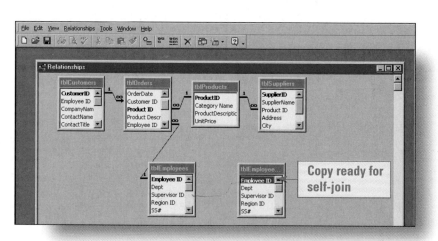

Step 7	*Repeat*	the method you learned earlier to join the Supervisor ID field in tblEmployees to the Employee ID field in tblEmployees_1
Step 8	*Exit*	Access, saving your changes

You have established relationships for several tables in the Dynamic database, as well as enforced referential integrity. Juanita, Kang, and Alan thank you for your help.

Summary

▶ A relationship links identical fields in separate tables.

▶ You can define three kinds of relationships among tables. A one-to-one relationship means each table has only one related field. A one-to-many relationship means the primary table can have more than one related record in the secondary table. A many-to-many relationship means each table can have many related records.

▶ To create a relationship between tables, draw a join line between the identical fields. A join line indicates that two fields in separate tables are related.

▶ Enforce referential integrity to ensure that related tables stay related even if you change the data in one table.

▶ Once you establish a relationship between tables, you can add a table to the relationship as long as the table includes a field that matches one in the other tables.

▶ A join is the actual link that defines the relationship between related tables.

▶ You can set up three different types of joins. An inner join matches the same field in two different tables. An outer join matches only records that are included in both tables. A self-join links copies of the same table.

Commands Review

Action	Menu Bar	Shortcut Menu	Toolbar	Keyboard
View a relationship	Tools, Relationships	Right-click, click Relationships	Double-click the join line	
Create a relationship			Click, hold, and drag between tables	
View a join	Relationships, Edit Relationship	Right-click, click Show All	Double-click the join line	
Create a join			Click join type	
Show a table	Relationships, Show Table	Right-click, click Show Table	🔲	
Set referential integrity	Relationships, Edit Relationship		Double-click a join line	
Add a table to a relationship	View, Show Table		🔲	ALT + V, H

chapter five

Turn in Monday 4/15/02

Concepts Review

SCANS

Circle the correct answer.

1. A relationship is a:
[a] way to print reports.
[b] combination of two tables.
[c] join between two tables.
[d] referential integrity definition.

2. You should identify relationships to:
[a] link information between two tables.
[b] create identical fields in different tables.
[c] look at the types of relationships that have been created.
[d] use the forms or queries in Access.

3. A one-to-many relationship links:
[a] one table with many entries.
[b] one field with many possible fields.
[c] several tables together.
[d] one database with many tables.

4. Referential integrity refers to the:
[a] accuracy of data entry.
[b] system of rules that ensures you don't accidentally delete or change related data.
[c] database design.
[d] orphans.

5. To add additional tables to a relationship, you must first:
[a] delete the original join line.
[b] show all of the tables you want to relate.
[c] close the Relationships window.
[d] click the Add New Table icon.

6. To edit a join you must:
[a] open the Join Properties dialog box.
[b] double-click the table that you want.
[c] click the referential integrity button.
[d] draw a line between two fields.

7. Creating a self-join is useful when:
[a] you want a table to update independently.
[b] you want to link tables that have different fields with the same type of information.
[c] each table has only one related field.
[d] you want to add other tables to a relationship.

8. Creating an outer join:
[a] automatically creates referential integrity.
[b] includes every record from one table and only matching records from another table.
[c] includes only the fields that match exactly.
[d] links tables in two different databases.

9. An inner join:
[a] is the most common type of join.
[b] eliminates referential integrity.
[c] is indicated by a dotted line.
[d] links two orphans.

10. Set referential integrity to:
[a] automatically create relationships.
[b] avoid orphaned records.
[c] join fields of those records that match exactly.
[d] link identical fields in separate tables.

Circle **T** if the statement is true or **F** if the statement is false.

T **F**   1. A relationship is the linking of tables.

T **F**   2. A many-to-many relationship is where many tables can be linked to many objects, such as forms or queries.

T **F**   3. Referential integrity checks the accuracy of the data you enter.

T **F**   4. Referential integrity will not allow you to delete a table that has been linked.

T **F**   5. An inner join matches the same field in two different tables.

T **F**   6. An outer join matches different fields in different tables.

T **F**   7. A self-join matches a field to itself.

T **F**   8. A one-to-one relationship has a field in one table that is related to one field in another table.

T **F**   9. Create a relationship to add new tables to a database.

T **F**   10. In a one-to-many relationship, one customer record could be related to many order records.

Skills Review

Exercise 1

1. If necessary, open the *mdbDynamicInc5* database created in this chapter.

2. View the tblDepartment and tblEmployees tables in Design view. Determine between which fields you can establish a relationship.

3. Relate tblDepartment and tblEmployees based on the Department ID field.

4. Save and close the Relationships window.

Exercise 2

1. If necessary, open the *mdbDynamicInc5* database created in this chapter.

2. View the relationship between the tblDepartment and tblEmployees tables.

3. Enforce referential integrity between the tables.

4. Save and close the Relationships window.

Exercise 3

1. If necessary, open the *mdbDynamicInc5* database created in this chapter.

2. View the relationship between the tblDepartment and tblEmployees tables.

3. Show the tblRegions table.

4. Set a one-to-many relationship between the Region ID field in tblRegions and tblEmployees.

5. Save and close the Relationships window.

chapter five

Exercise 4 C

1. If necessary, open the *mdbDynamicInc5* database created in this chapter.

2. View the relationships among the tblDepartment, tblEmployees, and tblRegions tables.

3. Set referential integrity for the relationship between tblEmployees and tblRegions.

4. Find out the types of joins used in each relationship.

5. Save and close the Relationships window.

Exercise 5 C

1. If necessary, open the *mdbDynamicInc5* database created in this chapter.

2. View the relationships among the tblDepartment, tblEmployees, and tblRegions tables.

3. Change the type of join from inner to outer join between two of the tables.

4. Save and close the Relationships window.

Exercise 6 C

1. If necessary, open the *mdbDynamicInc5* database created in this chapter.

2. Open the Relationships window and then hide the tblEmployees, tblEmployees_1, tblDepartment, and tblRegions tables by right-clicking a table and then choosing Hide Table.

3. Add tblCustomers_1 to the relationship window and, using a self-join, set a relationship between the Referred By field in the tblCustomers and the Customer ID field in the tblCustomers_1 table.

4. Save and close the Relationships window.

Case Projects

Project 1

Your work on setting up relationships in the *mdbDynamicInc5* was lost during a power outage. Maria Moreno wants you to set up new relationships. Use *mdbDynamic5Projects* for Projects 1-6. Start by creating a one-to-many relationship for the following tables:

- tblDepartment and tblEmployees
- tblProducts and tblCategories

Project 2

Use *mdbDynamic5Projects* to create a one-to-one relationship for the following tables:

- tblPayroll and tblEmployees

Project 3

Use *mdbDynamic5Projects* to create a one-to-many relationship for the tblOrders and tblProducts tables.

Project 4

Maria would now like to review the relationships. Search the Access online Help for instructions on printing the database relationship. Then follow the instructions to print the relationships in *mdbDynamic5Projects*.

Project 5

Set referential integrity for the relationship between tblDepartment and tblEmployees in *mdbDynamic5Projects*. Maria wants to protect this relationship so that any time you change a Department ID, Access automatically updates the Department ID in all related records in tblEmployees. You can do this by setting the Cascade Update option for the relationship between the two tables. In the Relationships window, double-click the relationship line for the relationship between tblDepartment and tblEmployees. Click the Cascade Update Related Fields check box to select it.

Project 6

Because the tblPayroll is also related to tblEmployees, Maria needs to turn on referential integrity with cascading updates and deletions for the tblPayroll relationship.

Maria also wants to protect these relationships so that any time you delete a record in tblDepartment, Access automatically deletes the related record in tblEmployees and tblPayroll. You can do this by setting the Cascade Delete option for the relationships between the three tables. In the Relationships window, double-click the relationship line for the relationship between the tables. Click the Cascade Delete Related Records check box to select it.

Project 7

Connect to your ISP and load the home page for a search engine. Search for an online computer dictionary or encyclopedia and find definitions for terms covered in this chapter, such as *referential integrity, relationships, one-to-many relationship,* and *joins.* Print at least two definitions or explanations. Close the browser and disconnect from your ISP.

Project 8

Using the Microsoft on the Web command on the Access Help menu, connect to the Microsoft Web site and look for tips and basic information about defining relationships in Access. Print at least two Web pages.

chapter five

Finding, Sorting, and Filtering Information

Chapter Overview

After you create a database and enter data, you use a database primarily to find information. In this chapter, you learn to find and replace values, and sort and filter records to make it easier to locate and use the information in your database.

► Use Access to locate data
► Find a record
► Sort records
► Filter records

Case profile

Alan Golden, the sales manager at Dynamic Inc., wants to view the most up-to-date product inventory so he can determine if there are enough products in stock to complete orders. Alan asks if you can train his staff to find, sort, and filter data in the Dynamic database.

chapter six

6.a Using Access to Locate Data

If you're familiar with other Office applications, you probably know how to use the <u>F</u>ind command on the <u>E</u>dit menu to find text in a document or other object. You can also use the <u>F</u>ind command in Access to perform simple searches. Access also offers more sophisticated tools for finding data, including sorting, filtering, querying, and reporting.

Sorting rearranges data on the screen so that it is easier to scan records to find the one you want. **Filtering** narrows down a list of records to eliminate the data you don't want. **Querying** creates a more formal filter with complex criteria, and **reporting** creates a printed report containing only the records that you want to see. This chapter explains how to use the find, sort, and filter features in Access.

6.b Finding a Record

Use the <u>F</u>ind command when you want to locate a record that contains a particular word or other value. You can also use it to quickly find or replace text or other values in your records. Alan asks you to locate all of the products in the Toy category. Your first task is to open the Find and Replace dialog box.

To open the Find and Replace dialog box:

Step 1	*Open*	mdbDynamicInc6
Step 2	*Open*	tblProducts
Step 3	*Click*	the Product Description field
Step 4	*Click*	<u>E</u>dit
Step 5	*Click*	<u>F</u>ind

Your screen should look similar to Figure 6-1.

The Find and Replace dialog box allows you to specify the information you want Access to locate in your database. You can do a broad search, such as looking for all records that include the word "Toy" in the product description, or you can be more specific, such as looking for a record that includes the words "Green Gremlin Toy."

QUICK TIP

To use the Find feature, you can also press the CTRL + F keys, or click the Find button on the Standard toolbar.

chapter
six

To specify search requirements in the Find and Replace dialog box:

Step 1	*Key*	Toy in the Find What: text box

Step 2	*Click*	the Match: list arrow

You now have three options. Choose **Whole Field** to search for data
that only matches what you key in the Find What: text box, such as
"Toy." Choose **Start of Field** to find data that begins with the letters
you key in the Find What: text box. For example, choose the Start of
Field option to find "Toy," "Toy Soldier," and "Toy Story." Choose **Any
Part of Field** to find data where the characters include "Toy" anywhere
in a field, as in "Infant Toys." You want to locate any product
description containing the word "toy."

Step 3	*Click*	Any Part of Field

Step 4	*Click*	More >>

The dialog box should look similar to Figure 6-2.

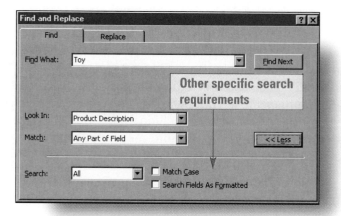

You can now enter other specific search requirements. In the Search: list box, you can choose to search Up, Down, or All of the current table. **Up** searches all of the records before the current one. For example, if you are working with record 15, choose Up to search only records 1–15. **Down** searches all of the records after the current one. For example, if you are working in record 15, choose Down to search from record 15 to the last record. **All**, the default, searches all of the records. For the Toy category search, you want to use All, the default option, so you do not need to change the option in the Search: list box.

You can also limit your search by matching the letter case or searching fields as formatted when you search. Check the Match Case check box to find "Toy" but not "toy." Check the Search Fields as Formatted check box if you do not want to find "**Toy**" because it is boldfaced. For the Toy category search, you do not need to limit the search with these options; you can use the defaults.

Step 5	*Click*	Find Next

Step 6	*Drag*	the Find and Replace dialog box out of the way, if necessary

Access leaves this dialog box open so you can continue using its features.

Access finds the next occurrence of "toy," which is in the second Child's plush toy record. Because Access is searching for all records by default, it begins its search with next record below the currently selected record.

You can also use the Find and Replace dialog box to replace text.

Replacing Text

To use the Find and Replace dialog box to replace text, click the Replace tab and use its options. Alan finds that a $35,000 automobile is incorrectly labeled as a toy car in the *mdbDynamicInc6* database. You can correct the mistake by replacing the text.

To replace text using the Find and Replace dialog box:

Step 1	*Click*	the Replace tab

Step 2	*Key*	Real in the Replace With: text box

Your screen should look similar to Figure 6-3.

If you click Replace, Access substitutes "Real" for the first occurrence of "Toy" that it locates in the database. If you click Replace All, Access substitutes "Real" for all occurrences of the word "Toy." Because you only want to replace one occurrence of "Toy" with "Real" for the record referring to the $35,000 automobile, continue clicking the Find Next button until you locate the right record.

chapter
six

FIGURE 6-3
Replace Tab

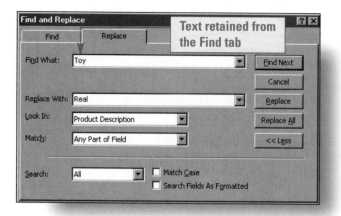

| Step 3 | *Click* | Find Next until you locate the correct record (Toy car-BMW) |

The replace button replaces the selected text and automatically finds the next occurrence of the word.

| Step 4 | *Click* | Replace |
| Step 5 | *Click* | Cancel to close the Find and Replace dialog box |

Using the Find command is a quick way to find a record or a value in one or more records. To find records by scanning a table, you can sort them first.

C   6.c Sorting Records

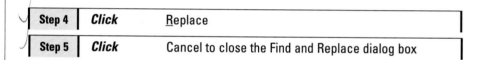

When you add records to your database, you do not necessarily enter them in a logical order for viewing. Instead, you later sort the records to find the ones you want. You can sort in Datasheet view or Form view, and can rearrange the records according to any fields you like.

Sorting Records on a Single Field

Alan asks you to sort the Dynamic products alphabetically according to category so he can view all the products in a particular category. You can therefore sort the records using a single field.

To sort records on a single field:

| Step 1 | *Verify* | tblProducts is open in Datasheet view |
| Step 2 | *Click* | the Category Name field |

Because Alan wants to sort alphabetically, you can sort the categories from A to Z.

| Step 3 | *Click* | the Sort Ascending button ⬛ on the Table Datasheet toolbar |

Access rearranges the records by the Category Name field. Your screen should look similar to Figure 6-4.

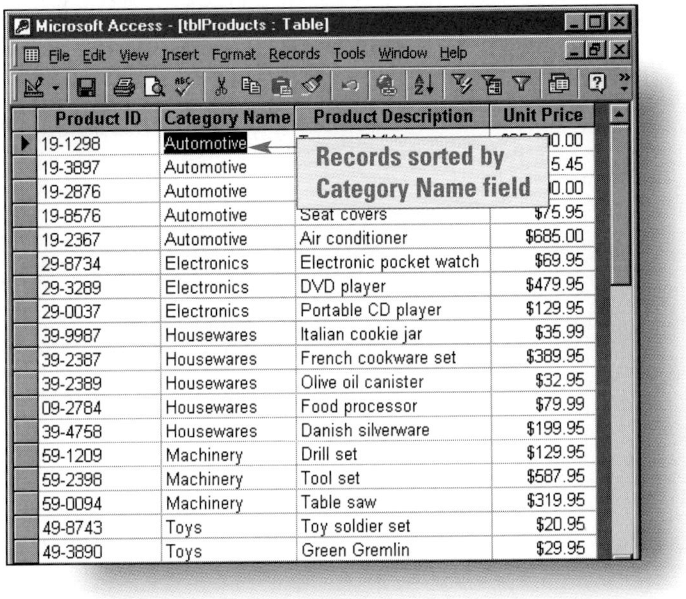

The original presorted order is based on the primary key. To restore the original order, choose the Remove Filter/Sort option on the Records menu. Otherwise, when you save the form or datasheet, the sort order is also saved.

| Step 4 | *Click* | Records |

| Step 5 | *Click* | Remove Filter/Sort |

You can also perform a more in-depth sort by using multiple fields.

Sorting Records on Multiple Fields

While you can sort on only one field at a time in a form, you can select two or more adjacent columns in a datasheet and then sort them. Access sorts the records starting with the leftmost selected column. In the tblProducts table, this is the Category Name field. Alan asks you to sort the product records alphabetically by category, and also alphabetically by product description within each category. This means that the first few records in the table will be in the Automotive category. Then each product in the Automotive category also sorts alphabetically, so you can find "Air conditioner" at the beginning of the Automotive product descriptions, and "Windshield wipers" near the bottom.

To sort records on multiple fields:

Step 1	**Drag**	the mouse pointer over the Category Name and Product Description fields headers to select the columns
Step 2	**Click**	the Sort Ascending button ![icon] on the Filter/Sort toolbar

Access rearranges the records according to the chosen fields. Your screen should look similar to Figure 6-5.

FIGURE 6-5
Results of a Multiple Sort

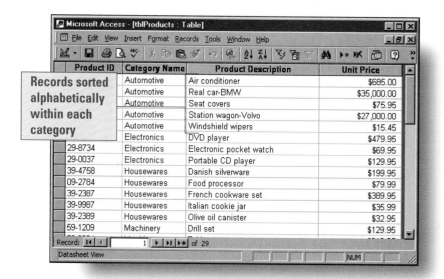

When you save the datasheet, Access saves the sort order. If you want to restore the original order, choose the Remove Filter/Sort option on the Records menu.

Step 3	**Remove**	the sort

6.d Filtering Records

Filter data when you want to view only specific records. You specify criteria, and Access shows only those records that meet the criteria. Filtering temporarily narrows down the number of the records that appear on your screen. There are three ways of adding filters: filter by selection, filter by form, and advanced filter/sort. This section covers the first two methods. You practice using the Advanced Filter/Sort feature in Case Projects 4 and 5.

Applying Filters by Selection

Filtering by selection, the easiest method of filtering, requires that you define a value; Access then finds all the records that include that value. For example, Alan asks you to find all the children's plush toys that Dynamic sells. Start by examining the values in a record that meet this criteria, such as the first record in the table.

To filter by selection:

Step 1	*Open*	tblProducts, if necessary
Step 2	*Find*	a Child's plush toy record

If necessary, use the Find command as explained in a previous section.

Step 3	*Right-click*	on the Product Description data in the record to open the shortcut menu
Step 4	*Click*	in the Filter For: text box
Step 5	*Key*	Child's plush toy

Your screen should look similar to Figure 6-6.

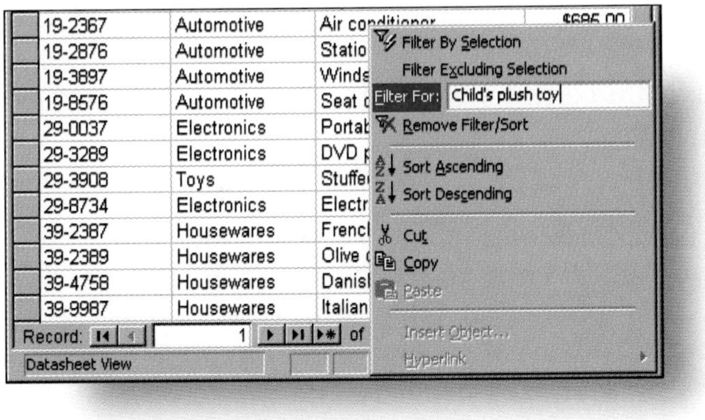

19-2367	Automotive	Air conditioner	$695.00
19-2876	Automotive	Statio	Filter By Selection
19-3897	Automotive	Winds	Filter Excluding Selection
19-8576	Automotive	Seat (	Filter For: Child's plush toy
29-0037	Electronics	Portab	Remove Filter/Sort
29-3289	Electronics	DVD p	
29-3908	Toys	Stuffe	Sort Ascending
29-8734	Electronics	Electr	Sort Descending
39-2387	Housewares	Frencl	Cut
39-2389	Housewares	Olive (	Copy
39-4758	Housewares	Danisl	Paste
39-9987	Housewares	Italian	

Record: 1 of   Insert Object...
Datasheet View   Hyperlink

FIGURE 6-6
Setting Up the Filter

Step 6	*Press*	the ENTER key

chapter
six

Your screen should look similar to Figure 6-7.

FIGURE 6-7
Filtered Records

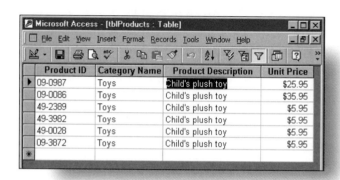

MENU TIP

To select the data you want to use as the criterion, such as the product description "Child's Plush Toy," click Records, click Filter, and then click Filter by Selection.

Access displays the records that match the selection criterion that you entered—you see the other records for children's plush toys. When you save a table or form, Access saves the filters you created. You can reapply the filters, if necessary, the next time you open the table or form.

Step 7	*Remove*	the filter

Step 8	*Close*	the tblProducts Table and do not save changes

When filtering by selection, you can filter on only one criterion at a time. However, you can apply other filters after the first one to narrow the list of matching records. For example, you could filter the list of children's plush toys to show only those that cost $5.95.

You can also filter by excluding records. To filter by excluding records, right-click the field and select Filter Excluding Selection. You then see all the records in the current list that do not include the selected text.

Applying Filters by Form

A more powerful filtering method than filtering by selection is filtering by form. **Filter by form** allows you to select several criteria to filter. You can also set up OR filters, which find records that match any one of several criteria. When filtering by form, you can also enter logical expressions. For example, you could search for records having an ID greater than 3456.

Alan thinks some of his staff incorrectly entered some children's plush toys as "stuffed animals." You can filter by form to find all the records that describe a product as either "Child's plush toy" or as "Stuffed animal." To filter by form:

Step 1	*Open*	tblProducts

Step 2	*Click*	the Filter By Form button on the Table Datasheet toolbar

Step 3	*Delete*	the contents of the Product ID field, if necessary

Your screen should look similar to Figure 6-8.

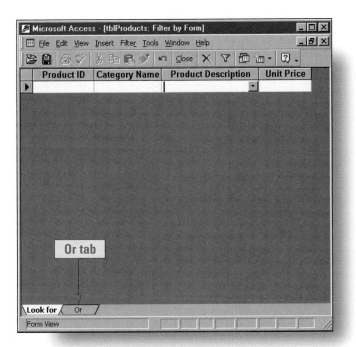

FIGURE 6-8
Filter by Form Dialog Box

MENU TIP

You can also click Filter, and then Filter by Form from the Records menu.

Step 4	*Click*	the Product Description field
Step 5	*Click*	the list arrow
Step 6	*Click*	Child's plush toy

This is the field you want to use to set the criterion. Alternatively, you can key this text directly into the field.

You can enter as many criteria as you like in various fields. Because you want to find either "Child's plush toy" or "Stuffed animal," set up an OR criterion.

| Step 7 | *Click* | the Or tab at the bottom of the tblProducts: Filter by form dialog box |

Notice that as you fill in the fields that you wish to filter, another Or tab appears at the bottom of the page.

Step 8	*Click*	the list arrow in the Product Description field
Step 9	*Click*	Stuffed animal
Step 10	*Click*	the Apply Filter button on the Filter/Sort toolbar

chapter
six

Your screen should look similar to Figure 6-9.

FIGURE 6-9
Records Filtered by Form

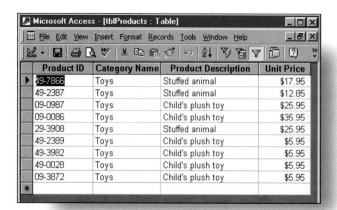

You applied a filter by selection and a filter by form. Now you can return the list to its previous state by removing the filter you applied.

Removing Filters

When you save a table or form, Access saves the filters you create. You can reapply the filters, if necessary, the next time you open the table or form. To return the list to its original, unfiltered state, you need to remove the filter.

Alan may want you to find other records for him, so you decide to remove the last filter you applied. When you remove a filter, you don't delete it—you stop showing records based on the criteria defined in a filter. You show all the records you saw before you applied the filter. You can reapply the filter if Alan needs to find the same records again as long as the table remains open. If you close the table and save it, you can always re-apply the filter. If you do not save the table, your filtering options will be lost.

To remove a filter and not save it:

| Step 1 | *Click* | the Remove Filter button $\boxed{\nabla}$ on the Table Datasheet toolbar |

Now you show the records that were displayed before you applied the filter.

| Step 2 | *Close* | the table without saving changes |

You are now ready to exit Access.

| Step 3 | *Exit* | Access |

Filters enable you to see only the specific records you want.

MOUSE TIP

You can also remove the filter by right-clicking the mouse in the field and selecting Remove Filter/Sort.

You can reapply the filter by clicking the Apply Filter button.

MENU TIP

You can also select Remove Filter/Sort from the Records menu.

Summary

▶ Use the Find command in Access to perform simple searches, such as those that find a word in your records or a record that contains a particular phrase. You can also replace values in your records. The Find and Replace tools are similar to those in other Office applications.

▶ Access also offers more sophisticated tools for finding data, including sorting and filtering.

▶ Sorting rearranges data on the screen so that it is easier to scan records to find the one you want. Filtering narrows down a list of records to eliminate the data you don't want. Filter your records when you need to find several records at once.

▶ You can sort in ascending order (as from A to Z) or descending order (as from Z to A) on either a single field or multiple fields. You can only sort in a datasheet on two or more adjacent columns of records. Access sorts the records starting with the leftmost selected column.

▶ Removing a sort on a datasheet causes the information to return to its original state. When you save a datasheet or form you sorted, Access saves the sort order. If you want to restore the original order, remove the sort before closing the datasheet or form.

▶ Filter data when you want to view only specific records. You specify criteria, and Access shows only those records that meet the criteria. Filtering temporarily narrows down the number of the records that appear on your screen. There are three ways of adding filters: filter by selection, filter by form, and advanced filter/sort.

▶ When you filter by selection, you define a value, and Access finds all the records that include that value. When you filter by form, you can select several criteria to filter.

▶ When you save a table or form, Access saves the filters you created. You can reapply the filters, if necessary, the next time you open the table or form. If you won't use a filter again, you can remove the filter.

chapter six

Commands Review

Action	Menu Bar	Shortcut Menu	Toolbar	Keyboard
Find data	Edit, Find		🔍	CTRL + F ALT + E, F
Replace data	Edit, Replace			CTRL + H ALT + E, R
Sort records ascending /descending	Records, Sort, Sort Ascending or Sort Descending	Sort Ascending or Sort Descending	↓A̲Z̲ or ↓Z̲A̲	ALT + R, S, A, or D
Filter by form	Records, Filter, Filter by Form	Filter by Form	▦	ALT + R, F, F
Filter by selection	Records, Filter, Filter by Selection	Filter by Selection	▽	ALT + R, F, S
Apply filter	Records, Apply Filter/Sort	Apply Filter/Sort	▽	ALT + R, Y
Remove filter or sort	Records, Remove Filter/Sort	Remove Filter/Sort	▽	ALT + R, R

Concepts Review

Circle the correct answer.

1. Use the Find command to:
[a] scan records until you find the one you want.
[b] find a record containing a particular word.
[c] narrow a list of records to eliminate the data you don't want.
[d] create a printed report containing the records you find.

2. Sort records to:
[a] find and replace text and other values in your records.
[b] conform to standard data integrity practices.
[c] find records containing a certain value.
[d] rearrange data on the screen so it's easier to find the record you want.

3. You can use the advanced search options on the Find dialog box when you want to:
[a] limit your search.
[b] broaden your search.
[c] replace text instead of find it.
[d] sort on two or more criteria.

4. Before you can sort on multiple records in a datasheet:
[a] select two or more adjacent columns.
[b] choose the Up, Down, or All option.
[c] switch to Form view.
[d] choose the type of sort you want: ascending or descending.

5. To filter a form:
[a] you must be in Datasheet view.
[b] you must be in Design view.
[c] switch to a table; you cannot filter a form.
[d] sort first, and then filter.

6. To remove filters and sorts, select the:
[a] field you filtered or sorted and then click Delete.
[b] Remove button on the toolbar.
[c] Remove Filter command from the Records menu.
[d] toolbox.

7. When you add a filter by form, you:
[a] add to the visual interest of the form.
[b] can select several criteria to filter.
[c] create a new form showing the results of the filter.
[d] filter on only one criterion at a time.

8. If you need to find several records at once:
[a] use the Find command.
[b] filter the data.
[c] sort on a single field.
[d] choose Whole Field, Start of Field, or Any Part of Field in the Find dialog box.

9. When you add a filter by selection, you:
[a] restore the table to its original appearance.
[b] can select several criteria to filter.
[c] delete all the records that don't match the criteria.
[d] filter on only one criterion at a time.

10. When you remove a filter, you:
[a] delete the filter.
[b] must apply it again later.
[c] sort on only one field.
[d] stop showing records based on the criteria defined in the filter.

Circle **T** if the statement is true or **F** if the statement is false.

T (F)   1. Sorting means changing the data in a field.

(T) F   2. Filtering is narrowing down the record choices.

(T) F   3. Removing a sort on a datasheet returns the information to its original state.

T (F)   4. Sorting is always the best choice.

(T) F   5. You can sort on multiple records.

T (F)   6. The entire purpose of creating filters is to make data entry easier.

T (F)   7. You should create a filter when you want to list records in alphabetical order.

T (F)   8. Once you remove a filter, you cannot use it again.

(T) F   9. You can find and replace values in your records.

T (F)   10. Filters let you display messages.

Skills Review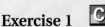

Exercise 1

1. If necessary, open the *mdbDynamicInc6* database.

2. In the tblEmployees table, find all the employees who live in Seattle.

3. Find only those employees who live in the 98052 zip code.

4. Close the tblEmployees table without saving.

Exercise 2

1. If necessary, open the *mdbDynamicInc6* database.

2. In the tblCustomers table, replace *Sales Agent* with *Sales Representative* in all the records.

3. Save and close the tblCustomers table.

chapter six

Exercise 3   C

1. If necessary, open the *mdbDynamicInc6* database.

2. In the tblCustomers table, sort alphabetically by city.

3. Restore the original order, and then close the tblCustomers table.

Exercise 4   C

1. If necessary, open the *mdbDynamicInc6* database.

2. In the frmEmployees form, sort in ascending order by last name.

3. Restore the original order, and then close the frmEmployees form.

Exercise 5   C

1. If necessary, open the *mdbDynamicInc6* database.

2. Open tblEmployees in Design view and change the order of the fields so you can sort first on Department ID and then on last name.

3. In the tblEmployees table, sort alphabetically in ascending order by Department ID and last name.

4. Close the tblEmployees table without saving changes.

Exercise 6   C

1. If necessary, open the *mdbDynamicInc6* database.

2. In the tblCustomers table, filter by selection to show all the customers from Spain.

3. Close the tblCustomers table and save the changes.

Exercise 7   C

1. If necessary, open the *mdbDynamicInc6* database.

2. Open the tblCustomers table and run the filter. Remove the filter.

3. Filter by form to show customers who have a contact title of Sales Representative or Sales Manager.

4. Close the tblCustomers table and save the changes.

Exercise 8   C

1. If necessary, open the *mdbDynamicInc6* database.

2. In the tblCustomers table, remove any filters.

3. Filter by selection to select all records except those in Mexico.

4. Remove the filter, and then close the tblCustomers table without saving.

Case Projects

Project 1

Alan wants a list of customers sorted by phone number so he can have his staff call them periodically. Sort the tblCustomers table in *mdbDynamicInc6* and print the results.

Project 2

Now Alan wants to sort the list of customers based on a number of fields. Examine the tblCustomers table and determine two or more fields you could logically sort. You may need to edit the table design so that all the fields are adjacent and in the proper order for sorting. Sort the tblCustomers table and print the results.

Project 3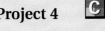

Alan needs to quickly review all the Seattle orders. Create a filter by selection for the frmOrders form that shows orders shipped to Seattle.

Project 4

Alan wants to filter the products in tblProducts to show only those in the Toys or Housewares category, and then wants to sort those by Product ID. Search the Access online Help for instructions on creating an Advanced Filter/Sort. Follow these instructions to filter and sort the tblProducts table to meet Alan's needs.

Project 5

Alan needs a list of items Dynamic sells that cost more than $10.00 each. Search the Access online Help for instructions on using an expression (greater than) in an Advanced Filter/Sort. Follow these instructions to filter the records in tblProducts to show only those items that cost more than $10.00.

Project 6

Alan needs to add a 10 percent surcharge to products shipped to customers outside of North America. You can add a calculated field to a form so that Alan's staff can correctly quote the higher charge. Create a form based on tblProducts. Then search the Access online Help for instructions on adding a calculated field. Follow these instructions to add a new field to the form that calculates the Unit Price * 0.10.

Project 7

Connect to your ISP and load the home page for a search engine. Search for an online computer dictionary or encyclopedia and find definitions for terms covered in this chapter, such as *sort, filter, find and replace* (or *search and replace*). Print at least three definitions or explanations. Close the browser and disconnect from your ISP.

Project 8

Using the Microsoft on the <u>W</u>eb command on the <u>H</u>elp menu, connect to the Microsoft Web site and look for information on sorting and filtering your records. Print at least two Web pages of information.

chapter six

Creating Basic Queries

Chapter Overview

In this chapter, you create a simple query. Like a filter, a query uses criteria you specify to select and display records. However, where a filter works with one table, a query can work with many tables. It can also perform actions on your data, such as updating or deleting records.

LEARNING OBJECTIVES

- ► **Understand queries**
- ► **Create a multi-table select query**
- ► **Modify a multi-table select query**
- ► **Save a query**
- ► **Specify criteria in a query**
- ► **Display related records in a subdatasheet**
- ► **Print the results of a query**

Case profile

An upcoming meeting at Dynamic Inc., concerns the company's European sales. One sales representative, Juanita Chavez, has been asked to prepare a presentation showing these sales' results. Although all of the information Juanita needs for her presentation is in the Dynamic database, she is unsure how to locate it quickly. She asks you to help her find the information she needs for her presentation. To do this, you create a query.

chapter seven

7.a Understanding Queries

A query is a question you ask about the data stored in your tables or a request you make to perform an action on the data, such as to calculate the sum of records. Although you can use sorts and filters to find and narrow your records in one table, a query can find and narrow records in a number of tables. In addition to helping you view the data you want, queries let you change and analyze data. You can also use them as the source of records for forms and reports.

Access lets you create different types of queries. The most common is a **select query**, which retrieves data from one or more tables by using criteria you specify and then displays it in the order you want. Juanita asks you to identify the customers in Europe who placed an order in the last year. To find this data, create a select query.

7.b Creating a Multi-Table Select Query

Use the Query Wizard to create a simple query, such as a select query. A select query can select records that meet Juanita's criteria— those that show which companies in which countries generate the most orders.

To create a simple query:

Step 1	**Open**	*mdbDynamicInc7*
Step 2	**Click**	Queries 🖦 on the Objects bar
Step 3	**Double-click**	Create query by using wizard

The Simple Query Wizard opens. Your screen should look similar to Figure 7-1.

Step 4	**Click**	Table: tblCustomers in the Tables/Queries list box
Step 5	**Move**	the CompanyName, City, and Country fields from the Available Fields: list box to the Selected Fields: list box

QUICK TIP

C You can use queries to delete records from a table. To do this, create a delete query. Working with Delete queries is covered in more detail in Chapter 11.

C

Do Tuesday

chapter seven

FIGURE 7-1
Simple Query Wizard

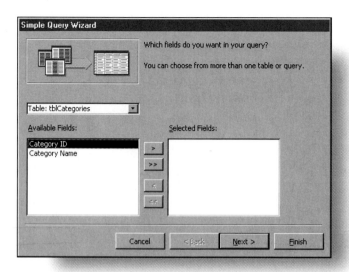

FIGURE 7-1
Simple Query Wizard

The tblCustomers table includes part of the information you want to see—companies and their countries. You can create a simple query based on only one table or on a number of tables. Because Juanita wants to see order information as well as company information, include a field from the tblOrders table in the query.

Step 6	*Click*	Table: tblOrders in the Tables/Queries list box

Step 7	*Move*	the Order Date field from the Available Fields: list box to the Selected Fields: list box

The Order Date field tells you that a company placed an order on that date.

Step 8	*Click*	Next >

You can now choose to show detailed or summary information in the query. Juanita wants to see all of the customer and order information, so accept the default to show detailed information.

Step 9	*Click*	Next >

Step 10	*Key*	qryCustomers as the query title

You want to open the query now, so accept the default option to open the query to view information.

Step 11	*Click*	Finish

Your screen should look similar to Figure 7-2.

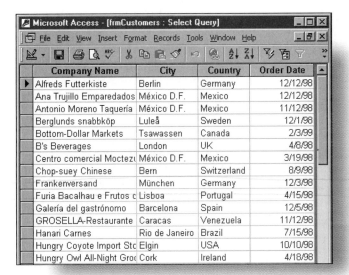

FIGURE 7-2
Simple Query Created with
a Wizard

QUICK TIP

 You can apply filters in a query's recordset, which, in effect, is a secondary filter. This allows you to retrieve and display more exactly the needed information.

You see all the records the query selected from the tblCustomers and tblOrders tables, showing only the Company Name, City, Country, and Order Date fields. Now you can sort these records to find more information.

7.c Modifying a Multi-Table Select Query

Once you create a select query, you can then modify it. For example, you can sort the query records, or you can remove unnecessary fields from it. Your first modification is to sort the query results alphabetically.

Sorting Records in a Query

Now that you created the qryCustomers query to generate a subset of the data in your database—a list of customers, their location, and the date on which they placed an order—you can sort the list alphabetically by country to see which countries are generating the most orders.

To sort the records in a query:

| Step 1 | *Click* | in the Country field |
| Step 2 | *Click* | the Sort Ascending button ⚏ on the Filter/Sort toolbar |

Your screen should look similar to Figure 7-3.

FIGURE 7-3
Records Sorted
Alphabetically by Country

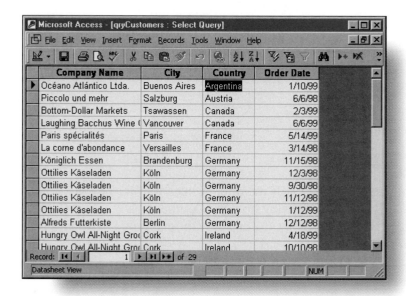

Now you can quickly scan the list to see which countries are generating the most orders—France, for example, has two.

To see all of the information Juanita needs—which customers in which countries are generating the most orders—you need to sort on multiple fields.

To sort on multiple fields in a query:

| Step 1 | *Switch* | to Design view |

Your screen should look similar to Figure 7-4.

To sort on more than one field, first arrange the fields in the design grid in the order you want to perform the sort. Access sorts on the leftmost field first, then on the next field to the right, and so on. To find which customers in which countries are generating the most orders, sort first on country, and then on customer.

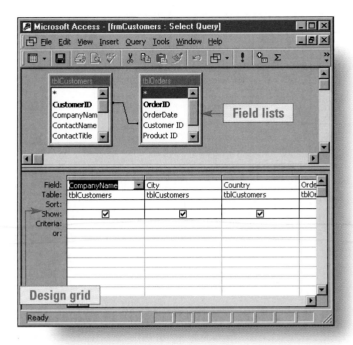

FIGURE 7-4
Select Query in
Design View

| Step 2 | *Click* | the selection bar above the Country field |

This selects the Country field and any criteria you set for it.

| Step 3 | *Drag* | the Country field to the left of the Company Name field |

Your screen should look similar to Figure 7-5.

FIGURE 7-5
Selecting Fields in the
Design Grid

**chapter
seven**

Step 4	**Click**	the list arrow in the Sort row of the Country field
Step 5	**Click**	Ascending
Step 6	**Click**	the list arrow in the Sort row of the CompanyName field
Step 7	**Click**	Ascending
Step 8	**Switch**	to Datasheet view

Scanning the records, you can see that one company in Germany is generating the most orders.

Now you can streamline the query to show only essential information. Juanita needs to know about countries, companies, and orders, not cities. You can remove the City field from the query.

Removing Fields from a Query

If your query is showing information you don't need, you can remove a field. When you remove a field, you're only removing it from the query. You're not deleting the field or its data from the table your query is based on.

To sort on multiple fields in a query:

Step 1	**Switch**	to Design view
Step 2	**Click**	the selection bar above the City field
Step 3	**Press**	the DELETE key

The City field is now deleted.

Now that you created a query to find exactly the information Juanita needs, you can save the query.

7.d   Saving a Query

Access saves the query when you close the Query window. You then see the query name in the Queries list on the Database window.

You can run a query at any time by opening it. If the data has changed since the last time you ran the query, it is automatically updated. For example, you can run the qryCustomers query once a month to provide Dynamic with up-to-date sales information.

To save and close the query:

Step 1	*Click*	the Close button
Step 2	*Click*	Yes to save the query changes

Juanita is pleased with how well the query provides her with the information she needs. Now she wants to add criteria to the query to provide more detailed information.

7.e Specifying Criteria in a Query

C

You can create a new query with multiple criteria using the Query Wizard, or you can modify an existing query to include additional criteria. In addition to the country, company, and order date, Juanita wants to know which products these customers are ordering. You can provide this information by adding a field to the query.

Adding Fields to the Query

After you create a query, you can modify it by adding other fields. Add only those fields whose data you want to view, set criteria on, group by, update, or sort. Because Juanita wants to see which products the customers are ordering, add the Product Description field from tblOrders to qryCustomers.

To add fields from other tables to an existing query:

Step 1	*Open*	qryCustomers in Design view, if necessary
Step 2	*Click*	Product Description in the field list of the tblOrders table
Step 3	*Drag*	the Product Description field to the first available column in the design grid

chapter
seven

Your screen should look similar to Figure 7-6.

You added all the necessary fields for your query. You now must set some criteria.

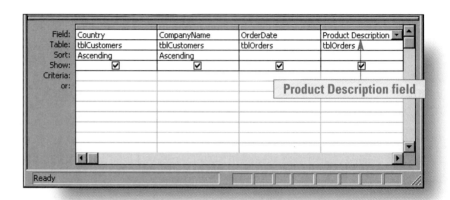

Product Description field

Setting Criteria

Criteria are restrictions you place on a query to identify the records you want to work with. Set criteria when you want to refine your queries to show specific information. For example, instead of viewing all of Dynamic's customers, you can show a list of only those in France. To do this, you set a criteria that limits the records the query retrieves to those where the country is France.

You set criteria in the query's design grid by entering an expression in the Criteria row for a field. An **expression** in a query is usually a combination of field names and symbols or words, called **operators**, that indicate what action to take. An expression can be as simple as one word, or more complex. For example, to retrieve records whose country is France, enter the expression "France" in the Criteria row for the Country field. To find those whose ID is greater than 100, enter the expression ">100."

You can use **comparison criteria** to find records by comparing their values. For example, you can find orders placed before January 1, 1999 or products that cost less than $10.00. Use **AND** or **OR** to show records based on multiple criteria, such as those whose customers reside in France or Germany (OR operator), or those who live in Germany and have bought toys (AND operator). You can also use **NULL** to retrieve records that have a field with no value, such as a customer without a fax number. Use **wildcard characters** to search for text patterns in your records, such as fields containing words that start with "Mac."

Setting Comparison Criteria

Use comparison criteria when you want to retrieve records with values that are greater than, greater than or equal to, less than, less than or equal to, or between values you specify.

For example, Table 7-1 shows you the criteria to enter to get a desired date.

Enter	For This Result
8/5/99	The exact date
<8/5/99	Before 8/5/99
>8/5/99	After 8/5/99
>=8/5/99	On or after 8/5/99
<=8/5/99	On or before 8/5/99
Not <8/5/99	Not before 8/5/99
Not >8/5/99	Not after 8/5/99

TABLE 7-1
Criteria for Selecting Records by Date

Juanita now wants information on customer orders in the current year. You need to set the criteria accordingly.

To set criteria for a query:

Step 1	*Open*	qryCustomers in Design view, if necessary
Step 2	*Click*	in the Criteria: row for the Order Date field
Step 3	*Key*	>12/31/98

Your screen should look similar to Figure 7-7.

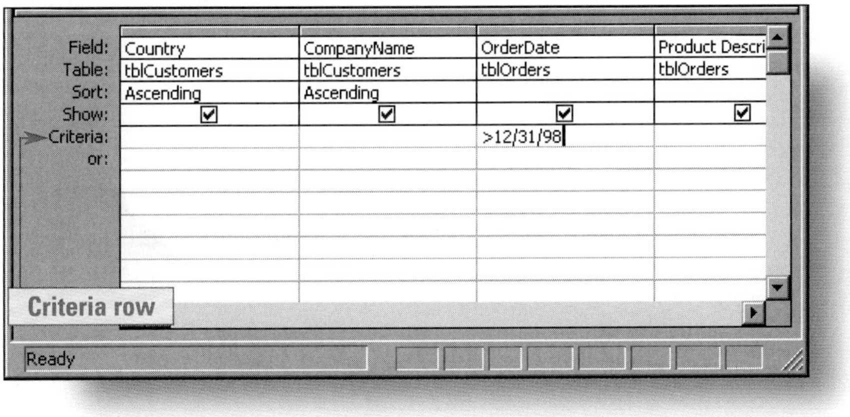

FIGURE 7-7
Entering Criteria in the Design Grid

This selects all the records where the order date is after the last day of 1998.

| Step 4 | *Switch* | to Datasheet view |

Your screen should now show all the orders placed after 12/31/98.

Specifying Criteria in Multiple Fields

Use the AND criteria when you want to select records where both conditions apply. For example, if you want to find records where the country is Germany and the product description is "Tool set," use the AND criteria. Use the OR criteria when you want to select records where either condition can apply. For example, if you want to know which customers are in Canada or Mexico, use the OR criteria.

In general, OR expands your selection—you choose records that contain one value or another. AND narrows your selection—you choose only those records that contain both values.

Juanita wants to find all the orders made by customers in France or in Germany. Use the OR criteria because you want to select records where the value in the Country field is France or Germany. Start by removing any other criteria you already applied.

To clear the current criteria:

Step 1	**Open**	qryCustomers in Design view, if necessary
Step 2	**Drag**	to select the criteria you set in the Order Date field
Step 3	**Press**	the DELETE key

Now you're ready to create new criteria to retrieve records based on the Country field.

To expand a query selection with an OR criteria:

Step 1	**Click**	in the Criteria: row of the Country field
Step 2	**Key**	France OR Germany
Step 3	**Press**	the ENTER key

Access formats the criteria to build an expression—it includes quotation marks around "France" and "Germany" after you press the TAB or ENTER keys.

Your screen should look similar to Figure 7-8.

Step 4	**Switch**	to Datasheet view to see the results of the query

You see all the orders made by companies in France and Germany. If you use the AND criteria, you do not retrieve any records—no record includes both France and Germany in its Country field.

QUICK TIP

You can also key the first criteria in the Criteria: row and key the second criteria in the "or:" row of the design grid.

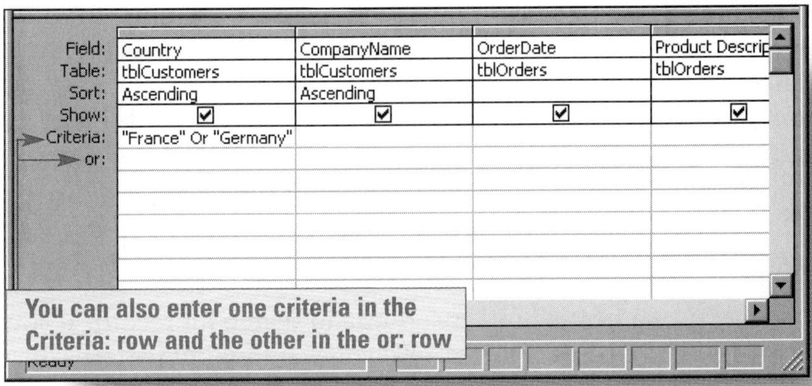

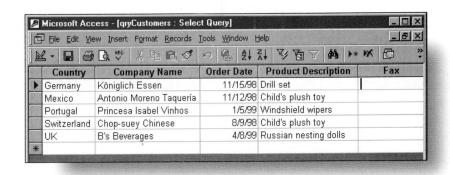

FIGURE 7-8
Query with OR criteria

Using the NULL Criteria

Use the NULL criteria when you want to find records where a field does not contain a value. Juanita likes to communicate with her customers by fax, though a few do not have fax numbers. She wants to identify those who don't have fax numbers so she remembers to communicate with them in other ways. You can set a NULL criteria to find the customers who don't have fax numbers.

Before you set a NULL criteria, clear all the current criteria from qryCustomers. Then add the Fax field to the query.

To add a field to the query:

Step 1	***Open***	the qryCustomers query in Design view, if necessary
Step 2	***Clear***	the current criteria by deleting it
Step 3	***Drag***	the Fax field from the tblCustomers field list to the first available column in the design grid
Step 4	***Click***	in the Criteria: row of the Fax field
Step 5	***Key***	Is Null
Step 6	***Switch***	to Datasheet view

Your screen should look similar to Figure 7-9.

Country	Company Name	Order Date	Product Description	Fax
Germany	Königlich Essen	11/15/98	Drill set	
Mexico	Antonio Moreno Taquería	11/12/98	Child's plush toy	
Portugal	Princesa Isabel Vinhos	1/5/99	Windshield wipers	
Switzerland	Chop-suey Chinese	8/9/98	Child's plush toy	
UK	B's Beverages	4/8/99	Russian nesting dolls	

FIGURE 7-9
Results of Query with Null Criteria

chapter seven

You see the list of customers who do not have a fax number. If you want to list those customers who do have a fax number, use the Not Null criteria.

The comparison, And, Or, and Null criteria retrieve records based on the complete information in a record. You use wildcards to retrieve records by specifying only partial information.

Using Wildcards in Queries

Use wildcard characters in query criteria to search for records if you only know part of the information, or if you want to find patterns of data. For example, you can search for customers whose names begin with *Mac* or end in *son*. A wildcard symbol (*) stands for unknown characters.

Juanita wants to contact a customer, but can only recall that the first word in his company is "Hungry." You can use a wildcard to find that record.

To use wildcards to set query criteria:

Step 1	***Switch***	to Design view
Step 2	***Clear***	the current criteria from qryCustomers
Step 3	***Click***	in the Criteria: row of the CompanyName field
Step 4	***Key***	Hungry*
Step 5	***Switch***	to Datasheet view

You see all the records where the Company Name starts with the word Hungry.

Step 6	***Close***	the query and save the changes

7.f Displaying Related Records in a Subdatasheet

Subdatasheets allow you to display related records from other tables while you work with a table or a query. For example, if you are in tblCustomers, you can view the orders for each customer in tblOrders, because the two tables are related. You can then easily view more detail about your data.

When browsing through orders for one customer, Juanita wants to see and enter other orders for that customer. You can create a subdatasheet that lets Juanita easily see and enter Order IDs, Order Dates, Customer IDs, and Product IDs for a particular customer when using the qryCustomers query.

To insert a subdatasheet in a query:

Step 1	*Open*	qryCustomers in Design view, if necessary
Step 2	*Delete*	Delete the current criteria
Step 3	*Switch*	Switch to Datasheet view
Step 4	*Click*	Insert on the menu bar
Step 5	*Click*	Subdatasheet

You see the Insert Subdatasheet dialog box, with tabs listing tables, queries, or both. Juanita wants to work with information from the tblOrders table—the Order ID, Order Date, Customer ID, and Product ID—so choose tblOrders as the object you want to insert. It's listed in the Both tab, which is displayed by default.

| Step 6 | *Click* | tblOrders |

The fields in the Link Child Fields: box and the Link Master Fields: box must match. In the Link Child Fields box, click the field you want to match in the Master Fields list. Choose the field that the two boxes have in common. For Juanita's subdatasheet, this field is Product Description.

Step 7	*Click*	the list arrow in the Link Child Fields: box
Step 8	*Click*	Product Description
Step 9	*Click*	the list arrow in the Link Master Fields: box
Step 10	*Click*	Product Description

The Insert Subdatasheet dialog box on your screen should look similar to Figure 7-10.

FIGURE 7-10
Insert Subdatasheet
Dialog Box

| Step 11 | *Click* | OK |

You see the results—a datasheet with a new first column. Click a plus sign in the first column of the datasheet to expand a subdatasheet and see the related information.

To expand and collapse the subdatasheet:

| Step 1 | *Click* | the plus sign in the first column for Paris spécialités |

Your screen should look similar to Figure 7-11.

FIGURE 7-11
Expanded Subdatasheet

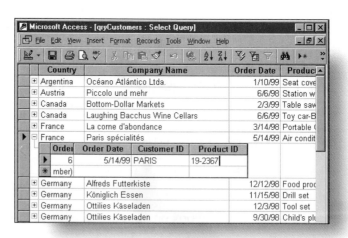

MENU TIP

To expand all the subdatasheets in the query, click Format, point to Subdatasheet, and then click Expand All. To collapse all the subdatasheets, click Format, point to Subdatasheet, and then click Collapse All.

You see the order, customer, and product information. You can also enter new information on the first blank line of the subdatasheet.

| Step 2 | *Click* | the minus sign in the first column for Paris spécialités to collapse the datasheet |

Juanita is ready to print the qryCustomers query.

7.g Printing the Results of a Query

The query results print like a datasheet—Access prints the query data in a table, similar to the one you see on your screen. Juanita wants to print the results of the qryCustomers query so she can show the data to her colleagues.

To print the query results:

Step 1	*Open*	qryCustomers in Datasheet view, if necessary
Step 2	*Click*	File
Step 3	*Click*	Print

The Print dialog box opens. You can now select print options, such as the number of copies to print. You can print only certain records by selecting the records first, and then clicking the Selected Records option button in the Print dialog box. You can also print the subdatasheets by expanding the ones you want to print before opening the Print dialog box. Juanita wants to print all the records without the subdatasheets, so you can accept the defaults.

| Step 4 | *Click* | OK to print the query |

The query is sent to the printer.

| Step 5 | *Close* | the query, saving your changes |
| Step 6 | *Exit* | Access |

Juanita will use the qryCustomer results in her presentation.

QUICK TIP

You can also press the CTRL + P keys to print.

chapter
seven

Summary

▶ A query is a question you ask about the data stored in your tables or a request you make to perform an action on the data, such as to calculate the sum of records. A query can find and filter records in a number of tables.

▶ A select query, the most common, retrieves data from one or more tables by using criteria you specify and then displays it in the order you want.

▶ Use the Query Wizard to create a simple select query.

▶ Once you run a query to generate a subset of the data in your database, you can sort the list in ascending or descending order. To sort on more than one field, first arrange the fields in the design grid in the order you want to perform the sort. Access sorts on the leftmost field first, then on the next field to the right, and so on.

▶ If your query is showing information you don't need, you can remove a field. When you do, you only remove it from the query. You do not delete the field or its data from the table your query is based on.

▶ Access asks if you want to save the query when you close the Query window. You then see the query name in the Queries list on the Database window.

▶ You can run a query at any time by opening it. If the data changed since the last time you ran the query, it is automatically updated.

▶ You can modify an existing query to include additional criteria by adding other fields. Add only those fields whose data you want to view, set criteria on, group by, update, or sort.

▶ Criteria are restrictions you place on a query to identify the records you want to work with. Set criteria when you want to refine your queries to show specific information.

▶ You set criteria in the query's design grid by entering an expression in the Criteria row for a field. An expression in a query is usually a combination of field names and symbols or words, called operators, that indicate what action to take. An expression can be as simple as one word, or more complex.

▶ You can use comparison criteria to find records by comparing their values.

▶ Use AND or OR to show records based on multiple criteria. In general, OR expands your selection—you choose records that contain one value or another. AND narrows your selection—you choose only those records that contain both values.

► You can also use NULL to retrieve records that have a field with no value.

► Use wildcards to search for text patterns in your records, or to find values based on some of the characters in the value. A wildcard symbol (*) stands for unknown characters.

► Subdatasheets allow you to display related records from other tables while you work with a table or a query.

► The query results print like a datasheet—Access prints the query data in a table, similar to the one you see on your screen.

Commands Review

Action	Menu Bar	Shortcut Menu	Toolbar	Keyboard
Sort a query in ascending order	Records, Sort, Ascending	Sort Ascending	![A Z↓]	ALT + R, S, A
Sort a query in descending order	Records, Sort, Descending	Sort Descending	![Z A↓]	ALT + R, S, C
Add a table to a query	Query, Show Table	Show Table	![icon]	ALT + Q, T
Run a query	Query, Run			ALT + Q, R

Concepts Review

Circle the correct answer.

1. A query is a:
- [a] way to display related records from other tables.
- [b] way of sorting and filtering data.
- [c] tool that is similar to tables.
- [d] tool that deletes information in your database.

2. Use a simple query to:
- [a] create messages that ask your users to answer questions.
- [b] accept data.
- [c] narrow down information.
- [d] insert information into a table.

3. Saving a query is:
- [a] part of backing up your data.
- [b] the purpose of a subdatasheet.
- [b] required before printing.
- [d] something Access does automatically.

4. A Query Wizard:
- [a] helps you create a simple query.
- [b] performs the same function as a table wizard.
- [c] checks for errors in your query.
- [d] analyzes your data before performing a query.

5. To see the results of a query:
- [a] you must be in Datasheet view.
- [b] click the Results button.
- [c] sort or filter it first.
- [d] click the Close button.

chapter seven

6. Add fields to a query when you want to:
[a] find records by comparing values.
[b] view, set criteria on, or sort the data in
the fields. (look in the Summary AI 48)
[c] modify the table the fields come from.
[d] quickly scan the data in the fields.

7. Which item is NOT used when setting criteria in a query?
[a] And
[b] Null
[c] Void
[d] wildcard

8. Use the OR criteria when you want to:
[a] narrow your selection.
[b] expand your selection.
[c] know the entire name of the field.
[d] find records where a field does not
contain a value.

9. Use the AND criteria when you want to:
[a] narrow your selection.
[b] expand your selection.
[c] know the entire name of the field.
[d] find records where a field does not
contain a value.

10. Create a subdatasheet when you want to:
[a] subtract values from the data.
[b] match records.
[c] view related data in other tables.
[d] find patterns of data in your records.

Circle **T** if the statement is true or **F** if the statement is false.

T F   1. You can press the CTRL + P keys to print a query.

T F   2. A subdatasheet lets you view or enter data in one table while working in another related table.

T F   3. Wildcards help you enter items by typing part of the item name.

T F   4. You can use comparison criteria to find records by comparing their values.

T F   5. Criteria are restrictions you place on a query.

T **F**   6. Use the Null criteria to enter <u>zero</u> values in your tables.

T **F**   7. You must remember to include quotation marks around the criteria you enter.

T F   8. A simple query is usually a select query.

T **F**   9. You can use the AND criteria to find customers in France or Germany, for example.

T F   10. A query can filter records from one or more tables.

Skills Review

SCANS

Exercise 1   C

1. If necessary, open the *mdbDynamicInc7* database.

2. Use the Query Wizard to create a simple select query that selects the ProductID, CategoryName, and ProductDescription fields from the tblProducts table and the CustomerID and OrderDate fields from the tblOrders table.

3. Choose to show detailed information in the query.

4. Save the query as qryProducts.

5. Print the query.

6. Close and save the query.

Exercise 2

1. If necessary, open the *mdbDynamicInc7* database.

2. Open the qryProducts query you created in Exercise 1.

3. Sort the records alphabetically in ascending order by Customer ID in Design view.

4. Close and save the query.

Exercise 3

1. If necessary, open the *mdbDynamicInc7* database.

2. Create a simple select query that selects all the fields from the tblEmployees table.

3. Show the detailed information.

4. Save the query as qryEmployees.

Exercise 4

1. If necessary, open the *mdbDynamicInc7* database.

2. Open the qryEmployees query you created in Exercise 3 in Design view.

3. Use the OR criteria to retrieve records of employees whose last names are Fuller or Yamamoto.

4. Close and save the query.

Exercise 5

1. If necessary, open the *mdbDynamicInc7* database.

2. Open the qryEmployees query you modified in Exercise 4 in Design view.

3. Clear all the current criteria.

4. Delete the SupervisorID, RegionID, SS#, and Photograph fields.

5. Find all the employees who live in Tacoma.

6. Close and save the query.

Exercise 6

1. If necessary, open the *mdbDynamicInc7* database.

2. Open the qryEmployees query you modified in Exercise 5 in Design view.

3. Clear all the current criteria.

4. Use the Null criteria to retrieve records where the employee does not have an e-mail address.

5. Close and save the query.

Exercise 7

1. If necessary, open the *mdbDynamicInc7* database.

2. Open the qryEmployees query you modified in Exercise 6 in Design view.

chapter seven

3. Clear all the current criteria.

4. Use a wildcard to retrieve records where the last name starts with *B*.

5. Close and save the query.

Exercise 8

1. If necessary, open the *mdbDynamicInc7* database.

2. Create a new query using the wizard to select all the fields from the tblOrders table and the supplier name and all address fields (address, city, state, and zip code) from the tblSuppliers table.

3. Save the query as qrySuppliers.

4. Create a subdatasheet that links the Product ID fields.

5. Expand one of the subdatasheets.

6. Print the query and then close and save it.

Case Projects

Project 1

Juanita Chavez needs a list of products that customers ordered. She also wants to know the price of each product. Create a query in the *mdbDynamicInc7* database called qryProducts that shows the Order ID, Order Date, Customer ID, Product ID, Product Description, Category Name, and Unit Price from tblOrders and tblProducts.

Project 2

Now Juanita wants to see the products sorted by category, and then by price. Rearrange the fields and then sort qryProducts to provide the information Juanita wants.

Project 3

Juanita needs to know who is ordering Dynamic's top-priced products, those costing more than $30.00. Clear any filters, sorts, or criteria. Then create a query using comparison criteria to show only product and order information for those products over $30.00.

Project 4

Juanita wants a list of all the toys Dynamic sold in 1998. Clear any filters, sorts, or criteria. Then create a query using criteria to list all the toys Dynamic sold in 1998. (Hint: Use the wildcard character "*" to query the date field.)

Project 5

Juanita also needs a list of all the electronic and houseware products Dynamic customers ordered. Clear any filters, sorts, or criteria. Then create a query using criteria to list electronic and houseware products.

Project 6

Juanita wants to filter the records you retrieved in Project 5 so that they display only products in the Electronics category. After you run the query in Project 5, click the Electronics category. To apply a filter to the query's recordset, click Filter by Selection on the toolbar, click Filter by Form on the toolbar, and then enter other criteria to filter the query's recordset.

Project 7

Using the Microsoft on the Web command on the Help menu, connect to the Microsoft Web site and look for information on queries. Print at least two Web pages that explain the basic concepts of queries.

Project 8

Using the Microsoft on the Web command on the Help menu, connect to the Microsoft Web site and look for information on criteria in queries. Print at least two Web pages about setting criteria, including using expressions or operators.

Designing and Using Basic Reports

Chapter Overview

A report is an effective way to present data in a printed format. In this chapter, you learn the different ways to create a report based on one or more tables or queries. You also learn how to modify a report, use the Print Preview toolbar, and save and print a report.

LEARNING OBJECTIVES

▶ Understand report types
▶ Create a report with AutoReport
▶ Create a report with the Report Wizard
▶ Preview a report
▶ Modify format properties
▶ Print a report

Case profile

The managers of Dynamic Inc., ask for your assistance in producing reports for the annual stockholders' meeting. Maria Moreno, Dynamic's owner, wants to provide a general report listing Dynamic employees. The accounting manager, Giang Hu, wants to print a report detailing the orders for the past year. The warehouse manager, Kang Leing, needs a report listing Dynamic's products.

chapter eight

8/29/02 ✓

8.a Understanding Report Types

A report is an Access database object that presents information in a printed format. For example, you can create and print a sales summary, phone list, or mailing label. Because you have control over the size and appearance of everything on the report, you can display the information the way you want to see it.

Most of the information in a report comes from an underlying table or query, which is where the report finds its information. Other information is stored in the report's design.

You can choose from a number of different report types. Each type uses the same data, but a different design. The two most common report types are columnar and tabular. A **columnar report** arranges each record's data vertically—each field for each record appears on a line by itself. A **tabular report** arranges the data for each record horizontally, with each field appearing in a column.

A **detail report** lists record details. A **grouped report** organizes records into groups and then subtotals the groups. A **label report** creates mailing labels. A **chart report** includes a chart or graph comparing numeric data.

You can create reports using AutoReport, the Report Wizard, or Design view. Use AutoReport to create a simple report based on a single table or query. Use the Report Wizard to specify the kind of report you want to create, and have Access guide you step by step. You can modify the report later in Design view if you like.

Create your first report for Maria using AutoReport.

8.b Creating a Report with AutoReport

You can create a very simple columnar or tabular report using AutoReport. **AutoReport** assists you in quickly creating a report based on a single table or query. (You can modify and improve the report design later in Design view.)

Start by creating a report for Maria listing Dynamic's employees and their departments. Because you do not want to include all of the information from tblEmployees, base the report on qryEmployees, which lists only the employee names and their departments.

To create a report using AutoReport:

| Step 1 | *Open* | *mdbDynamicInc8* |

Step 2	*Click*	Reports 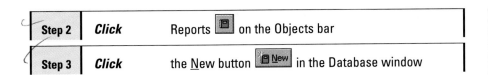 on the Objects bar
Step 3	*Click*	the <u>N</u>ew button in the Database window

The New Report dialog box on your screen should look similar to Figure 8-1.

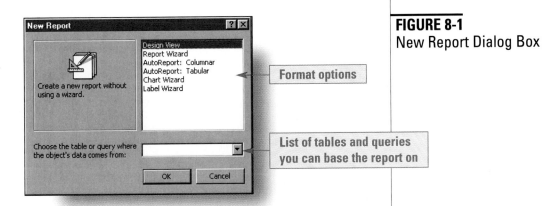

FIGURE 8-1
New Report Dialog Box

This dialog box offers you several options for producing reports. You want to create a simple, tabular report, which lists the information Maria wants.

Step 4	*Click*	AutoReport: Tabular

In this type of report, the fields in each record appear on one line, and the labels print once at the top of each page. If you choose AutoReport: Columnar, each field appears on a separate line with a label to its left. You can also use the New Report dialog box to create a report with a chart or to create mailing labels.

Step 5	*Click*	qryEmployees in the Choose the table or query where the object's data comes from: list box
Step 6	*Click*	OK

chapter
eight

Access automatically creates the report. Your screen should look similar to Figure 8-2.

FIGURE 8-2
Simple Tabular Report
Created with AutoReport

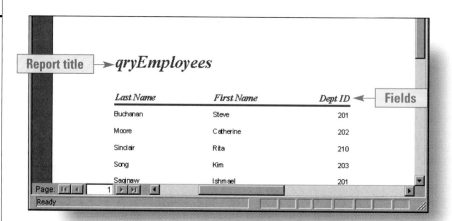

Notice that the report title is the title of the query that you used to create it. Later in this chapter, you learn how to modify and enhance a report before printing it.

Step 7	*Click*	the Close button

Access asks if you want to save the report.

Step 8	*Click*	Yes

The Save As dialog box opens.

Step 9	*Key*	rptEmployees as the name of the report
Step 10	*Click*	OK

Use AutoReport to create a report from one table or query. If you want to create a report from more than one source, however, you can use the Report Wizard.

8.c Creating a Report with the Report Wizard

If you want to choose a number of options to determine the format and content of your report, use the **Report Wizard**. You can use the Report Wizard to create the report for Giang which shows the orders Dynamic received in the last year.

To create a report using the Report Wizard:

| Step 1 | *Click* | Reports 🔲 on the Objects bar, if necessary |
| Step 2 | *Double-click* | Create report by using wizard |

You see the first Report Wizard dialog box, where you can select the fields you want in the report. The fields can come from one or more tables or queries. Giang wants to see the customer name and ID, the products ordered, and their order date.

Step 3	*Click*	Table: tblCustomers in the Tables/Queries list box
Step 4	*Move*	the CustomerID and CompanyName fields into the Selected Fields: text box
Step 5	*Click*	Table: tblOrders in the Tables/Queries list box
Step 6	*Move*	the OrderDate and Product Description fields into the Selected Fields: text box
Step 7	*Click*	Next >

You can now select how you want to view your data. The wizard looks at the relationship between the tables you selected and then groups the records in your report based on these relationships. For example, you can group the CustomerID and CompanyName data together, separate from the information that came from tblOrders. You can also group all the data together, which is what Giang suggests.

To complete the Report Wizard:

| Step 1 | *Click* | by tblOrders |
| Step 2 | *Click* | Next > |

You can now add grouping levels, if you like. For now, create a simple report without grouping. For more information on groups, see "Grouping Data in a Report" later in this chapter.

| Step 3 | *Click* | Next > |

You can now choose how to sort the information in the report. Giang wants the orders sorted by customer, so choose to sort the CustomerID field in descending order.

M O U S E   T I P

Click the Show me more information button in the Report Wizard dialog box to see tips on grouping your data.

chapter
eight

Step 4	*Click*	CustomerID in the list box
Step 5	*Click*	the Sort button [↕️] to switch to descending order
Step 6	*Click*	Next >

You can now choose a layout for your report. The default layout is tabular and portrait, which is fine for Giang's report. To see a preview of the other layouts you can use, click an option and check the preview box. If you want to include a lot of fields, you can use a landscape orientation, which treats the page as 11-inches wide and 8½-inches long.

| Step 7 | *Click* | Next > to accept the default layout |

Now choose a style for the report. Click a style name, such as Bold, to see a preview. The style you choose sets options such as the font, font style, and line spacing for the report.

Step 8	*Click*	Corporate
Step 9	*Click*	Next >
Step 10	*Key*	Dynamic Annual Orders as the title of the report
Step 11	*Click*	Finish

Your report should look similar to Figure 8-3.

CAUTION TIP

It is always a good idea to be specific when naming a report so the viewer knows its content at a glance.

FIGURE 8-3
Report Created with the Report Wizard

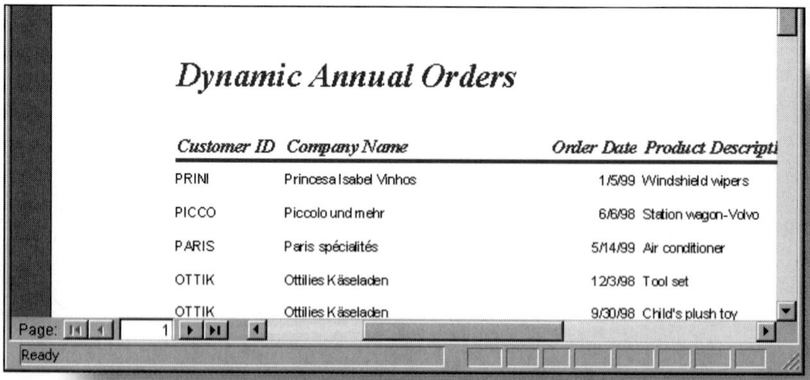

QUICK TIP

[C] One method for creating reports is to use Design view. Using Design view takes more time, but will allow a more customized report. Once you create a report (using any method), you use Design view to modify it.

Now that you created a report, you can see how it looks when you print it.

8.d Previewing a Report

You can preview a report to see how it looks on the printed page. Giang wants to see the content and layout of the report before printing, especially because his report is longer than one page. You can use the Print Preview toolbar to look at the report in a variety of ways, including using different magnifications and viewing two or more pages at a time.

After you create a report using the Report Wizard, Access automatically shows you the report in Print Preview.

To preview a report:

| Step 1 | Click | the Two Pages button on the Print Preview toolbar |

Your screen should now look similar to Figure 8-4.

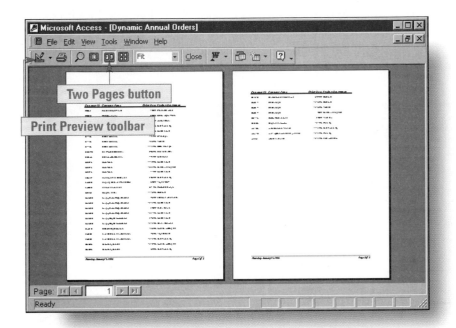

| Step 2 | Click | the Zoom button 🔍 on the Print Preview toolbar to increase the magnification of the report |
| Step 3 | Click | the Zoom button 🔍 again to decrease the magnification |

MOUSE TIP

You can view any report in Print Preview from the Database window or from Design view. In the Database window, click Reports, select the report you want to preview, and then click the Preview button on the Database window toolbar. In Design view, click the Print Preview button on the Report Design toolbar.

QUICK TIP

You can use the navigation buttons at the bottom of the Print Preview window to move between pages.

FIGURE 8-4
Two-Page View of Report in Print Preview

chapter eight

Step 4	*Click*	the Close button to close the report

You see that the Report Wizard creates a useful report for Giang's Accounting department.

You are now ready to assist Kang with his report. He already created it but wants to improve its appearance. You can do that by modifying the report in Design view.

C 8.e Modifying Format Properties

Once you create a report, you can modify it. For example, you can change the **labels** (the names of each field), customize the headers and footers, and modify the overall format. You can also customize headers and footers for both the page and the entire report, and group and sort data. Each of these elements—labels, fields, and headers and footers—are included in different sections of the report.

Kang already created a report listing Dynamic's products, as shown in Figure 8-5.

FIGURE 8-5
Original rptProducts Report

Incomplete report title →

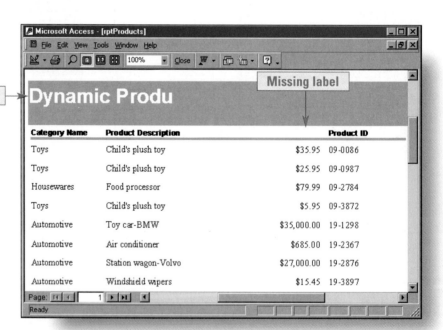

You want to improve the content and format of Kang's report. You start by modifying the page header.

Using Report Sections

The information in a report is divided into sections. Each section has a different purpose and prints in a particular order. First, Access prints the **report header** at the top of the first page of the report. The report header is usually the title of the report. Next, Access prints the **page header**, which appears at the top of each page of the report. The page header usually includes the column headings. Below the page header, Access prints the **detail**, which displays the data from the fields for each record. The **page footer** appears at the bottom of each page of the report, and usually shows the page number. You can also include a **report footer**, which appears at the bottom of the last page of the report. Use it to display items such as report totals. Figure 8-6 shows the sections of a report.

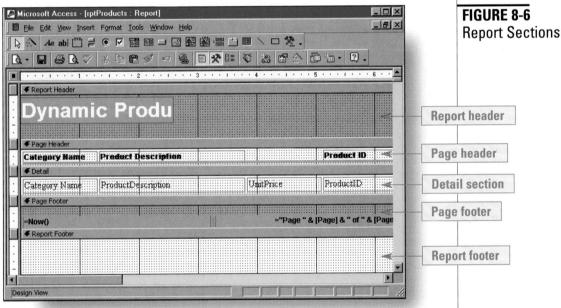

FIGURE 8-6
Report Sections

You determine where information appears in every section by including controls such as labels and text boxes.

Using the Control Toolbox to Add Controls

A label shows the name of an item, such as a field. Fields are shown in text boxes. Kang's report includes a field for UnitPrice, but not a label. You can create a label for this field using the toolbox and then adjust the label's position so it aligns with the other labels on the report.

chapter
eight

To add a label to the report:

| Step 1 | *Click* | Reports 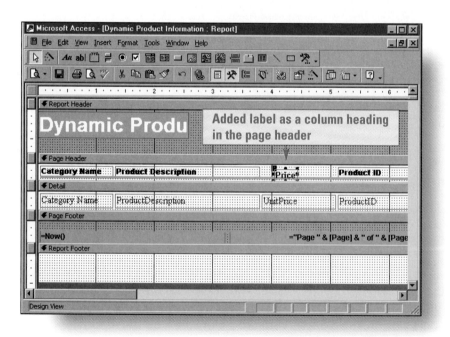 on the Objects bar, if necessary |
| Step 2 | *Double-click* | rptProducts |

Kang's Product report opens in Print Preview.

Step 3	*Switch*	to Design view
Step 4	*Close*	the Field List dialog box, if necessary
Step 5	*Click*	the Toolbox button on the Report Design toolbar, if necessary, to open the toolbox
Step 6	*Click*	the Label button on the toolbox
Step 7	*Click*	in the Page Header section above the UnitPrice field
Step 8	*Key*	Price
Step 9	*Press*	the ENTER key to complete the entry and select the label

Your screen should look similar to Figure 8-7.

FIGURE 8-7
Adding a Label to a Report

Once you add a label, you can move it. Adjust the position of the Price label to align it with the other labels in the page header.

You see the selection handles for the label, which let you move and size it.

To move the Price label:

| Step 1 | *Point to* | the edge of the Price label |

When the mouse pointer changes to an open hand, you can move the label.

| Step 2 | *Drag* | the label to align it with the other labels |

You can also format a label by changing its size, background color, or font, for example. The Price label in rptProducts doesn't match the other labels. You can use the Format Painter to use the same format as the other labels.

To format the Price label to match the other labels:

| Step 1 | *Click* | the Product Description label |

You can also click any label that has the formatting you want.

| Step 2 | *Click* | the Format Painter button 🖌 on the Report Design toolbar |

| Step 3 | *Click* | the Price label |

The Price label now matches the formatting of the other page header labels.

Now you're ready to work on other sections of the report. You can resize the report title in rptProducts and add a report footer to show the total price of the products.

chapter
eight

Setting Section Properties

The headers and footers in a report include information such as the report title and the page number. You can format and size items in the headers and footers as you do in any other section of the report. You can also add controls, such as one that calculates the sum of the fields. In Kang's report, you need to resize the report title to see the complete text. The title is contained in a text box, which you can quickly size by clicking and dragging. Then add a control to the report footer to show the total price of the products.

To resize the report title:

Step 1	*Click*	the title in the report header

You see the selection handles for the title's text box, which let you size it.

Step 2	*Point to*	the right-center selection handle

When the mouse pointer changes to a double-headed arrow, you can resize the title.

Step 3	*Drag*	the text box to the right until you see the entire title—Dynamic Product Information

After deselecting the label, your screen should look similar to Figure 8-8.

FIGURE 8-8
Report with Resized Title

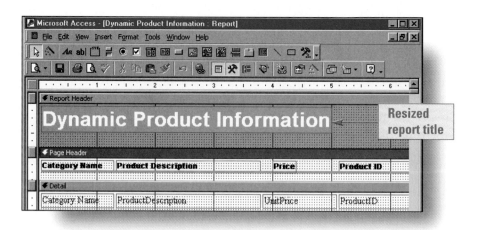

QUICK TIP

If you don't see the report footer section, you can open it by increasing the height of its section. Point to the bottom edge of the section. When you see a double-headed arrow, drag down to increase the height of the section.

Now that you changed the report header, you can add a calculated control to the report footer.

Using a Calculated Control in a Report

A **calculated control** allows you, for example, to determine the sum of the fields. In this report, you add a text box that calculates the total of all the UnitPrice fields listed in the report.

To add a calculated control to the report footer:

| Step 1 | *Click* | the Text Box button 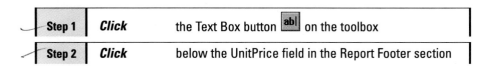 on the toolbox |
| Step 2 | *Click* | below the UnitPrice field in the Report Footer section |

When you insert a text box, you insert a **compound control**, which means it has two parts—an attached label for the text and the text itself. The label initially shows boldfaced placeholder text, such as Text11, and the text box shows the value.

Step 3	*Click*	in the text box label
Step 4	*Select*	the existing label text
Step 5	*Key*	Grand Total:
Step 6	*Click*	in the text box

Because Kang wants to show the sum of the Price fields, enter an expression to create a calculated control.

| Step 7 | *Key* | =Sum([UnitPrice]) |

Your screen should look similar to Figure 8-9.

QUICK TIP

 You can enter a value in the text box or you can enter an expression that calculates a value for you. If you enter an expression, the text box becomes a calculated control—it calculates values in your report.

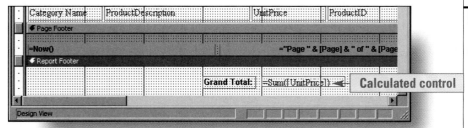

FIGURE 8-9
Inserting a Calculated Control

Now you can see the results of your changes.

| Step 8 | *Switch* | to Print Preview |
| Step 9 | *Click* | the Two Pages button 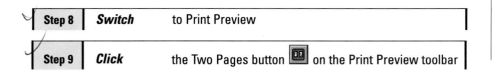 on the Print Preview toolbar |

chapter
eight

Your screen should look similar to Figure 8-10.

FIGURE 8-10
Redesigned Report

Complete report title

Added label

Calculated control

Kang's report is much easier to read, but you can still improve it by grouping information. You can group the records by category, for example, and show subtotals for each.

Grouping Data in a Report

By grouping records that share a common value, you can calculate subtotals and make a report easier to read. You can also add a group header to identify the records in the group. For Kang's report, you can group the records by category, as well as add a group header and footer to show a group name and subtotals for the products in each category.

To group records in a report:

Step 1	*Switch*	to Design view
Step 2	*Click*	the Sorting and Grouping button [≡ on the Report Design toolbar

The Sorting and Grouping dialog box opens.

| Step 3 | *Click* | the list arrow in the first row of the Field/Expression column |

You can now choose the field you want to group.

Step 4	*Click*	Category Name

Note that Access sorts this field in ascending order by default. (You set the sort order for other data later in this chapter.)

Step 5	*Click*	in the Group Header row and then click the list arrow
Step 6	*Click*	Yes to add a group header for the field
Step 7	*Click*	in the Group Footer row and then click the list arrow
Step 8	*Click*	Yes to add a group footer for the field
Step 9	*Close*	the Sorting and Grouping dialog box
Step 10	*Switch*	to Print Preview

You see the report with a new group header and footer divisions. Recall that you may need to use the Zoom button on the Print Preview toolbar to magnify your report.

Now you can add a label to the group header to identify the group and a text box to calculate subtotals for each group. Do so by moving a label and field to another section.

Moving a Label and Field to a Different Section

You can enter information in a group header and footer by adding labels, text boxes, or other controls. You can also enter information by moving controls from other sections. Kang's report is now grouped by Category Name. Instead of repeating the category name for every product in a group, move the Category Name label and field to the group header. The category name, such as Housewares, becomes the title of the group.

To move a field label to the group header section:

Step 1	*Switch*	to Design view
Step 2	*Click*	the Category Name field in the Detail section

You see the selection handles for the text box when you click the field.

Step 3	*Point to*	the Category Name text box until the pointer changes to an open hand
Step 4	*Drag*	the control to the Category Name Header

QUICK TIP

C To make small adjustments to the placement of a control, hold down CTRL and then click the UP, DOWN, LEFT, or RIGHT ARROW keys to precisely place the control.

chapter
eight

You decide to also move the label and field that calculates field totals to the group footer. The field then calculates the subtotal for each group, so you can see the total price for all the individual product types. To move a text box to the group footer:

Step 1	*Click*	the text box containing the =Sum formula

Because this field is a compound control, you see the selection handles for both the label and the text box when you click the field.

Step 2	*Verify*	that both the field and its label are selected
Step 3	*Point to*	the control until the pointer changes to an open hand
Step 4	*Drag*	the control to the Category Name Footer

Your screen should look similar to Figure 8-11.

FIGURE 8-11
Report with Labels and Fields in New Sections

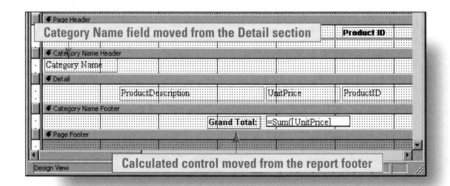

Now that your groups are set, you can sort the data in the report. Kang wants to see the products sorted according to price, with the most expensive items first.

Sorting Data in a Report

You can sort on one or more fields in a report. Kang wants to sort according to product price within each group.

To sort records in a report:

Step 1	*Click*	the Sorting and Grouping button [≡] on the Report Design toolbar

You see the Sorting and Grouping dialog box.

Step 2	*Click*	the list arrow in the second Field/Expression row
Step 3	*Click*	UnitPrice
Step 4	*Click*	in the Sort Order column and then click the list arrow
Step 5	*Click*	Descending

Recall that descending order sorts from Z to A or 9 to 0.

Step 6	*Close*	the Sorting and Grouping dialog box
Step 7	*Switch*	to Print Preview
Step 8	*Click*	the Zoom button 🔍 on the Print Preview toolbar to increase the magnification of the report

Your screen should look similar to Figure 8-12.

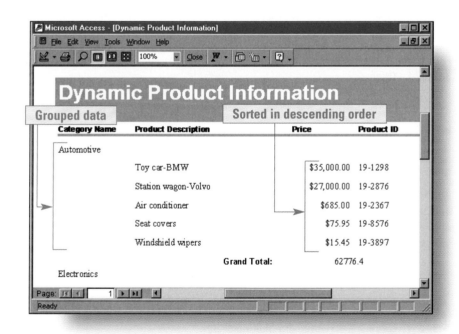

FIGURE 8-12
Sorted Report

Now that you grouped and sorted the data in the report, you can refine its format. You can change the format of Kang's report so it matches the format of other Dynamic reports.

Modifying Report Properties

You can modify the format of a report by applying a predefined format and by setting the properties for individual sections or controls. Choose a different predefined format for Kang's report and change the background color of the Detail section. You can also change the format of the calculated field.

To apply a predefined format to the report:

Step 1	*Switch*	to Design view
Step 2	*Click*	Edit on the menu bar
Step 3	*Click*	Select All
Step 4	*Click*	the AutoFormat button ▦ on the Report Design toolbar

Choose the format you want from the list. Click a name to see a preview of the format in the Preview box. Kang wants his report to match the other Dynamic reports, which use the Corporate format.

Step 5	*Click*	Corporate, if necessary
Step 6	*Click*	OK

Now you can refine the appearance of the report by setting properties for sections and controls.

Modifying Control Properties

To add a background color to the Detail section of Kang's report, you change the Fill/Back Color property for the section. To change the background color of the Detail section:

Step 1	*Right-click*	the background of the Detail section
Step 2	*Point to*	Fill/Back Color in the shortcut menu
Step 3	*Click*	the light blue color box

Now the details of the report stand out against the light blue background. Your next change is to modify the calculated totals field so it automatically displays a dollar amount.

Step 4	*Double-click*	the =Sum([UnitPrice]) field
Step 5	*Click*	the list arrow in the Format field on the Format tab in the Properties dialog box

Step 6	**Click**	Currency
Step 7	**Close**	the Properties dialog box
Step 8	**Click**	the Print Preview button on the Report Design toolbar

Your screen should look similar to Figure 8-13.

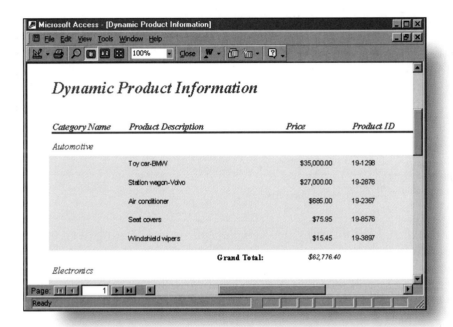

Microsoft Access - [Dynamic Product Information]

File Edit View Tools Window Help

100%   Close

Dynamic Product Information

Category Name	Product Description	Price	Product ID
Automotive			
	Toy car-BMW	$35,000.00	19-1298
	Station wagon-Volvo	$27,000.00	19-2876
	Air conditioner	$685.00	19-2367
	Seat covers	$75.95	19-8576
	Windshield wipers	$15.45	19-3897
	Grand Total:	$62,776.40	
Electronics			

Page: 1

Ready

MENU TIP

To save the report with a different name or in a different location, click <u>F</u>ile and then click Save <u>A</u>s.

FIGURE 8-13
Reformatted rptProducts Report

Now that you modified the report, you are ready to save it.

Saving a Report

You should save your report as you change your report design. Access also automatically saves the report when you close it.

To save the report:

| Step 1 | **Click** | <u>F</u>ile |
| Step 2 | **Click** | <u>S</u>ave to save the report with its default name |

Now you're ready to print the report.

QUICK TIP

C You can enhance reports by inserting graphics. Graphics can provide a visual reminder, for example, of the company producing the report or of the information contained in the report. An overuse of graphics, however, can detract from the report's appearance.

chapter eight

8.f # Printing a Report

After you create and save a report, you can print it. Before you print a report for the first time, check the report in Print Preview. You can print a report from Design view or Print Preview. You can also select the report in the Database window and then follow the steps below.

To print the report:

Step 1	*Click*	File
Step 2	*Click*	Print

You see the Print dialog box where you can specify a printer, the range of pages you want to print, the number of copies you want, and whether they should be collated.

Step 3	*Click*	OK

The printed report provides Kang an easy-to-read listing of all of Dynamic's products.

Step 4	*Close*	the report
Step 5	*Close*	Access

MOUSE TIP

To bypass the Print dialog box when printing a report, click the Print button on the Database or Print Preview toolbar.

Summary

▶ A report is an Access database object that presents information in a printed format. Because you have control over the size and appearance of everything on the report, you can display the information the way you want to see it.

▶ Most of the information in a report comes from an underlying table or query, which is where the report finds its information. Other information is stored in the report's design.

▶ You can choose from a number of different report types. Each type uses the same data, but a different design. The two most common report types are columnar and tabular. A columnar report arranges each record's data vertically—each field for each record appears on a line by itself. A tabular report arranges the data for each record horizontally, with each field appearing in a column.

▶ You can create reports using AutoReport, the Report Wizard, or Design view. Use AutoReport to create a simple report based on a single table or query. Use the Report Wizard to specify the kind of report you want to create, and have Access guide you step by step. You can modify the report later in Design view if you like.

▶ You can preview a report to see how it looks on the printed page. Use the Print Preview toolbar to look at the report in a variety of ways, including using different magnifications and viewing two or more pages at a time.

▶ Once you create a report, you can modify it by changing the labels (the names of each field), customizing the headers and footers, and changing the overall format. You can also customize headers and footers for both the page and the entire report, and group and sort data. Each of these elements—labels, fields, and headers and footers—are included in different sections of the report.

▶ The information in a report is divided into sections. Each section has a different purpose and prints in a particular order. First, Access prints the report header at the top of the first page of the report. The report header is usually the title of the report. Next, Access prints the page header, which appears at the top of each page of the report. The page header usually includes the column headings. Below the page header, Access prints the detail, which displays the data from the fields for each record. The page footer appears at the bottom of each page of the report, and usually shows the page number. You can also include a report footer, which appears at the bottom of the last page of the report. Use it to display items such as report totals.

chapter eight

▶ By grouping records that share a common value, you can calculate subtotals and make a report easier to read. You can add a group header to identify the records in the group. You can also sort on one or more fields in a report.

▶ You can enter information in a group header and footer by adding labels, text boxes, or other controls. You can also enter information by moving controls from other sections.

▶ You can modify the format of a report by applying a predefined format and by setting the properties for individual sections or controls.   *ques. 10*

▶ Save your report as you change your report design. Access also automatically saves the report when you close it.

▶ After you create and save a report, you can print it. Before you print a report for the first time, check the report in Print Preview. You can print an open report from Design view or Print Preview. You can also first select the report in the Database window and then print it.

Commands Review

Action	Menu Bar	Shortcut Menu	Toolbar	Keyboard
Create a report	Insert, Report or AutoReport		New	ALT + I, R or A
Preview a report	File, Print Preview	Print Preview		ALT + F, V
Save a report	File, Save	Save		CTRL + S ALT + F, S
Print a report	File, Print	Print		CTRL + P ALT + F, P

Concepts Review

Circle the correct answer.

1. A report is a(n):
   [a] printed version of the data in a database.
   [b] way of sorting and filtering data.
   [c] Access feature that is similar to tables.
   [d] tool that deletes information in your database.

2. Create a report to:
   [a] share data.
   [b] accept data.
   [c] narrow down information.
   [d] customize tables and queries.

3. You can create different kinds of reports in Access, including a:
   [a] spreadsheet.
   [b] columnar report.
   [c] form report.
   [d] two-page view.

4. Use the Report Wizard to:
   [a] create a simple report based on a single table or query.
   [b] set the properties of the report footer.
   [c] create a report by starting with a blank design.
   [d] choose a number of options to determine the format and content of your report.

5. Use AutoReport to:
[a] create a simple report based on a single table or query.
[b] set the properties of the report footer.
[c] create a report by starting with a blank design.
[d] choose a number of options to determine the format and content of your report.

6. Use the tools on the Print Preview toolbar to:
[a] change the print options.
[b] choose a format for the report.
[c] see the content and layout of the report before you print it.
[d] modify the report design.

7. Include a label in a report to:
[a] show the name of a field.
[b] calculate the sum of fields.
[c] adjust the alignment of other report elements.
[d] sort the data.

8. Group data in a report to:
[a] customize the headers and footers.
[b] insert page numbers.
[c] keep common fields together.
[d] sort the data.

9. The report header section usually shows:
[a] the column headings.
[b] the data from the fields for each record.
[c] report totals.
[d] the title of the report.

10. You can modify the format of a report by:
[a] applying a predefined format.
[b] sorting the data.
[c] saving it with a new name.
[d] viewing it in Print Preview.

Circle **T** if the statement is true or **F** if the statement is false.

T F   1. You can press the CTRL + P keys to print a report.
T F   2. AutoReport assists you in creating a report based on <u>two or more</u> queries. *one*
T F   3. You can choose how to sort report data in the Report Wizard or the Sorting and Grouping dialog box.
T F   4. Click the Zoom button to see two pages in a multi-page report side by side.
T F   5. Grouping records helps the user see relevant information.
T F   6. You cannot sort grouped reports.
T F   7. A field label must match the field name.
T F   8. An AutoReport is usually in a tabular or columnar report format.
T F   9. Once you insert a label and field in one section, you cannot move it to another section.
T F   10. One of the format properties you can set is the background color of a report section.

Skills Review

SCANS

Exercise 1

1. If necessary, open the *mdbDynamicInc8* database.

2. Use AutoReport to create a columnar report based on the tblOrders table.

3. Name the new report rptOrders.

4. Save, print, and close the new report.

chapter eight

Exercise 2

1. If necessary, open the *mdbDynamicInc8* database.

2. Use the Report Wizard to create a new report based on the tblDepartment and tblEmployees tables. Use only the following fields in the report: Department Name from tblDepartment, and Dept., FirstName, LastName, and Email from tblEmployees.

3. Choose to view the data by tblDepartment. Sort the report by last name.

4. Choose an outline layout and the Bold format for the report.

5. Name the new report rptDepartment.

6. Save and print the new report.

Exercise 3

1. If necessary, open the *mdbDynamicInc8* database.

2. Open the rptDepartment report you created in Exercise 2.

3. Preview the report in Print Preview. Increase and decrease the magnification. Choose a different magnification percentage from the Zoom list box.

4. Close the report.

Exercise 4

1. If necessary, open the *mdbDynamicInc8* database.

2. Open the rptDepartment report you created in Exercise 2.

3. In Design view, change the title of the report to *Dynamic Departments*. Change the e-mail label to *E-mail Address*.

4. Resize any labels as necessary.

5. Preview, save, print, and close the rptDepartment report.

Exercise 5

1. If necessary, open the *mdbDynamicInc8* database.

2. Open the rptDepartment report you modified in Exercise 4.

3. In Design view, add a control to the report footer to calculate the total number of employees. The label can be *Total Employees*. The calculated field should be *=Count([LastName])*.

4. Move and resize the controls, if necessary.

5. Preview, save, and print the report.

6. Close the report.

Exercise 6

1. If necessary, open the *mdbDynamicInc8* database.

2. Open the rptOrders report you created in Exercise 1 in Design view.

3. Group the data by the Customer ID field.

4. Move the controls as necessary to improve the appearance of the report. Delete the Customer ID control (label and text box) from the Detail section.

5. Preview, save, and print the report.

Exercise 7

1. If necessary, open the *mdbDynamicInc8* database.

2. Open the rptOrders report you modified in Exercise 6.

3. Sort the data in each group by the Order Date field in descending order.

4. Preview, save, and print the report.

Exercise 8

1. If necessary, open the *mdbDynamicInc8* database.

2. Open the rptOrders report you modified in Exercise 7 in Design view.

3. Copy the Customer ID control (label and text box) from the Customer ID Header section to the Detail section.

4. Move and resize the controls as necessary.

5. Preview, save, and print the report.

6. Close the report.

Case Projects

Project 1

Using the Office on the <u>W</u>eb command on the <u>H</u>elp menu, open the Microsoft home page and then link to pages that provide basic information about Access reports. Print at least two of the Web pages.

Project 2

Search the Access online Help for information about creating and modifying reports. Link to a Web page that provides more information or examples. Print at least two pages.

Project 3

Maria Moreno, the owner of Dynamic Inc., asks you to add a graphic showing Dynamic's logo on her rptEmployees report. Insert the *Logo.bmp* graphic from the Data Disk to the rptEmployees report. Open the report in Design view, and then click the Unbound Object Frame button in the toolbox. Click where you want to insert the graphic, and then choose the *Logo.bmp*.

Project 4

Giang wants to change his Dynamic Annual Orders report to add a line to the top of the report. You can use the Control toolbox to add the line to Giang's report. Search the Access online Help for instructions on using the toolbox to add a line to a report. Then follow these instructions to draw a line at the top of Giang's report and format it to make it thicker.

Project 5

Kang wants to include order information when he prints rptProducts for the sales department, but doesn't want to include it when he prints the report for customers. You can accomplish this by using conditional formatting in Kang's rptProducts report. Search the Access online Help for instructions on using conditional formatting. Then follow these instructions to include the Order ID and Order Date information in one version of the report, but not in another.

Project 6

Maria wants you to create a report showing a list of Dynamic's suppliers. To create this report in Design view, click Reports on the Object Bar, click New on the Database window, and then click Design View. Click the tblSuppliers table and click OK. Drag the Supplier ID, name, address (including city and state), and ZIP code fields from the Field List to the report. Resize and rearrange the controls as desired. Save the report as rptSuppliers.

Project 7

In Design view, open the rptSuppliers report you created in Project 6. Modify the report by changing its properties. Right-click in the Page Header section, point to Fill/Back Color, and select a background color for this section. Select all the labels and then click Properties in the Report Design toolbar. Change the Border Style to dashes to include a border around the labels.

Project 8

In Design view, open the rptSuppliers report you modified in Project 7. Maria wants you to insert a subreport that shows product information from rptProducts. Make sure the Control Wizards button on the toolbox is selected, and then click the Subform/Subreport button. Click where you want to place the subreport, and then follow the steps in the Wizard dialog boxes. Make sure you have defined relationships for the tables used in rptSuppliers and rptProducts—if you have, Access automatically synchronizes the report and subreport.

chapter eight

Creating and Using Data Access Pages

Chapter Overview

In this chapter, you learn how to create and modify a data access page. You also learn how to use them for sharing data across an intranet or the Internet, and for publishing on the Web.

LEARNING OBJECTIVES

- ▶ Define data access pages
- ▶ Create a data access page
- ▶ Use the group and sort features of data access pages
- ▶ Modify data access pages
- ▶ Build order forms for the Internet
- ▶ Use data access pages for Web publication

Case profile

Dynamic Inc., recently created a new group within its advertising department, which is responsible for creating and maintaining a Web presence for the company. Janet Washington, the head of the group, already created the basic site. Now Janet wants your help in linking data from the Dynamic database to the Web site. To do that, you create data access pages.

chapter
nine

9.a Defining Data Access Pages

Data access pages (DAPs) are HyperText Markup Language (HTML) pages based on Access tables or queries but stored as separate files. People who do not have Access on their computers can then interact with the Access database information. You can also more easily e-mail DAPs than an entire database. However, to view DAPs, you need to use **Microsoft Internet Explorer 5**, which is Microsoft's latest version of its Web browser.

You can use AutoPage, the Page Wizard, or Design view to create a data access page. AutoPage is the simplest method, and creates a page that displays all the fields and records from a table or query. Use the Page Wizard to select fields from more than one table or query and to have Access guide you step by step. Use Design view to modify the DAPs you create, or to create a new one on your own.

Janet wants you to list Dynamic product information on the Web site. Because this information is included in a single table, you can create the first DAP for Janet using AutoPage.

9.b Creating a Data Access Page

C

AutoPage allows you to create a basic data access page that displays all fields (except those that store pictures) and records from a table or query. Because the first DAP Janet requested is based on the tblProducts table, create her first DAP using AutoPage.

To create a DAP with AutoPage:

Step 1	*Open*	mdbDynamicInc9
Step 2	*Click*	Pages on the Objects bar
Step 3	*Click*	the New button in the Database window

The New Data Access Page dialog box opens.

You can use the dialog box to create a new data access page in Design view, from an existing Web page, with the Page Wizard, or using AutoPage. You want to create a simple, columnar page, which lists the information Janet wants, so you can use AutoPage.

chapter
nine

Step 4	*Click*	AutoPage: Columnar in the list box
Step 5	*Click*	tblProducts in the Choose the table or query where the object's data comes from: list box
Step 6	*Click*	OK

Now you see a list of all the fields in tblProducts, with one record per page. Your screen should look similar to Figure 9-1.

FIGURE 9-1
Data Access Page Created
with AutoPage

Field names

Navigation toolbar

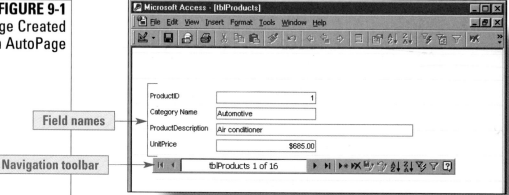

You can use the Navigation toolbar to see all the records.
Now that you created a DAP, save it before you close it.
To save a DAP:

Step 1	*Click*	File on the menu bar
Step 2	*Click*	Save As

You see the Save As dialog box, where you can enter a name for your DAP.

Step 3	*Key*	dapProducts
Step 4	*Click*	OK

You see the Save As Data Access Page dialog box, where you can select a location for the DAP. (Remember, DAPs are stored as files separate from the database.)

QUICK TIP

When you save a data access page, Access stores the HTML file in the folder you specified and adds a shortcut to the page in the Database window.

Step 5	*Locate*	your Data Disk, if necessary
Step 6	*Click*	Save
Step 7	*Close*	the DAP window

Now Janet is ready to create a second data access page that will list Dynamic's employees and e-mail addresses.

9.c Using the Group and Sort Features of Data Access Pages

The **Page Wizard** allows you to create a data access page by choosing fields from one or more tables or queries and options for determining the format of the page. Janet creates a query that retrieves the names of the Dynamic employees and related information, including their e-mail addresses. You can use this query when you create Janet's second DAP using the Page Wizard.

To create a DAP using the Page Wizard:

Step 1	*Double-click*	Create data access page by using wizard

The Page Wizard, which looks similar to other Access wizards, opens.

Step 2	*Click*	Table: tblEmployees from the Tables/Queries list box, if necessary
Step 3	*Double-click*	the LastName, FirstName, and Email fields to select them
Step 4	*Click*	the Table: tblDepartment in the Table/Queries list box
Step 5	*Double-click*	Department Name to include it in the DAP
Step 6	*Click*	Next >

You can now group the information on the data access page. A **grouped data access page** groups the information according to a field. If you group the page by department, you see each employee listed in the department to which they belong. Janet doesn't need to group the employees this way.

chapter
nine

Because she wants a simple, ungrouped DAP, you won't need to add grouping levels at this time.

| Step 7 | *Click* | Next > |

You can now select a sort order. You can sort on any field in ascending or descending order. Janet wants to list the employees alphabetically by last name.

| Step 8 | *Click* | LastName in the first list box |

The default sort is ascending order, which sorts from A to Z or 0 to 9.

| Step 9 | *Click* | Next > |
| Step 10 | *Key* | dapEmployees as the title for the data access page |

You can also choose to open the page or modify it. Janet wants to see what the DAP looks like, so you can open the page.

| Step 11 | *Click* | the Open the page option button, if necessary |
| Step 12 | *Click* | Finish |

Access creates and opens your data access page. Your screen should look similar to Figure 9-2.

FIGURE 9-2
Data Access Page Created with the Page Wizard

Records sorted in ascending order by LastName field

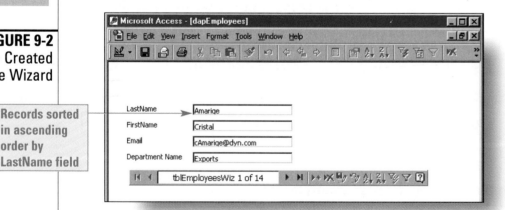

Step 13	*Close*	the dapEmployees window
Step 14	*Save*	Save the DAP page as dapEmployees.htm in the folder where the database is stored

Janet wants to improve the appearance of the DAP. You can now modify dapEmployees in Design view.

9.d Modifying Data Access Pages

Once you create a data access page, you can change its design in Design view. As you and Janet review dapEmployees, you decide to rearrange the fields, modify the font, add a title, and resize the fields. You also want to apply a theme to the page.

Your first task is to add a title and instructions for using the data access page. You can do so by replacing the placeholder text in Design view.

To replace placeholder text in a DAP:

Step 1	*Open*	dapEmployees in Design view
Step 2	*Close*	the Field List, if necessary

Your screen should look similar to Figure 9-3.

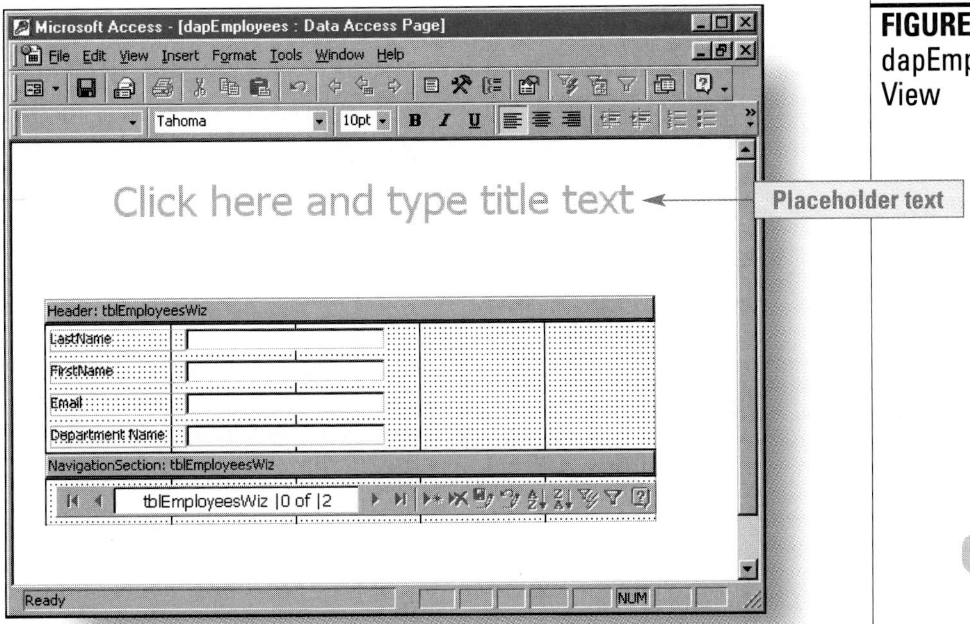

FIGURE 9-3
dapEmployees in Design View

chapter
nine

Step 3	*Click*	in the title text area
Step 4	*Key*	Dynamic Employees E-mail List
Step 5	*Press*	the ENTER key
Step 6	*Key*	Use the arrow buttons on the Navigation toolbar to find the employee you want.

Now that you replaced the placeholder text, you can increase the font size of the field names to make them easier to read. Start by selecting the fields you want to format.

To modify the font in a DAP:

Step 1	*Click*	the LastName field
Step 2	*Click*	the Font Size list arrow on the Formatting toolbar
Step 3	*Click*	10 pt
Step 4	*Repeat*	Steps 1–3 for the FirstName, Email, and Department Name fields

MOUSE **TIP**

If you don't see the Formatting toolbar, right-click in the toolbar area and then choose Formatting (Page) from the shortcut menu.

Your screen should look similar to Figure 9-4.

FIGURE 9-4
dapEmployees with Title
and Reformatted Fields

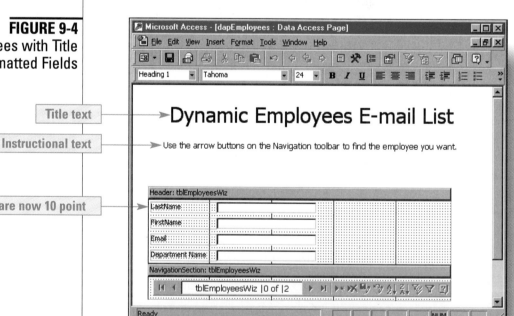

Title text

Instructional text

Field names are now 10 point

You and Janet also want to rearrange the fields so the DAP is easier for users to scan online. You can move the FirstName and LastName fields next to each other on the same line. Start by making room for both fields by resizing the field area.

To resize the field area:

| Step 1 | *Click* | the header bar to select the entire header area |

You see white selection handles in the border around the entire field.

| Step 2 | *Point to* | the right-center selection handle until the pointer changes to a double-headed arrow |
| Step 3 | *Drag* | right to increase the size of the field area |

Your screen should look similar to Figure 9-5.

Drag the center-right selection handle to resize the field area

FIGURE 9-5
dapEmployees with
Resized Field Area

Now you can move the LastName and FirstName fields.
To move the fields:

| Step 1 | *Click* | the box part of the LastName field |

You see white selection handles in the border around the field.
As in a report, the field name and box are a compound control, which means it has two parts—an attached field name and a box where the user enters information.

| Step 2 | *Point to* | the field until the pointer changes to a four-headed arrow |
| Step 3 | *Drag* | the LastName field to the right edge of the page |

chapter
nine

Now you can resize the LastName field before moving the FirstName
field next to it.

Step 4	*Click*	the LastName field label

You see white selection handles around the field name.

Step 5	*Point to*	the left-center selection handle until the pointer changes to a double-headed arrow
Step 6	*Drag*	right to make the label area smaller
Step 7	*Repeat*	Steps 1–3 above to move the FirstName field next to the LastName field
Step 8	*Repeat*	Steps 1–3 to move the Email and Department Name fields to locations similar to that shown in Figure 9-6

FIGURE 9-6
dapEmployees with
Rearranged Fields

Rearranged
fields

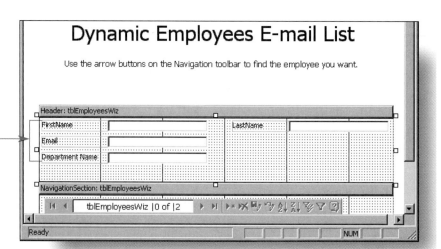

You made the data access page easier to use. Now you can also make
it more visually appealing by applying a theme—a professionally
designed format that combines colors, backgrounds, and text to create
an inviting page.

To apply a theme:

Step 1	*Click*	Format on the menu bar
Step 2	*Click*	Theme

The Theme dialog box opens. The Theme dialog box lists the designs you can apply to your data access page. Click a theme to see a sample. You and Janet decide to use the Blends theme for all of your data access pages because it matches your corporate image.

Step 3	*Click*	Blends in the Choose a Theme: list box
Step 4	*Click*	OK
Step 5	*Switch*	to Page view

After resizing the fields if necessary, your screen should look similar to Figure 9-7.

FIGURE 9-7
Redesigned dapEmployees

You and Janet are satisfied with the data access page. You are ready to close it.

| Step 6 | *Close* | the dapEmployees page |
| Step 7 | *Save* | the dapEmployees page |

Your final task for Janet's Web group is to build an order form that they can use with Internet customers.

chapter
nine

9.e Building Order Forms for the Internet

An order form is a way for people to enter data. You can create an online order form by creating a data access page. People can then enter information on the Web that you can add to your Access database. To create a DAP order form, you can use the Page Wizard.

Janet wants to create an order form based on tblCustomers that customers can use to enter their mailing information.

To create an order form using the Page Wizard:

missing some fields

Step 1	**Double-click**	Create data access page by using wizard
Step 2	**Click**	Table: tblCustomers from the Table/Queries list
Step 3	**Double-click**	the CompanyName, ContactName, ContactTitle, Address, Region, City, and Country, PostalCode, Phone, and Fax fields to select them
Step 4	**Click**	Next >

You can now group the information. Grouping, however, is not appropriate for order forms because grouped data access pages are read-only; users cannot enter information or otherwise interact with the DAP.

Step 5	**Click**	Next >

You can sort the fields, but you don't need to in an order form. You generally do not want users to navigate through records in an order form—they should see their own form, but no one else's.

Step 6	**Click**	Next >
Step 7	**Key**	dapNewCustomers as the title for the data access page

You can now modify the page's design and apply a theme.

Step 8	**Click**	the Modify the page's design option button, if necessary
Step 9	**Click**	the Do you want to apply a theme to your page? check box
Step 10	**Click**	Finish

You see the Theme dialog box. For consistency, choose the Blends theme.

Step 11	*Click*	Blends in the Choose a Theme: list box
Step 12	*Click*	OK
Step 13	*Close*	the FieldList dialog box, if necessary

Access creates your data access page and opens it in Design view.

For your order form, you want users to enter their own data but not see any information from tblCustomers, such as the names and addresses of other customers. You can accomplish this by editing the properties of the Navigation toolbar.

To edit the properties of the Navigation toolbar:

Step 1	*Right-click*	the Navigation toolbar
Step 2	*Click*	Properties on the shortcut menu

You see a list of properties for the Navigation toolbar.

Step 3	*Click*	the All tab, if necessary, to see all the properties

To prevent users from seeing the records of other Dynamic customers, you must eliminate the navigation buttons ShowDelButton, ShowFilterBySelectionButton, ShowFirstButton, ShowHelpButton, ShowLastButton, ShowNextButton, ShowPrevButton, ShowSortAscendingButton, ShowSortDescendingButton, and ShowToggleFilterButton, ShowUndoButton. To do this, make the condition for these navigation tools "False."

Step 4	*Click*	the list arrow in the text area of ShowDelButton
Step 5	*Click*	False
Step 6	*Repeat*	Steps 4 and 5 for the other navigation buttons

> **CAUTION TIP**
>
> Be sure the ShowNewButton and ShowSaveButton are set to True.

Looking at the DAP, you decide you want to change one other item. You want to modify the RecordSetLabel to create a more informative label.

Step 7	*Click*	in the text box for the RecordsetLabel
Step 8	*Select*	the existing text in the RecordSetLabel property field
Step 9	*Key*	Welcome Dynamic Customers

chapter
nine

Your screen should look similar to Figure 9-8.

FIGURE 9-8
Properties Box for
Navigation Toolbar

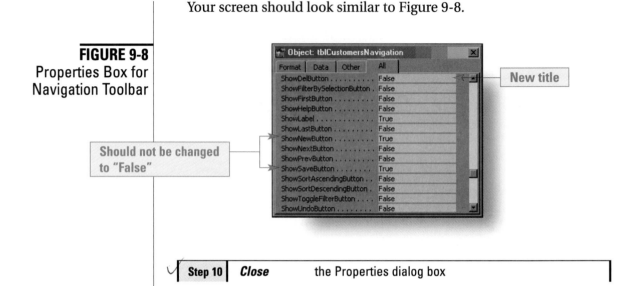

Should not be changed
to "False"

New title

| Step 10 | *Close* | the Properties dialog box |
| Step 11 | *Switch* | to Page view |

If you now click the New Record button on the Navigation toolbar, you see a blank form with the button for writing the information to the database active. When users enter new data, they click the Save button to enter the information to the Access database.

You now decide to add instructions that tell customers what to do. Your assistant adds a title and instructions to the data access page and rearranges fields. The completed DAP is illustrated in Figure 9-9.

FIGURE 9-9
dapNewCustomers

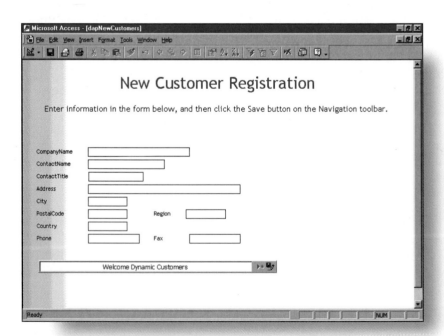

CAUTION TIP

To see how the DAP appears on the Web, click File and then Web Page Preview. The DAP opens in your Web browser.

Now that you created the DAP, you are ready to upload it to the Web.

9.f Using Data Access Pages for Web Publication

Access makes it easy for anyone to publish DAPs to a server. If your company is running Microsoft **Internet Information Server (IIS)**, network software that lets you publish on the Web, you can also export your Access database as a dynamic Web page, allowing users to interact with it. Otherwise, the DAP will be static, restricting users to only reading the page.

To save the page to the IIS server on your network, you must know the location of the server, have access to the server (gained from your Internet/intranet administrator), and know the structure of the server (where to save your pages). You can then use the Export command to save the page to the IIS server.

To upload a DAP to a server, open the DAP. From the Access File menu, choose Export. Locate the server and the appropriate folder on the network. Then save the DAP to this location.

You can now save and close dapNewCustomers and exit Access.

To save dapNewCustomers and exit Access:

Step 1	*Click*	File on the menu bar
Step 2	*Click*	Save and save the data access page as dapNewCustomers
Step 3	*Click*	the Save button
Step 4	*Close*	dapNewCustomers
Step 5	*Exit*	Access

Janet can publish the New Customers data access page to Dynamic's Web site.

chapter
nine

Summary

▶ Data access pages (DAPs) are HyperText Markup Language (HTML) pages based on Access tables or queries but stored as separate files. You can display these pages on the Internet in a Web browser or in an intranet in a network browser.

▶ To view DAPs, you need to use Microsoft Internet Explorer 5, which is Microsoft's latest version of its Web browser.

▶ You can use AutoPage, the Page Wizard, or Design view to create a data access page. AutoPage allows you to create a basic data access page that displays all fields (except those that store pictures) and records from a table or query. Use the Page Wizard to select fields from more than one table or query and to have Access guide you step by step. Use Design view to modify the DAPs you create, or to create a new one on your own.

▶ When you save a data access page, Access stores the HTML file in the folder you specified and adds a shortcut to the page in the Database window.

▶ You can group the information on the data access page when you want to keep related fields together. A grouped data access page groups the information according to a field. Grouping is not appropriate for order forms because grouped data access pages are read-only.

▶ You can also sort on any field in a DAP in ascending or descending order. Sort information on a data access page when you want to help users find information.

▶ Access makes it easy for anyone to publish DAPs to a server. If your company is running Microsoft Internet Information Server (IIS), network software that lets you publish on the Web, you can also export your Access database as a dynamic Web page, allowing users to interact with it. Otherwise, the DAP will be static, restricting users to only reading the page.

Commands Review

Action	Menu Bar	Shortcut Menu	Toolbar	Keyboard
Select a button on the Record Navigation toolbar			Click the left or right arrow button	LEFT ARROW or RIGHT ARROW
Add a control to a section			Click a button on the toolbox	SHIFT + ENTER
To move the selected control to the right			Drag to the right	CTRL + RIGHT ARROW
To move the selected control to the left			Drag to the left	CTRL + LEFT ARROW
To move the selected control up			Drag up	CTRL + UP ARROW
To move the selected control down			Drag down	CTRL + DOWN ARROW
Add fields to the DAP			Drag from Field List	ALT + A and ENTER
Apply a theme to a DAP	Format, Theme			ALT + F, H

Concepts Review

Circle the correct answer.

1. HTML means:
[a] Hyperlink MetaLanguage.
[b] HyperText Markup Language.
[c] HyperText MetaLanguage.
[d] Hyperlink Markup Language.

2. The main purpose of a data access page is to:
[a] format data on a page.
[b] share information.
[c] group data together.
[d] insert information into a table.

3. Besides using the Page Wizard or Design view to create a data access page, you can also use:
[a] AutoWizard.
[b] the Form Wizard.
[c] AutoPage.
[d] a Web server.

4. Group data on a data access page if you want to:
[a] sort the data.
[b] publish to the Internet.
[c] change the Navigation toolbar.
[d] keep fields together that logically belong together.

5. Though you can group data on a data access page, the published page will be:
[a] ungrouped.
[b] read-only.
[c] unsorted.
[d] without visual interest.

6. Use the Page Wizard to create a data access page when you want to:
[a] apply a theme to the page.
[b] save the resulting HTML file in a new location.
[c] select fields from one or more tables or queries.
[d] create a read-only Web page.

chapter nine

7. A theme is:
- [a] a set of professionally designed backgrounds, colors, bullets, and other design elements.
- [b] the underlying meaning of a data access page.
- [c] the list of tables or queries that supply the data to a DAP.
- [d] a collection of fonts you can apply to the DAP.

8. To build an Internet order form:
- [a] you must add a title to the data access page.
- [b] create a data access page.
- [c] save your HTML file in the default folder.
- [d] rearrange the fields before saving.

9. After you create a data access form:
- [a] you can modify it in Design view.
- [b] Access publishes it to your Web site automatically.
- [c] you cannot convert it to an Internet order form.
- [d] you can no longer apply a theme.

10. If you save data access pages to an Internet Information Server, you:
- [a] cannot make any more changes to them.
- [b] can export your Access database as a dynamic Web page.
- [c] can let users only read the pages.
- [d] cannot save the pages on your own computer.

Circle **T** if the statement is true or **F** if the statement is false.

T (F) 1. Data access pages are based on forms.

(T) F 2. Data access pages are based on tables or queries.

T (F) 3. Grouped data access pages are write only.

T (F) 4. You can only create data access pages using your Web browser.

(T) F 5. You can change a number of controls in a data access page to improve how it works and looks.

(T) F 6. You must edit the data access page in Design view.

T (F) 7. You can apply a theme to a data access page only after you publish it.

(T) F 8. A theme provides consistency and visual appeal to a data access page.

T (F) 9. You must save a data access page to an IIS server.

(T) F 10. You can send a data access page to others even if they don't use Access.

Skills Review

Exercise 1

1. If necessary, open the *mdbDynamicInc9* database.

2. Use AutoPage to create a data access page based on the tblOrders table.

3. Save the new data access page as dapOrders.

4. Save and close the new data access page.

Exercise 2

1. If necessary, open the *mdbDynamicInc9* database.

2. Use the Page Wizard to create a new data access page based on the tblCategories and tblProducts tables. Use only the following fields in the report: Category ID from tblCategories, and Category Name, Product ID, Product Description, and Unit Price from tblProducts.

3. Do not group the data, but sort the report by category name.

4. Name the new data access page dapCategories and save it.

Exercise 3

1. If necessary, open the *mdbDynamicInc9* database.

2. Open the dapCategories data access page you created in Exercise 2 in Design View.

3. Rearrange and resize the fields to make the data access page more attractive and easier to use.

4. Save and close the data access page.

Exercise 4

1. If necessary, open the *mdbDynamicInc9* database.

2. Open the dapCategories data access page you revised in Exercise 3.

3. In Design view, change the title of the report to *Dynamic Product Categories*. Add appropriate instructions. Change the field labels to include space between words. (Hint: Click the label once to select it and again to position the insertion point in the label.)

4. Save and close the dapCategories data access page.

Exercise 5

1. If necessary, open the *mdbDynamicInc9* database.

2. Open the dapCategories data access page you modified in Exercise 4.

3. Change the theme of dapCategories.

4. Preview and save the data access page.

Exercise 6

1. If necessary, open the *mdbDynamicInc9* database.

2. Open the dapOrders data access page you created in Exercise 1.

3. Change the design to make it an appropriate order form. For example, increase the font size of the field labels and make them bold so the page is easier to read online.

4. Preview and save the data access page.

Exercise 7

1. If necessary, open the *mdbDynamicInc9* database.

2. Use the Page Wizard to create a data access page based on tblSuppliers.

3. Sort the data by Supplier Name.

4. Preview and save the data access page as dapSuppliers.

chapter nine

Exercise 8

1. If necessary, open the *mdbDynamicInc9* database.

2. Open the dapSuppliers data access page you created in Exercise 7.

3. Change the text displayed in the Navigation toolbar to Suppliers Information.

4. Apply the Canvas theme with vivid colors and add the title "Dynamic Inc. Suppliers" to the page.

5. Navigate through the records with the Navigation toolbar.

6. Preview and save the data access page.

Case Projects

Project 1

Using the Office on the <u>W</u>eb command on the <u>H</u>elp menu, open the Microsoft home page and then link to pages that provide basic information about data access pages. Print at least two of the Web pages.

Project 2

Connect to the Internet and load a search engine. Search for Web sites that provide advice about designing Web pages or online order forms. Print at least two pages.

Project 3

Maria Moreno, the owner of Dynamic, Inc., asks you to add a hyperlink to the dapEmployees data access page you created. She wants users to be able to click the hyperlink and go to a page on the Dynamic Web site that provides answers to common questions. The address for this Web page is *www.dynamic.com/QA*. Search the Access online Help for instructions on adding a hyperlink to a data access page. Then follow these instructions to insert the hyperlink Maria wants to dapEmployees.

Project 4

Maria also wants users to be able to send her e-mail messages from the dapEmployees data access page on the Dynamic Web site. Her e-mail address is *mMoreno@dyn.com*. Search the Access online Help for instructions on sending an e-mail message to a data access page. Then follow these instructions to insert the e-mail link Maria wants to dapEmployees.

Project 5

Janet Washington wants to add a box around the fields in dapEmployees. You can use the Toolbox to add the box to Janet's data access page. Search the Access online Help for instructions on using the toolbox to draw a box or rectangle in a report. Then follow these instructions to draw a box around the fields in dapEmployees.

Project 6

Maria wants you to create a data access page for Dynamic's suppliers. You can quickly create this data access page in Design view. Search the Access online Help for instructions on creating a data access page in Design view. Then follow these instructions to create a data access page called dapSuppliers that includes Supplier ID and name, address, and fax information.

Project 7

In Design view, open the dapSuppliers report you created in Project 6. Search the Access online Help for instructions on modifying the properties of a data access page, including the fields and the Navigation toolbar. Then follow these instructions to modify the data access page properties to improve its appearance and usability.

Project 8

Maria also wants to provide a way for prospective employees to apply to Dynamic. Build an order form users can complete as an online employment form.

Advanced Form Features

Chapter Overview

In this chapter you focus on more advanced form features: creating and using subforms, merging tables, and adding hyperlinks.

Case profile

Alan Golden, sales manager at Dynamic Inc., wants you to create a form that makes order entry more efficient for his staff. His staff wants to enter all the order data, which is then recorded in several database tables, using a one-page form. Giang Hu, the accounting manager, also wants to see invoice and order information as he and his staff work with the product form. To provide the information Alan and Giang need, you can use subforms.

chapter
ten

10.a Planning Subforms

A **subform** is a smaller form within a form. The **main form**, or outer form, is the primary form and contains the subform. Use subforms when you want to show data from tables or queries that have a one-to-many relationship—one field in the subform is related to many fields in the main form. For example, Alan wants to add a subform to the frmCustomers form to show order data. The data in the tblCustomers table is the "one" side of the relationship. The data in the tblOrders table is the "many" side of the relationship—each customer can have many orders.

The main form and subform in this type of form are linked so that the subform displays only records that are related to the current record in the main form. For Alan, this means that when you display the main frmCustomers form, you see the orders this customer placed in the subform.

A main form can have any number of subforms. You can also nest a subform within a subform. You could create a form for Alan that shows customers, a subform that displays orders, and another subform within the first one that displays order details.

Before you create a main form and subforms, plan what to include and how to use them. Alan wants his staff to fill out orders as they speak to customers on the phone. When a customer calls, Alan wants a customer service representative to open the customer's record, see the products they ordered in the past, and then enter new order information. He also wants to verify billing address information and change it if necessary. You know Alan wants his staff to work with the frmCustomers form and the frmOrders form the same time. You and Alan sketch how the forms are related, as shown in Figure 10-1.

FIGURE 10-1
Sketch of Form and Subform

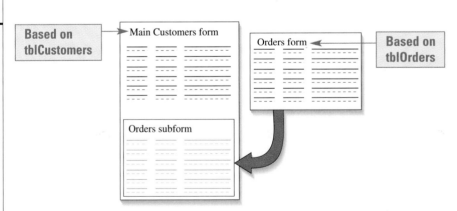

The sketch shows that the tblCustomers table serves as the basis for the main form and the tblOrders table for the subform. That way, Alan's staff can open a customer's form, check existing orders and enter new ones, and verify customer information. You can use the Form Wizard to add the frmOrders form to frmCustomers as a subform.

10.b Creating a Form with Subforms

You can create a form with subforms in a number of ways. You can use the Form Wizard to create a form and a subform at the same time based on existing tables. Even if you already created the forms that serve as the main form and the subform, use the Form Wizard if you want Access to guide you through the steps of creating a form with subforms. The Form Wizard is also the best choice if you already set up a one-to-many relationship between the tables or queries you want to use to create the form and subform.

If you already created the main form, open it in Design view, and then use the Control Wizard to add the subform. Once you become familiar with forms and subforms, you can add an existing form to another form in Design view to create a subform. You can also modify the design of any form with subforms in Design view. If you created a subform with a datasheet layout, you can modify its layout in Form view.

You are now ready to create your first subform.

Using the Form Wizard to Create a Form and Subform

Because this is the first time you create a subform for Dynamic, use the Form Wizard to create a form and subform at the same time.

To create a form with subforms using the Form Wizard:

Step 1	**Open**	*mdbDynamicInc10* located on the Data Disk

Step 2	**Click**	Forms 🔲 on the Objects bar

Step 3	**Click**	the <u>N</u>ew button 🔲 New on the Database toolbar

The New Form dialog box opens.

Step 4	**Double-click**	Form Wizard

In the first wizard dialog box, select a table or query that is the basis for the main form. Alan's main form is based on tblCustomers and includes all the fields.

| Step 5 | *Click* | Table: tblCustomers in the Tables/Queries: list box |
| Step 6 | *Click* | >> to move all fields to the Selected Fields: list box |

Now select the table or query that is the basis for the subform. Alan's subform is based on tblOrders and includes those fields not shown in tblCustomers.

| Step 7 | *Click* | Table: tblOrders in the Tables/Queries: list box |

notes
Although you first selected the table for the main form and then the table for the subform, you can select the tables or queries for the form and subform(s) in any order.

| Step 8 | *Move* | the OrderID, OrderDate, Product ID, and Product Description fields to the Selected Fields: list box |
| Step 9 | *Click* | Next > |

Because the two tables are related, the wizard asks which table or query you want to view the data by. Alan wants tblCustomers to provide the data for the main form. You then choose formats and themes for the form and subform.
To complete the Form Wizard:

| Step 1 | *Click* | by tblCustomers, if necessary |

In this same wizard dialog box, indicate that you want to create a form with a subform.

| Step 2 | *Click* | the Form with subform(s) option button, if necessary |
| Step 3 | *Click* | Next > |

Now you can choose the format for the subform. Click a format to see a preview. Alan wants to use the Datasheet format, the default, because his staff is most familiar with that one.

| Step4 | *Verify* | that Datasheet is selected |
| Step 5 | *Click* | Next > |

Now you can select the style or theme for the form. To be consistent with the other forms, use Sumi Painting.

| Step 6 | *Click* | Sumi Painting |
| Step 7 | *Click* | Next > |

Now enter names for the form and subform.

Step 8	*Key*	frmCustomer Orders as the name of the main form
Step 9	*Key*	frmOrders subform as the name of the subform
Step 10	*Click*	Finish

Your opened form should look similar to Figure 10-2.

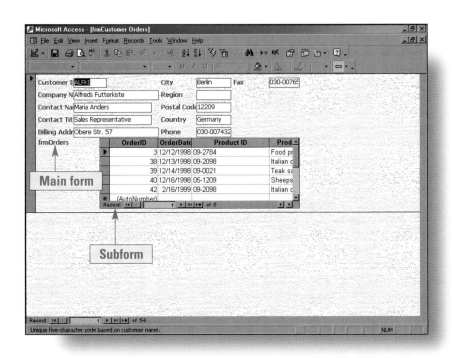

FIGURE 10-2
New Form and Subform

Once you create the form and subform, you can fine-tune the layout in Form view and Design view.

Modifying Form Properties

After you create a form with a subform, you can change the layout of a subform displayed as a datasheet in either Form view or Design view. Use Form view to modify how the subform presents data. You can change the width of a column, the order of the columns, and the height of the rows. You can also hide, show, or freeze a column.

Alan notices that some columns in the frmOrders subform are too narrow. You can resize the columns in Form view.

To modify the layout of the subform in Form view:

| Step 1 | *Point to* | the column divider between the OrderDate and Product ID fields until the pointer becomes a double-headed arrow |
| Step 2 | *Drag* | right to widen the OrderDate column |

Alan wants to size all the columns to fit their data. Access can determine the best fit for you.

| Step 3 | *Double-click* | the column separator between OrderDate and Product ID |
| Step 4 | *Repeat* | Step 3 for the remaining columns |

Now Alan wants to move the Product Description field to the left of the Product ID field.

| Step 5 | *Click* | the Product Description column heading |
| Step 6 | *Drag* | the Product Description column heading to the left of the Product ID column |

Your screen should look similar to Figure 10-3.

Alan also wants to adjust the size of the subform and move it lower in the main form. You can make these adjustments in Design view.

To size and position the subform:

| Step 1 | *Switch* | to Design view |
| Step 2 | *Click* | the border of the subform |

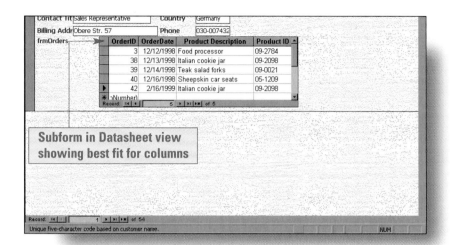

FIGURE 10-3
Form with
Reformatted Subform

You see selection handles around the subform.

Step 3	*Point to*	the left middle selection handle of the subform until the pointer becomes a double-headed arrow
Step 4	*Drag*	left to increase the width of the subform
Step 5	*Point to*	the border of the subform until the pointer becomes an open hand
Step 6	*Drag*	to move the subform down

Your screen should look similar to Figure 10-4.

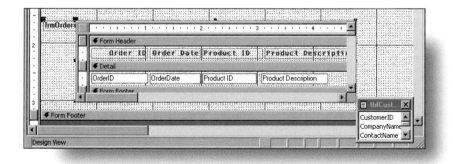

FIGURE 10-4
Form with Enlarged and
Moved Subform

| Step 7 | *Close* | the form, saving your changes |

Now that you created a subform in a form and fine-tuned its design, you can show related records in the subform.

C Synchronizing Forms

If you already created a one-to-many relationship between two tables and used them to create a form and subform with the Form Wizard, the subform automatically shows related records on the main form. In Alan's frmCustomer Orders, the main form shows customer information and the subform shows the products a customer has ordered.

If you do not use the Form Wizard to create a form and subform, you can still show related records in the subform. Do so by linking (also called **synchronizing**) the main form and the subform. Alan already created a main form using fields from tblProducts. To add a subform, he dragged frmSuppliers from the Database window onto frmProducts in Design view. Then he saved the new form as frmProducts and Suppliers. Alan wants to see related supplier information when he's working with information about a particular product. For example, when he or his staff looks up information about the Dynamic electronic pocket watch, he also wants to see which company supplies the watch to Dynamic. You can show related records by linking the Suppliers subform to the Products main form.

To synchronize a subform and form:

Step 1	*Click*	Forms on the Objects bar, if necessary
Step 2	*Double-click*	frmProducts and Suppliers
Step 3	*Switch*	to Design view

You see the main form for the products information and the subform for the suppliers information. Now you can set the subform properties to make sure the forms are linked, and, if they are not, you can then link them.

Step 4	*Right-click*	the border of the subform to open the shortcut menu
Step 5	*Click*	Properties
Step 6	*Click*	the All tab, if necessary

You see the Properties list for the subform. The Link Child Fields property box should show the name of the field in the subform that links to the same field in the main form. The Link Master Fields property shows the name of this field in the main form.

| Step 7 | *Click* | the Link Child Fields property box |

You see the ellipsis button, which helps you enter appropriate information in this property box.

| Step 8 | *Click* | the ellipsis button |

Your dialog box should look similar to Figure 10-5.

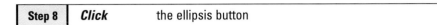

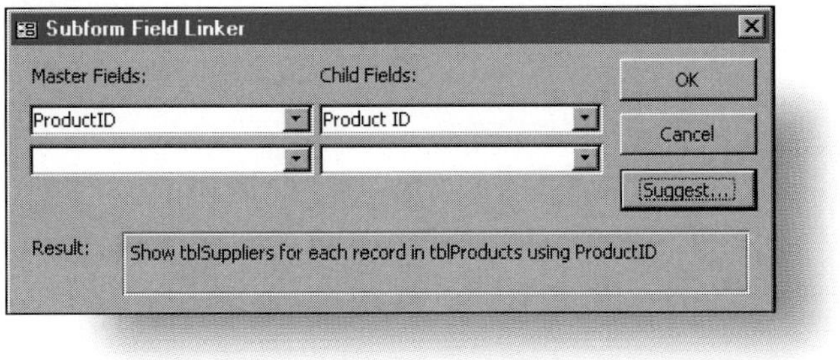

FIGURE 10-5
Subform Field Linker
Dialog Box

This dialog box lets you select the linking fields from lists of fields in the main form and subform. You and Alan are not sure what the current selection means—you see Product ID in both the Master and Child fields. You can let Access help you make your decision.

| Step 9 | *Click* | Suggest |

Access checks any relationships you already set up for the underlying tables or queries in the main form and subform and suggests which fields you should link. It also interprets what the link means—that you show the data from tblSuppliers for each record in tblProducts using a Product ID. This is the result you and Alan want.
To complete synchronizing the form and subform:

Step 1	*Click*	Show tblSuppliers for each record in tblProducts using Product ID
Step 2	*Click*	OK
Step 3	*Click*	OK to exit from the Subform Field Linker dialog box

The Link fields (Link Child Fields and Link Master Fields) now indicate that the form and subform are related by the Product ID field.

| Step 4 | *Close* | the Properties box |
| Step 5 | *Switch* | to Form view |

Now the main products form shows related supplier records in the subform. Your screen should look similar to Figure 10-6.

FIGURE 10-6
Linked Form and Subform

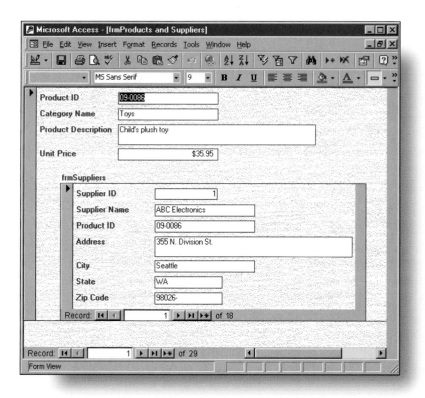

| Step 6 | *Close* | the form, saving your changes |

Next, you create a subform by merging two tables.

 10.c Using the Subform Control

You can also create and add a subform to an existing form by merging two tables. Giang uses the frmProducts form to keep track of Dynamic's products. He wants you to add a subform showing invoice and order information. You can do this by merging two tables to create a subform.

To create a subform by merging two tables:

Step 1	*Click*	Forms 📇 on the Objects bar, if necessary
Step 2	*Double-click*	frmProducts
Step 3	*Switch*	to Design view

Use the Control Wizard to merge the tblInvoices and tblOrders tables to create a subform. Make sure the Control Wizards button on the toolbox is selected.

Step 4	*Click*	the Control Wizards button ▨ on the toolbox to select it, if necessary
Step 5	*Click*	the Subform/Subreport button ▦ on the toolbox
Step 6	*Click*	below the last field in the frmProducts form

The first Subform Wizard dialog box opens. The Subform Wizard, similar to other wizards, guides you step-by-step through the process of merging two tables to create a subform.

To use the Subform Wizard:

| Step 1 | *Click* | the Use existing Tables and Queries option button, if necessary |
| Step 2 | *Click* | Next > |

Now you can choose one or more tables and select the fields you want to include on the subform.

Step 3	*Click*	Table: tblInvoices in the Tables/Queries list box
Step 4	*Double-click*	the InvoiceID, CustomerID, EmployeeID, InvoiceDate, and ShipDate fields to select them
Step 5	*Click*	Table: tblOrders in the Tables/Queries list box
Step 6	*Double-click*	the OrderID, OrderDate, and Product Description fields to select them
Step 7	*Click*	Next >

Now the wizard asks if you want to define the fields to link your main form to the subform yourself, or choose from the list. Let Access help you by choosing from the list.

| Step 8 | *Click* | Show tblOrders for each record in tblProducts using Product ID, if necessary |

This option best describes how Giang wants to set up his main form and subform—he sees related order information in the subform for each product in the main form. These forms are linked by the Product ID field.

chapter
ten

Step 9	*Click*	<u>N</u>ext >

Now you can enter a name for the new form.

Step 10	*Key*	frmProduct Details
Step 11	*Click*	<u>F</u>inish
Step 12	*Switch*	to Form view

Your screen should look similar to Figure 10-7.

FIGURE 10-7
Form with Merged-Tables
Subform

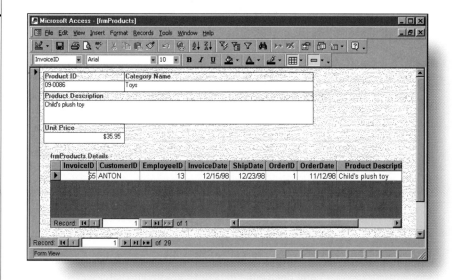

Step 13	*Close*	the form, saving your changes

Alan and Giang are pleased with how you created forms with subforms for their departments. Now they ask you to create hyperlinks to further customize forms.

10.d Creating Hyperlinks

You can include a hyperlink in a form to "jump" to other destinations. A **hyperlink** is text or graphics that users can click to go to another destination, such as an Access table or a site on the Web. Access lets you add hyperlinks to an existing file or Web page, an object in the database, or an e-mail address. You can also create a new document when you click the hyperlink.

Giang wants his accounting staff to have as much information as possible as they work with frmProducts. They often need to know about products Dynamic is advertising at special rates on its Web site. They want to look up information in other tables. They are also the ones who send out the invoices; they want to include a note to some customers explaining discounts or special charges. Alan wants to know about any comments customers make, which the accounting staff often hear as they check invoice and order information. You can provide all this information to Giang and Alan using hyperlinks.

Adding a Link to a Web Page

You can add a link to a form that users can click to open a page on the Web. Because Giang's staff needs to know about specials advertised on the Dynamic Web site, add a hyperlink to the Dynamic Web site from the frmProducts form.

To create a hyperlink to a Web page:

Step 1	*Click*	Forms 📇 on the Objects bar, if necessary
Step 2	*Double-click*	frmProducts
Step 3	*Switch*	to Design view
Step 4	*Click*	the Hyperlink button 🖼 on the Form Design toolbar
Step 5	*Click*	Existing File or Web Page in the Link to: column, if necessary

The Insert Hyperlink dialog box on your screen should look similar to Figure 10-8.

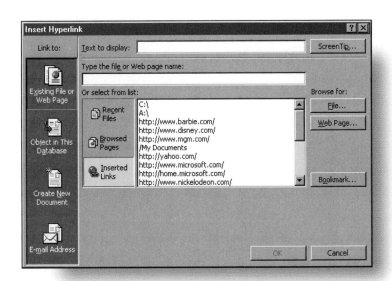

FIGURE 10-8
Insert Hyperlink
Dialog Box

Step 6	*Key*	Dynamic Web Site in the Text to display: text box
Step 7	*Key*	www.dynamic.com in the Type the file or Web page name: text box
Step 8	*Click*	OK to see the form with the hyperlink
Step 9	*Drag*	the hyperlink object to the right of the UnitPrice field

Now Giang's staff can click the hyperlink to go the Dynamic Web site and look up advertised specials.

Adding a Link to an Object in the Database

You can add a link to a form that users can click to open another object in the current database, such as a table, query, or another form. Because Giang's staff often wants to look up supplier information, you can add a hyperlink that opens the tblSuppliers table. Make sure the link to the Web page is not selected before you create a hyperlink to an object in the database.

To create a hyperlink to an object in the database:

Step 1	*Click*	the Hyperlink button 🔲 on the Form Design toolbar
Step 2	*Click*	Object in This Database in the Link to: column

You see a list of objects you can link to.

Step 3	*Key*	Suppliers in the Text to display: text box
Step 4	*Click*	the plus sign (+) next to Tables to expand the list of tables in *mdbDynamicInc10*
Step 5	*Double-click*	tblSuppliers
Step 6	*Drag*	the hyperlink object to the right of the Dynamic Web Site link

This adds a link to the form that Giang's staff can click to open the tblSuppliers table.

Adding a Link to Create a New Document

You can add a link to a form that users can click to create a new data access page or other document, such as a Word document. Because Giang's staff wants to include notes and reminders with invoices, you can add a hyperlink to frmProducts that creates a new Word document. Make sure the link to the object in the database is not selected before you add a hyperlink to create a new document.

To create a hyperlink that creates a new document:

Step 1	*Click*	the Hyperlink button on the Form Design toolbar
Step 2	*Click*	Create New Page in the Link to: column
Step 3	*Key*	Word in the Text to display: text box
Step 4	*Key*	Note.doc as the name of the document you want to create
Step 5	*Click*	the Edit the new document later option button
Step 6	*Click*	OK
Step 7	*Drag*	the hyperlink to the right of the Suppliers hyperlink

This adds a link to the form that Giang's staff can click to create a new Word document.

Adding a Link to an E-Mail Address

You can also add a link to a form that users can click to send a message to a particular e-mail address. Alan wants to know about any comments customers make when they speak to Giang's staff. You can add a hyperlink to Alan's e-mail address so the staff can quickly send him messages. Make sure the link to create a new document is not selected before you create a hyperlink to an e-mail address.

To create a hyperlink that links to an e-mail address:

Step 1	*Click*	the Hyperlink button on the Form Design toolbar
Step 2	*Click*	E-mail Address in the Link to: column
Step 3	*Key*	Sales Manager in the Text to display: text box
Step 4	*Key*	AGolden@dyn.com as the e-mail address
Step 5	*Key*	Customer Comment as the Subject
Step 6	*Click*	OK
Step 7	*Drag*	the hyperlink to the right of the Word hyperlink

This adds a link to the form that Giang's staff can click to send Alan an e-mail message.

Now you can view the results of your work.

chapter
ten

| Step 8 | *Switch* | to Form view |

Your screen should look similar to Figure 10-9.

FIGURE 10-9
frmProducts with
Added Hyperlinks

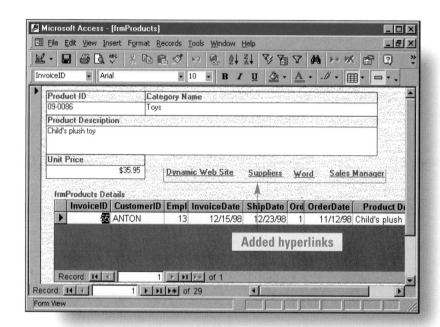

The hyperlinks appear underlined and in a bright color, such as bright blue. After you click them, they display in a different color, such as light purple.

You created a number of forms and subforms and added hyperlinks to them to make them more useful. You're ready to exit Access.

To close the form and exit Access:

| Step 1 | *Close* | frmProducts, saving your changes |
| Step 2 | *Exit* | Access |

The forms and subforms you created will make order entry much more efficient for the Dynamic sales and accounting staffs.

Summary

► A subform is a smaller form within a form. The main form contains the subform. Use subforms when you want to show data from tables or queries that have a one-to-many relationship—one field in the subform is related to many fields in the main form.

► The main form and subform can be linked so that the subform displays only records that are related to the current record in the main form.

► A main form can have any number of subforms. You can also nest a subform within a subform.

► You can use the Form Wizard to create a form and a subform at the same time based on existing tables. The Form Wizard is also the best choice if you already set up a one-to-many relationship between the tables or queries you want to use to create the form and subform.

► If you already created the main form, open it in Design view and then use the Control Wizard to add the subform. Once you become familiar with forms and subforms, you can add an existing form to another form in Design view to create a subform.

► After you create a form with a subform, you can change the layout of a subform displayed as a datasheet in either Form view or Design view. Use Form view to modify how the subform presents data. You can change the width of a column, the order of the columns, and the height of the rows. You can also hide, show, or freeze a column. Modify subforms displayed as forms in Design view.

► If you already created a one-to-many relationship between two tables and used them to create a form and subform with the Form Wizard, the subform automatically shows related records on the main form.

► If you do not use the Form Wizard to create a form and subform, you can still show related records in the subform. Do so by linking (also called synchronizing) the main form and the subform. The linking fields don't have to appear in the main form or subform, but they must be included in the underlying tables or queries.

► Once you create a form with a subform, you can use the main form and the subform to add records. The information you enter on the main form is stored in its underlying table; the information you enter on the subform is also stored in its underlying table.

► When you use a form with a subform to enter new records, Access saves the current record in the main form when you enter the subform. It also automatically saves each record as you add it to the subform.

chapter ten

▶ Besides using the Form Wizard to create a form with a subform, you can also add a subform to an existing form by merging two tables. The Subform Wizard guides you step by step through this process.

▶ You can include a hyperlink in a form to "jump" to other destinations. A hyperlink is text or graphics that users can click to go to another destination, such as an Access table or a site on the Web. Access lets you add hyperlinks to an existing file or Web page, an object in a database, or an e-mail address. You can also create a new document when you click the hyperlink.

Commands Review

Action	Menu Bar	Shortcut Menu	Toolbar	Keyboard
Move from the last field in the main form to the first field in the subform			Click the first field in the subform	TAB
Move from the first field in the subform to the last field in the main form			Click the last field in the main form	CTRL + SHIFT + TAB
Set properties for subforms and controls	View, Properties	Properties	Double-click the subform or control	ALT + V, P
Insert a hyperlink	Insert, Hyperlink	Hyperlink		CTRL + K ALT + I, H

Concepts Review

Circle the correct answer.

1. A subform is:
- [a] a link to a Web site.
- [b] a way to set a one-to-many relationship.
- [c] a smaller form within a form.
- [d] the primary form.

2. Use a subform to:
- [a] print a form.
- [b] give instructions to users within the form.
- [c] provide a way for Access users to work with customers on the phone.
- [d] show data from other tables or queries.

3. A main form and subform should be _____ to the data being entered.
- [a] unrelated
- [b] masked
- [c] related
- [d] merged

4. To create a subform you can use the _____ process that you do for any form.
- [a] same
- [b] opposite
- [c] reverse
- [d] corollary

5. To modify a subform:
- [a] you can be in either Form or Design view.
- [b] you must be in Design view.
- [c] use the Subform Wizard.
- [d] make sure the Control Wizard button is pressed down.

6. If you want to show related records in a subform:
- [a] link the main form and subform.
- [b] add a hyperlink to the main form.
- [c] add a record to the subform.
- [d] merge two tables.

7. One way to add a subform to an existing form is to:

[a] use the Query Wizard to create the underlying queries.

[b] merge two tables into a form.

[c] add records to the subform first.

[d] add a link to a new document in the main form.

8. To add a new record to the subform:

[a] click the New Record button on the subform Navigation toolbar.

[b] click the New Record button on the main form Navigation toolbar.

[c] switch to Design view.

[d] use the Subform Wizard.

9. Create a hyperlink in a form to:

[a] insert text or graphics.

[b] open another object in a database.

[c] make sure fields in the main form and subform are related.

[d] merge two tables into a form.

10. One way to send e-mail messages from a form is to:

[a] add a hyperlink to an e-mail address.

[b] insert a subform.

[c] modify the design of a form.

[d] add a hyperlink to a new document.

Circle **T** if the statement is true or **F** if the statement is false.

T   F   1. To see the contents of a subform, click the plus sign to expand the form.

T   F   2. You must use Design view to change the layout of a subform displayed as a datasheet.

T   F   3. You can use the Form Wizard if you set up a many-to-many relationship between two tables.

T   F   4. The Subform Wizard is exactly the same as the Form Wizard.

T   F   5. You can create forms that allow you to enter information from different tables.

T   F   6. The subform always automatically shows records related to those on the main form.

T   F   7. You can only link a form and a subform using the Form Wizard.

T   F   8. When you enter information on a subform, Access stores the data in a new table.

T   F   9. You can include a hyperlink even if you don't have a connection to the Internet.

T   F   10. You can use the Control Wizard to add a hyperlink to a form.

Skills Review

Exercise 1

1. If necessary, open the *mdbDynamicInc10* database.

2. Use the Form Wizard to create a form based on the tblEmployees table and a subform based on the tblOrders table. Use all the fields from the tables except Employee ID from tblOrders.

3. Choose to display the subform as a Datasheet.

4. Name the new main form frmOrders by Employee. Name the new subform frmOrder Details.

5. Save and close the new form.

chapter ten

Exercise 2

1. If necessary, open the *mdbDynamicInc10* database.

2. Open the frmOrders by Employees form you created in Exercise 1.

3. Move one column and change the width of all the columns in the subform to the "best fit."

4. Position and size the fields in the main form as necessary to make a useful and appealing form.

5. Save and close the form.

Exercise 3

1. If necessary, open the *mdbDynamicInc10* database.

2. Open the frmOrders by Employees form you modified in Exercise 2.

3. Add one record to the main form to add a new employee and another to the subform to add a new order for the new employee. Use the data listed below:

Main Form
ID: 300
Dept: 201
Supervisor ID: 102
SS#: 555-12-1234
First Name: Virgil
Last Name: Stevens

Subform
Order Date: 3/18/99
Customer ID: ANTON
Product ID: 09-0086
Product Description: Child's Plush Toy
Invoice ID: 300

4. Save and close the form.

Exercise 4

1. If necessary, open the *mdbDynamicInc10* database.

2. Open the frmInvoices form in Design view.

3. Use the Subform Wizard to merge tblCategories (use Category ID and Category Name fields) and tblOrders (use OrderID, Order Date, Customer ID, Product ID, Product Description fields) to create a subform.

4. Save the subform as frmCategories Subform and close it.

Exercise 5

1. If necessary, open the *mdbDynamicInc10* database.

2. Open the frmNew Products form.

3. Verify that the subform and main form are linked so the subform shows related records.

4. Save and close the form.

Exercise 6

1. If necessary, open the *mdbDynamicInc10* database.

2. Open the frmNew Products form.

3. Add a hyperlink to the Microsoft Web site: *www.microsoft.com*

4. Save and close the form.

Exercise 7

1. If necessary, open the *mdbDynamicInc10* database.

2. Open the frmNew Products form you modified in Exercise 6.

3. Add a hyperlink users can click to go to the tblOrders table.

4. Save and close the form.

Case Projects

Project 1

Using the Office on the Web command on the Help menu, open the Microsoft home page and then link to pages that provide information about subforms. Print at least two of the Web pages.

Project 2

Dynamic wants to include a hyperlink on their frmOrders form that users can click to contact companies that provide international shipping. Connect to the Internet and load a search engine. Search for Web sites that provide information and services for people who want to ship products like Dynamic's around the world. Print information on at least two companies.

Project 3

Giang Hu, the accounting manager of Dynamic, wants to use a subform to calculate a total for a group of records. Search the Access online Help for instructions on calculating a total in a subform and displaying it on a form. Then follow these instructions to insert a subform that calculates the number of orders on the frmCustomer Orders form. Use the COUNT function in your calculation. (Hint: You must set the Default View property in the subform's Form property dialog box to Continuous Forms.)

Project 4

Maria Moreno, the owner of Dynamic, wants to make the frmProducts form more useful and informative by adding a title and the current date. You can do this by adding text to the form header and a control to the form footer. To add a title, open the form in Design view and then view the header section. Click the Label tool in the toolbox, click the header section, and then type the title text. To add the current date, click the footer section. On the Insert menu, click Date and Time, and then check the Include Date check box.

Project 5

Now Maria wants to customize the form sections to make frmProducts more visually appealing. She wants to change the color of the fields in the Detail section so that they are red. Open the form in Design view. On the Edit menu, click Select All to select all the fields. Right-click a field, click Font/Fore Color, and then click the red on the color palette.

chapter ten

Project 6

Maria wants to create more forms and subforms on her own, but she wants to know more about how Access links main forms and subforms. Search the Access online Help for information about how Access links main forms and subforms. Print this information. Then summarize this information in a Word document.

Project 7

Maria wants to create a form from which users can open other forms or reports. This type of form is called a switchboard. To create a switchboard that lists all the other forms and reports in *mdbDynamicInc10*, click the Tools menu, point to Database Utilities, and then click Switchboard Manager. Use the Edit Switchboard Page dialog box to add items to the switchboard listing the forms and reports in *mdbDynamicInc10*.

Project 8

Alan Golden, the sales manager at Dynamic, wants to add a subform to the frmOrders subform in frmCustomer Orders. Search the Access online Help for information about creating a form with a subform that contains another subform. Then follow these instructions to add another subform with employee information (just name, ID, and Dept. ID) to the one in frmCustomer Orders) for Alan.

Creating Action Queries

Chapter Overview

In this chapter, you create advanced queries. You first design a parameter query and then create several action queries. Action queries let you change a number of records all at once.

LEARNING OBJECTIVES

▶ Create a parameter query
▶ Create an action query

Case profile

The sales department at Dynamic Inc., wants to be able to update the order status, from pending to completed or deleted. Juanita Chavez, a sales representative, asks you to find this information using a parameter query. Juanita and Giang Hu, the accounting manager, also want to make other permanent changes to the database. Juanita wants to remove all deleted orders and change the tax rate. Giang wants to create a table summarizing the year's sales, and then add any new orders to it. You make these changes with action queries.

chapter
eleven

11.a Creating a Parameter Query

A query is a way to ask questions of the data in your database. In a query you specify criteria to retrieve the data you want. A **parameter query** is an advanced select query that asks you to enter search criteria in a dialog box—you don't have to specify it in the query's design grid. When you open a query, you see the Enter Parameter Value dialog box asking you to enter specific information, such as the order status you want. Access then displays the data that matches your criteria.

Parameter queries are also handy when used with forms, reports, and data access pages. For example, you can create a monthly orders report based on a parameter query. When you print the report, Access displays a dialog box asking for the month that you want the report to include. You enter a month, and Access prints the appropriate report.

Juanita asks for an easy way to update order status. One way to do this is to locate all of the orders that are pending. Use a parameter query to quickly locate these orders.

To create a parameter query:

Step 1	**Open**	mdbDynamicInc11
Step 2	**Click**	Queries ▦ on the Objects bar
Step 3	**Double-click**	qryOrders Query
Step 4	**Switch**	to Design view

Your screen should look similar to Figure 11-1.

| Step 5 | **Click** | in the Criteria: cell for the Status field |

You are now ready to enter brief instructions enclosed in square brackets. These instructions are the prompt you see in the Enter Parameter Value dialog box. Because Juanita is looking for order status, you can use "Enter status request" as the prompt.

| Step 6 | **Key** | [Enter status request] |

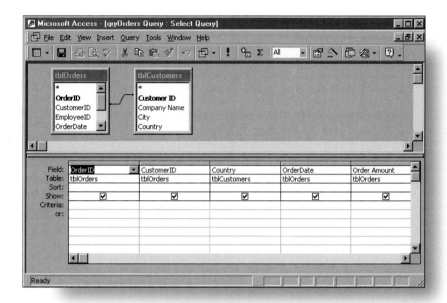

FIGURE 11-1
qryOrders Query in
Design View

Now you can define the data type for each query parameter. Access uses this data type to validate the information entered in the Enter Parameter Value dialog box. By default, Access uses Text as the data type for parameters, but you can choose the one that matches the data you want to retrieve. The Status field in qryOrders Query uses the Text data type. To define the data type, open the Query Parameters dialog box.

To define a query parameter:

Step 1	*Click*	the Query command on the menu bar
Step 2	*Click*	Parameters

The Query Parameters dialog box on your screen should look similar to Figure 11-2.

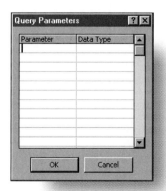

FIGURE 11-2
Query Parameters
Dialog Box

chapter
eleven

| Step 3 | *Key* | Enter status request in the first empty cell in the Parameter column |
| Step 4 | *Click* | in the Data Type column |

The Text data type is inserted as the default.

| Step 5 | *Click* | OK |

Now you can test the parameter query you created.
To test the parameter query:

Step 1	*Close*	qryOrders Query
Step 2	*Click*	Yes to save your changes
Step 3	*Double-click*	qryOrders Query in the Database window

You see the Enter Parameter Value dialog box asking you to enter the status request. The status can be P for pending, C for complete, or D for deleted.

| Step 4 | *Key* | P |
| Step 5 | *Click* | OK |

You see all the pending order records.
You created and tested a parameter query. Now you can add other parameters to the same query.

Creating Multiple Parameters

You can create queries that prompt for several parameters to find exactly the data you want. You can specify parameters in a number of different fields, or you can enter multiple parameters in one field. When you run a query with multiple parameters, Access prompts you to enter criteria for each parameter you set in successive dialog boxes.

Juanita wants to find customer order records with a certain status and in a certain country, such as all the pending orders from customers in Italy.

MOUSE TIP

You can also test a query by clicking the Run button on the Query Design toolbar.

To create a query with multiple parameters:

Step 1	*Switch*	to Design view

Step 2	*Click*	in the Criteria: cell for the Country field

Step 3	*Key*	[Enter country]

Now you can define the query parameter's data type.

Step 4	*Click*	Query on the menu bar

Step 5	*Click*	Parameters

Step 6	*Key*	Enter country in the second row of the Parameter column

Notice that Access adds the brackets as necessary.

Step 7	*Click*	in the Data Type column

Access inserts the Text data type for you. The dialog box on your screen should look similar to Figure 11-3.

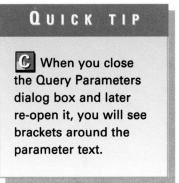

QUICK TIP

When you close the Query Parameters dialog box and later re-open it, you will see brackets around the parameter text.

FIGURE 11-3
Query Parameters Dialog Box with Multiple Parameters

Step 8	*Click*	OK

Now you can test the query.

chapter
eleven

To test a multiple parameter query:

Step 1	*Click*	the Run button ![!] on the Query Design toolbar
Step 2	*Key*	P in the first Enter Parameter Value dialog box
Step 3	*Click*	OK
Step 4	*Key*	Italy in the second Enter Parameter Value dialog box
Step 5	*Click*	OK

You see all the pending orders for customers in Italy.

After testing the query, Juanita realizes it is more efficient to enter the country first and then the status. You change the order of the parameters next.

Changing a Parameter Order

The parameter listed first in the Query Parameters dialog box is the first parameter the user is asked to enter. You change the parameter order in the Query Parameters dialog box by rekeying the information and changing data types, if necessary.

Juanita and her staff want to enter the country before the status. To do this, change the order of the parameters in the Parameter column—you don't need to change the data type, because both are Text data types.

To change the order of parameters:

Step 1	*Switch*	to Design view
Step 2	*Click*	Query on the menu bar
Step 3	*Click*	Parameters
Step 4	*Key*	Enter country in the first row of the Parameter column
Step 5	*Key*	Enter status request in the second row of the Parameter column
Step 6	*Click*	OK
Step 7	*Close*	qryOrders Query, saving your changes

Now when you run this query, Access first prompts you to enter the country, and then prompts you for the order status.

Now that you created a parameter query, you are ready to create another advanced query type: an action query.

11.b Creating an Action Query

Unlike a select query, which retrieves records based on criteria you specify, an **action query** changes many records in just one operation. For example, you can create new tables or permanently change data in existing tables. There are four types of action queries: delete query, update query, make-table query, and append query.

A **delete query** removes a group of records from one or more tables. For example, use a delete query to remove discontinued products. An **update query** makes global changes to a group of records in one or more tables. For example, you can automatically raise prices by 10 percent for all toys, or you can raise salaries by 5 percent for the people within a certain job category. A **make-table query** creates a new table from all or part of the data in one or more tables. An **append query** inserts a group of records from one or more tables to the end of one or more different tables. For example, suppose that Dynamic acquires new customers. If you receive an Access database table containing information on those customers, you could simply append it to the current tblCustomers.

Juanita and the other sales representatives spend a lot of time tracking cancelled orders. She wants to create a delete query to remove all cancelled orders.

Creating a Delete Query

You can create a delete query to remove all deleted orders from tblOrders. However, since you cannot retrieve records once the delete query removes them, it is often a good idea to make a copy of the table first. Once you are satisfied with the delete query results, you can then delete the copied table as well.

To create a copy of tblOrders:

Step 1	*Click*	Tables 🔲 on the Objects bar
Step 2	*Right-click*	tblOrders

chapter
eleven

Step 3	*Click*	Copy from the shortcut menu
Step 4	*Right-click*	in the Database window
Step 5	*Click*	Paste

You are prompted to rename the table.

| Step 6 | *Key* | tblOrders1 |
| Step 7 | *Click* | OK |

With a backup copy of tblOrders, you can now modify qryOrders Query to make it a delete query.

To create a delete query:

Step 1	*Click*	Queries ⊞ on the Objects bar
Step 2	*Open*	qryOrders Query in Design view
Step 3	*Delete*	the country criteria [Enter country]
Step 4	*Open*	the Query Parameters dialog box and delete the [Enter country] parameter
Step 5	*Click*	OK to close the Query Parameters dialog box
Step 6	*Run*	the query and enter D in the status request text box to retrieve deleted orders
Step 7	*Switch*	to Design view
Step 8	*Click*	the Query Type list arrow ⊞▾ on the Query Design toolbar

Your screen should look similar to Figure 11-4.

FIGURE 11-4
Query Type Options

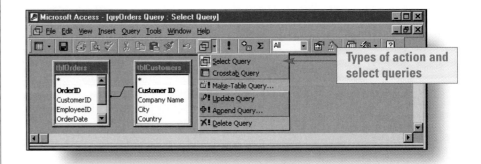

| Step 9 | *Click* | D̲elete Query |

The Query window adds a Delete: row in the design grid.

| Step 10 | *Drag* | the asterisk (*) from the tblOrders field list to the first field in the design grid to identify the table which will have records deleted |

This adds a new column with tblOrders. The asterisk (*) is the field, tblOrders is the table, and Delete: From illustrates where items meeting the delete criteria will be removed from.

Now you can save the query.

| Step 11 | *Close* | qryOrders Query |
| Step 12 | *Click* | Yes to save the design changes |

Notice in the Database window that Access uses an exclamation point to indicate action queries.

Now if you reopen qryOrders Query and use "D" as the parameter, Access deletes all records with the status of D from the tblOrders table. Access shows a warning before it runs the delete query.

Now Juanita wants to create an update query to help her change the tax rate information.

Creating an Update Query

The tax rates just increased from 8.0 percent to 9.0 percent. To change all the current orders easily, you can create an update query. Juanita already created a select query for the tax rate; you simply need to modify it. Remember that you made a backup copy of tblOrders, so you still have the original copy in case the update query changes your records in tblOrders incorrectly.

To create an update query:

Step 1	*Right-click*	qryOrders Update Tax Rate Query in the Database window
Step 2	*Click*	Design View
Step 3	*Click*	the Query Type list arrow 🔲▾ on the Query Design toolbar
Step 4	*Click*	U̲pdate Query

chapter
eleven

The Query window adds an Update To: row in the design grid. Enter text in this row that you want the query to use for updating. Juanita wants to update the query with the new tax rate of 9.0 percent.

| Step 5 | *Key* | 9.0 in the Update To: cell for the Tax Rate field |

Your screen should look similar to Figure 11-5.

FIGURE 11-5
Updating the Sales Tax
Rate in the Update To: Row

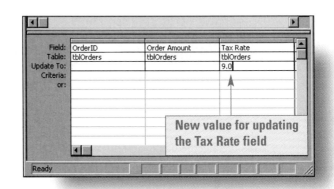

Now you can run the update query.

| Step 6 | *Click* | the Run button [!] on the Query Design toolbar |

Access reminds you that you cannot undo this query.

Step 7	*Click*	Yes
Step 8	*Close*	the qryOrders Update Tax Rate query
Step 9	*Click*	Yes to save the design changes

Now you can check the changes the query made by opening the tblOrders table.

| Step 10 | *Click* | Tables [▦] on the Objects bar |
| Step 11 | *Double-click* | tblOrders |

You see that the update query changed the tax rate from 8.0 percent to 9.0 percent.

Step 12	*Close*	tblOrders

Now the accounting department wants to use a make-table query to create a table summarizing the year's sales.

Creating a Make-Table Query

Giang wants to create a table summarizing the year's sales. You can do this by creating a make-table query based on qryOrders Query. Because you do not want to modify qryOrders Query, you first have to copy the query and then rename it. Remember, both copies still include the parameter query to select records by status.

To copy the qryOrders Query query:

Step 1	*Click*	Queries 🖳 on the Objects bar, if necessary
Step 2	*Right-click*	qryOrders Query
Step 3	*Click*	Copy in the shortcut menu
Step 4	*Right-click*	in the Database window
Step 5	*Click*	Paste in the shortcut menu
Step 6	*Key*	qryOrders Create Table
Step 7	*Click*	OK

Now you're ready to create the make-table query for Giang.
To create a make-table query:

Step 1	*Click*	qryOrders Create Table, if necessary
Step 2	*Click*	Design 📝 on the Objects bar
Step 3	*Delete*	the first column in the design grid (contains tblOrders.*)

Now you can change the query type to a make-table query.

Step 4	*Click*	Query on the menu bar
Step 5	*Click*	Make-Table Query

Access asks you to name the new table that you create.

> **M O U S E   T I P**
>
> You can also click the Query Type list arrow on the Query Design toolbar, and then click Make-Table.

chapter
eleven

| Step 6 | *Key* | tblEnd of Year Orders in the Table Name: list box |

| Step 7 | *Click* | OK |

Now you can run the query to make the new table.

| Step 8 | *Click* | the Run button ⚑ on the Query Design toolbar |

You see the Enter Parameter Value dialog box.

| Step 9 | *Key* | C to select only the completed orders |

| Step 10 | *Click* | OK |

Access tells you how many rows you are adding to a new table, and reminds you that once you run the query, you cannot undo any changes.

| Step 11 | *Click* | Yes |

Now you can view the new table.
To view the new tblEnd of Year Orders table:

| Step 1 | *Close* | qryOrders Create Table, saving your changes |

| Step 2 | *Click* | Tables ▦ on the Objects bar |

| Step 3 | *Double-click* | tblEnd of Year Orders |

| Step 4 | *Sort* | the OrderID field in ascending order |

Your screen should look similar to Figure 11-6.

FIGURE 11-6
New Table Created with
the Make-Table Query

| Step 5 | *Close* | the table and save the change |

Once you create a table, you can add new records to it with the append query.

Creating an Append Query

Giang realizes he must also add any deleted orders to tblEnd of Year Orders because they should be included in the end of year totals. You can add these records by creating an append query based on qryOrders Query, which already contains much of the information you need for the append query.

To create an append query:

Step 1	*Click*	Queries [icon] on the Objects bar
Step 2	*Copy*	qryOrders Create Table Query in the Database window
Step 3	*Paste*	the copied query as qryAppend End of Year
Step 4	*Open*	qryAppend End of Year in Design view

You are ready to use this select query to create an append table query.

| Step 5 | *Click* | the Query Type list arrow on the Query Design toolbar |
| Step 6 | *Click* | Append Query |

Now you can locate the table you want to append.

| Step 7 | *Click* | tblEnd of Year Orders in the Table Name: list box |
| Step 8 | *Click* | OK |

The Query window adds an Append To: row in the design grid. You are now ready to run the query and then review the results.

| Step 1 | *Click* | the Run button [!] on the Query Design toolbar |
| Step 2 | *Key* | D to select all the deleted records and click OK |

C A U T I O N   T I P

If you deleted records from the tblOrders table using the delete query created earlier in this chapter, you must delete the tblOrders table and rename the backup table, tblOrders1, to tblOrders before you can run the append query you create in this section.

chapter
eleven

Access reminds you that once you append the following rows, you cannot undo the change to the tblEnd of Year Orders table.

Step 3	*Click*	Yes
Step 4	*Close*	qryAppend End of Year, saving your changes
Step 5	*Click*	Tables ▦ on the Objects bar
Step 6	*Double-click*	tblEnd of Year Orders

Review the changes that you made. You should see items with the Status "D" in addition to the "C" items that were there previously. Once you are satisfied the changes were made correctly, close the table and then exit Access.

Step 7	*Close*	tblEnd of Year Orders
Step 8	*Exit*	Access

You have created parameter and action queries to help Dynamic employees locate information, as well as permanently change it, in the database. Juanita and Giang thank you for your help.

Summary

▶ A parameter query is an advanced select query that asks you to enter search criteria in a dialog box. When you open a query, the Enter Parameter Value dialog box asks you to enter specific information, such as the order status you want. Access then displays the data that matches your criteria.

▶ You can create queries that prompt for several parameters to find exactly the data you want. You can specify parameters in a number of different fields, or you can enter multiple parameters in one field. When you run a query with multiple parameters, Access prompts you to enter criteria for each parameter you set in successive dialog boxes.

▶ The parameter listed first in the Query Parameters dialog box is the first parameter the user is asked to enter. You change parameter order in the Query Parameters dialog box by rekeying the information and changing data types, if necessary.

▶ Action queries change many records in just one operation. There are four types of action queries: delete query, update query, make-table query, and append query.

▶ A delete query removes a group of records from one or more tables.

▶ An update query makes global changes to a group of records in one or more tables.

▶ A make-table query creates a new table from all or part of the data in one or more tables.

▶ An append query inserts a group of records from one or more tables to the end of one or more different tables.

chapter eleven

Commands Review

Action	Menu Bar	Shortcut Menu	Toolbar	Keyboard
Create a make-table query	Query, Make Table Query	Query Type, Make-Table Query		ALT + Q, K
Create an update query	Query, Update Query	Query Type, Update Query		ALT + Q, U
Create an append query	Query, Append Query	Query Type, Append Query		ALT + Q, P
Create a delete query	Query, Delete Query	Query Type, Delete Query		ALT + Q, D
Create an action query	Query, [query type]	Query Type		ALT + Q
Run a query	Query, Run			ALT + Q, R

Concepts Review

SCANS

Circle the correct answer.

1. A parameter is a:
[a] question.
[b] way of sorting and filtering data.
[c] tool that is similar to tables.
[d] request for criteria.

2. The purpose of a delete query is to:
[a] narrow down information.
[b] accept data.
[c] delete records from a database.
[d] insert information into a table.

3. Use action queries to:
[a] back up a select query.
[b] permanently change data in the database.
[c] enter search criteria in a dialog box.
[d] retrieve requested records from the database.

4. Enter multiple parameters in a field when you want to:
[a] create multiple fields.
[b] update records in successive tables.

[c] prompt users to enter criteria for each parameter.
[d] append records to a selected table.

5. Use an update query to:
[a] display the current date and time.
[b] find records that meet multiple criteria.
[c] permanently delete records from the database.
[d] make global changes to a group of records in one or more tables.

6. Use a make-table query to:
[a] create a new table from all or part of the data in one or more tables.
[b] make global changes to a group of records in one or more tables.
[c] append records to a selected table.
[d] prompt users to enter criteria for each parameter.

7. **Change the order of parameters in the Query Parameter dialog box when you want to change the:**
   [a] order of the parameters requested in the Enter Query Parameter dialog box.
   [b] sort order of the data in the query.
   [c] data types associated with the parameter.
   [d] type of dialog box you see when you select the query.

8. **Use an append query to:**
   [a] create a new table from all or part of the data in one or more tables.
   [b] make global changes to a group of records in one or more tables.
   [c] add records to a selected table.
   [d] prompt users to enter criteria for each parameter.

9. **Action queries are different from select queries because they:**
   [a] permanently change the data in the database.
   [b] retrieve records based on multiple criteria.
   [c] use backup copies of tables instead of originals.
   [d] require you to use parameters.

10. **Make a backup copy of a table:**
    [a] before running an action query that changes the data in the table.
    [b] each time you exit Access.
    [c] after you create a parameter query.
    [d] after you run a delete query.

Circle **T** if the statement is true or **F** if the statement is false.

T   F   1. An action query changes many records in just one operation.

T   F   2. You should not make copies of your tables before you create an action query.

T   F   3. A make-table query creates a new table from all or part of the data in one or more tables.

T   F   4. Set parameters when you want to secure your data.

T   F   5. Setting parameters is one way of narrowing the information.

T   F   6. An append query adds groups of records to the beginning of your tables.

T   F   7. You can specify parameters in a number of different fields, but you cannot enter multiple parameters in one field.

T   F   8. An action query is a type of select query.

T   F   9. An action query is what the query wizard uses when creating a query.

T   F   10. You can specify a data type when you create a parameter.

chapter eleven

Skills Review

Exercise 1

1. If necessary, open the *mdbDynamicInc11* database. Make a backup of tblOrders.

2. Open qryOrders Query in Design view, change the query to a Select Query, and clear all criteria in the Design grid and in the Parameters dialog box.

3. Create a parameter query to retrieve records based on the Customer ID.

4. Prompt the user to *Enter the Customer ID*.

5. Test the parameter query by entering *PARIS* when prompted.

6. Save and close the query.

Exercise 2

1. If necessary, open the *mdbDynamicInc11* database.

2. Open the qryOrders Query you modified in Exercise 1 in Design view.

3. Add another parameter query to retrieve customer order records based on the Order Date.

4. Prompt the user to *Enter the Order Date*. Choose Date/Time as the data type.

5. Test the parameter query by entering *PARIS* when prompted for the Customer ID and 12/22/98 when prompted for the order date.

6. Save and close the query.

Exercise 3

1. If necessary, open the *mdbDynamicInc11* database.

2. In Design view, open qryOrders Query, which you modified in Exercise 2.

3. Change the order of the parameters in the query.

4. Test the parameter query by entering the same information you did in Exercise 2.

5. Save and close the query.

Exercise 4

1. If necessary, open the *mdbDynamicInc11* database.

2. Make a backup copy of tblOrders named tblOrdersBackup, and a backup of tblCustomers called tblCustomersBackup.

3. Open the qryOrders Query you modified in Exercise 3 in Design view. Delete all existing parameters and criteria and remove the tblCustomers table.

4. Create a delete query to remove all the records for customers with the ID *PICCO*.

5. Run the delete query to test it.

6. Save and close the query.

Exercise 5 [C]

1. If necessary, open the *mdbDynamicInc11* database.

2. Open the qryOrders Query you modified in Exercise 4 in Design view and delete all existing criteria.

3. Create an update query in qryOrders Query to change the Customer ID from *CHOPS* to *CHINE*.

4. Run the query to test it.

5. Save and close the query.

Exercise 6 [C]

1. If necessary, open the *mdbDynamicInc11* database.

2. Open the qryOrders Query you modified in Exercise 5 in Design view and delete all existing criteria. Add the OrderID, Order Amount, Status, and Order Date fields from the tblOrders table to the design grid. Add the tblCustomers table to the query and add the country field from the tblCustomers to the design grid. Position the Order ID field as the first field and the country field to follow the Customer ID field.

3. Create a make-table query to make a table called tblEurope Orders by using *Italy* as the criteria for the Country field.

4. Run the query to test it.

5. Save and close the query.

Exercise 7 [C]

1. If necessary, open the *mdbDynamicInc11* database.

2. Open the qryOrders Query you modified in Exercise 6 in Design view and create an append query to add records from customers in France to tblEurope Orders.

3. Run the query to test it.

4. Save and close the query.

Exercise 8 [C]

1. If necessary, open the *mdbDynamicInc11* database.

2. Open the qryOrders Query you modified in Exercise 7 in Design view and delete all the action queries. Change the query type to a *Select Query*. Delete all criteria and parameters.

3. Save and close the query.

chapter eleven

Case Projects

Project 1

Using the Office on the <u>W</u>eb command on the <u>H</u>elp menu, open the Microsoft home page and then link to pages that provide information about action queries. Print at least two of the Web pages.

Project 2

Connect to your ISP and load the home page for a search engine. Search for an online computer dictionary or encyclopedia and find definitions for terms covered in this chapter, such as *parameter, query, append,* and *action query*. Print at least three definitions or explanations. Close the browser and disconnect from your ISP.

Project 3

Juanita Chavez, a sales representative at Dynamic, wants to produce a report that shows orders by country. Search the Access online Help for instructions on using a parameter query to produce reports. Then follow these instructions to create a parameter query Juanita can use to produce a report that shows orders by country. Print one report for a particular country, such as France.

Project 4

Juanita also wants to calculate the average total of all the orders. You can do this by creating a totals query and using the Avg calculation. Create a select query based on the Order ID and Order Amount fields in tblOrders. Open the query in Design view and then click the Totals button on the Query Design toolbar. In the Total cell under Order ID, select Count. In the Total cell under Order Amount, select Avg. Click the Datasheet View button to see the recordset.

Project 5

Now Juanita wants to change the caption of a field in the query result you created in Project 4. Changing a caption changes the text in the field's column header. You can change a caption by modifying the query properties. Open the query in Design view and then click the field whose caption you want to change. Click Properties in the Query Design toolbar and then type the new caption.

Project 6

Juanita also wants to create queries that prompt her for a Customer ID, and then update information in those records. Create a parameter query in qryOrders Query to prompt for Customer ID. Add an update query to change the "P" status to "C."

Project 7

Maria Moreno, the owner of Dynamic, wants you to present a report on action queries to the sales and accounting staffs. In a Word document, provide the following information:

- Differences between action queries and select queries

- Typical scenarios for using delete, update, make-table, and append queries.

Save and print this information.

Project 8

Juanita expects to have tens of thousands of orders in the future, along with a few thousand customers. The queries that reference a Company Name will work more quickly if the company name in the tblCustomers table is indexed. She also wants to prevent any of her staff from entering the Company Name twice in the tblCustomers table. Open the tblCustomers table in Design view. Select the Company Name field and change the Indexed Property to Yes (No Duplicates).

Designing Advanced Queries

Chapter Overview

I n this chapter, you learn how to create and use advanced queries. You create a multiple table query, set a crosstab query, and use calculated fields and concatenation in queries.

LEARNING OBJECTIVES

► Create multiple table queries
► Set a crosstab query
► Create a calculated field
► Use concatenation in queries

Case profile

The department managers at Dynamic Inc., are now comfortable working with Access queries and find that they want to do more with them. Giang Hu wants to produce order reports for each of the company's customers. Alan Golden wants to combine two name fields into a single column, as well as perform a variety of calculations on the order data. He also wants to know which customers each employee serves, and how much revenue is generated. You can use advanced queries to provide this information.

chapter
twelve

12.a Creating Multiple Table Queries

You can create queries that retrieve records from more than one table. To do so, you add the tables to the query, making sure the tables join to each other. Joining the tables shows Access how to connect the information in the tables. You can create a **multiple table query** to join the tables and then query them to find the information you want.

To produce the orders report for Giang, first create a multiple table query that retrieves customer information from tblCustomers and order information from tblOrders. Before you create or run the query, join the tables you want to use.

Specifying Join Properties for Relationships

Whenever you add more than one table to a query, Access needs to know how to join the information in the tables. If you already joined the tables using a wizard or the Relationships window, you see one or more join lines between the tables you add to your query. The join lines show which fields are connected. If you don't see the join lines, you can add them in Design view.

To add and join tables in a query:

Step 1	*Open*	mdbDynamicInc12
Step 2	*Click*	Queries on the Objects bar
Step 3	*Double-click*	Create query in Design view
Step 4	*Double-click*	tblCustomers and tblOrders in the Show Table dialog box
Step 5	*Click*	Close to close the Show Table dialog box
Step 6	*Click*	Customer ID in the tblCustomers field list
Step 7	*Drag*	to the CustomerID field in the tblOrders field list

This joins the two tables.

Now you're ready to set up the query to retrieve customer and order information for Giang's report.

To create a multiple table query:

Step 1	*Double-click*	the Customer ID and the Company Name fields in the tblCustomers field list

CAUTION TIP

If you don't join the tables in a query, Access doesn't know which records are associated with which, so it displays every combination of records between the two tables. For example, if both unjoined tables had 10 records, the resulting query would produce 100 (10 × 10) records.

If you want to join two numeric fields, make sure both have FieldSize property settings of Byte, Integer, or Long Integer.

Step 2	**Double-click** the OrderDate field in the tblOrders field list

Step 3	**Switch** to Datasheet view

This query shows all customers who placed an order. Your screen should look similar to Figure 12-1.

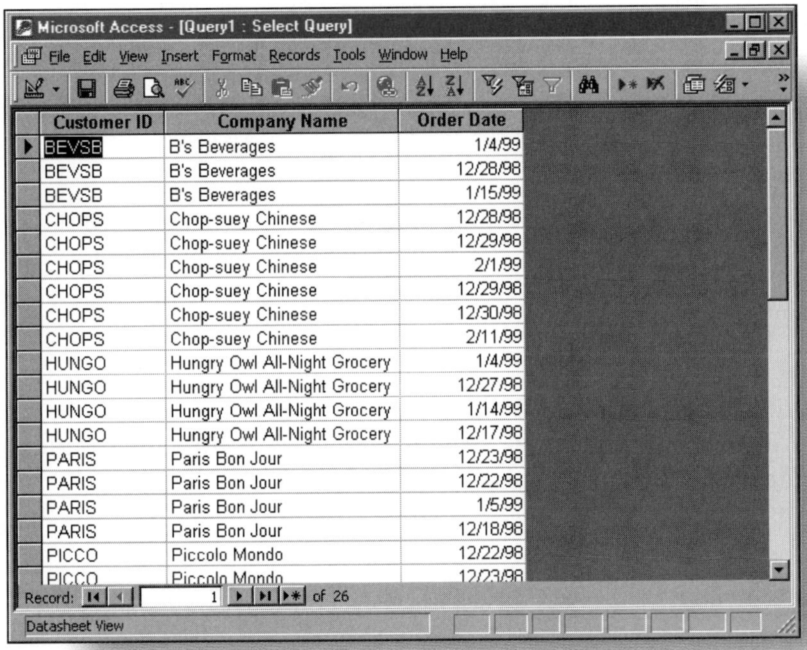

FIGURE 12-1
Customer Orders

Microsoft Access - [Query1 : Select Query]

File Edit View Insert Format Records Tools Window Help

Customer ID	Company Name	Order Date
BEVSB	B's Beverages	1/4/99
BEVSB	B's Beverages	12/28/98
BEVSB	B's Beverages	1/15/99
CHOPS	Chop-suey Chinese	12/28/98
CHOPS	Chop-suey Chinese	12/29/98
CHOPS	Chop-suey Chinese	2/1/99
CHOPS	Chop-suey Chinese	12/29/98
CHOPS	Chop-suey Chinese	12/30/98
CHOPS	Chop-suey Chinese	2/11/99
HUNGO	Hungry Owl All-Night Grocery	1/4/99
HUNGO	Hungry Owl All-Night Grocery	12/27/98
HUNGO	Hungry Owl All-Night Grocery	1/14/99
HUNGO	Hungry Owl All-Night Grocery	12/17/98
PARIS	Paris Bon Jour	12/23/98
PARIS	Paris Bon Jour	12/22/98
PARIS	Paris Bon Jour	1/5/99
PARIS	Paris Bon Jour	12/18/98
PICCO	Piccolo Mondo	12/22/98
PICCO	Piccolo Mondo	12/23/98

Record: 1 of 26

Datasheet View

Step 4	**Save** the query as qryOrder Date

Now you want to see a list of all customers whether or not they placed an order. You can change the join properties to do this.

Step 5	**Switch** to Design view

Step 6	**Double-click** the join line between tblOrders and tblCustomers

Step 7	**Click** option 2 and click OK

Step 8	**Run** the query

This query shows all customers, whether or not they have placed an order.

Step 9	**Close** the query without saving changes

Now that you added a join to create a multiple table query, you can learn how to remove one.

chapter
twelve

Removing Joins in a Query

The relationships you establish by adding joins in the Query Design window remain established until you remove the join. Giang wants to join a field in the tblOrder Details table and then remove it.

To remove a join:

Step 1	*Open*	qryOrder Date in Design view
Step 2	*Click*	the Show Table button ⊞ on the Query Design toolbar
Step 3	*Double-click*	tblOrder Details

You see the tblOrder Details field list in the Query Design window.

Step 4	*Click*	Close to close the Show Table dialog box

Notice that tblOrders and tblOrder Details are already joined by the OrderID field. Giang decides he doesn't want to include information from the tblOrder Details table. You need to remove the join.

To remove the join:

Step 1	*Right-click*	the join line between tblOrders and tblOrder Details
Step 2	*Click*	Delete
Step 3	*Right-click*	the field list for the tblOrders Detail table
Step 4	*Click*	Remove Table
Step 5	*Click*	File
Step 6	*Click*	Save As
Step 7	*Save*	the query as qryOrder Details and close it

Now that you created one kind of advanced query, you're ready to create another. This query, a crosstab query, indicates which customers each employee serves, and how much revenue is generated.

12.b Setting a Crosstab Query

Crosstab queries take a large amount of complex data and summarize some or all of the information into a row-and-column format. This format helps you make comparisons and see trends in your data. You can also use a crosstab query as the basis for a report.

Alan, the sales manager, wants to know which customers each employee serves, and how much revenue each customer generates. A select query (see Figure 12-2) produces a long list of information, making comparisons difficult due to the amount of scrolling needed. A crosstab query (see Figure 12-2), on the other hand, summarizes the same information in a more compact way.

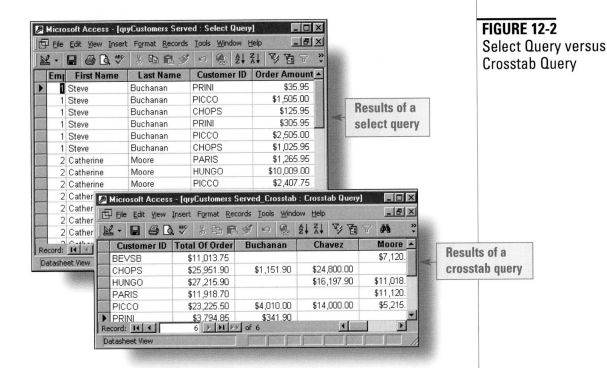

FIGURE 12-2
Select Query versus
Crosstab Query

Use the Crosstab Query Wizard to guide you through the steps of creating a crosstab query.

To create a crosstab query:

| Step 1 | *Click* | Queries 🖼 on the Objects bar, if necessary |

| Step 2 | *Click* | the New button 🔲New on the Database toolbar |

The New Query dialog box opens.

| Step 3 | *Double-click* Crosstab Query Wizard |

The Crosstab Query Wizard dialog box on your screen should look similar to Figure 12-3.

chapter
twelve

FIGURE 12-3
Crosstab Query Wizard
Dialog Box

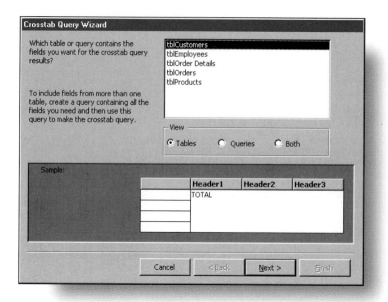

Step 4	*Click*	the Queries option button in the View section
Step 5	*Click*	qryCustomers Served in the list box
Step 6	*Click*	Next >

You can now choose the field values you want to use as the row headings. Alan wants to see which customers his employees serve, so choose the Customer ID field.

Step 7	*Double-click*	CustomerID
Step 8	*Click*	Next >

QUICK TIP

You can modify the column headings after you complete the wizard by modifying the ColumnHeadings property. After you complete the query, open it in Design view, and then right-click the background to see the property list for the query.

You can now choose the field values to use as column headings. Because Alan wants to compare customers and employees, choose the LastName field, which shows the last name of the employee. You then indicate the number you want to calculate for each column and row intersection. Alan wants to see how much revenue each employee generates, so you want to show the total order amount for each.
To complete the Crosstab Query Wizard:

Step 1	*Click*	LastName
Step 2	*Click*	Next >

| Step 3 | *Click* | Order Amount in the Fields: list |

| Step 4 | *Click* | Sum in the Functions: list |

Your screen should look similar to Figure 12-4.

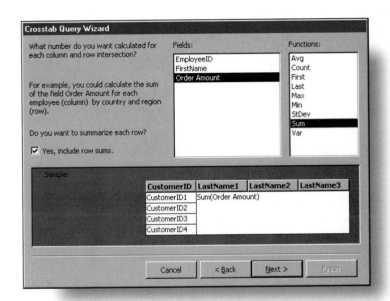

FIGURE 12-4
Fields Selected for
Crosstab Query

| Step 5 | *Click* | Next > |

| Step 6 | *Click* | Finish to accept the name of the query (qryCustomers Served_Crosstab) |

Your screen should look similar to Figure 12-5.

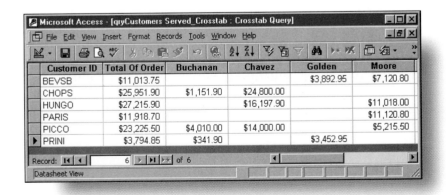

FIGURE 12-5
Results of Crosstab Query

Customer ID	Total Of Order	Buchanan	Chavez	Golden	Moore
BEVSB	$11,013.75			$3,892.95	$7,120.80
CHOPS	$25,951.90	$1,151.90	$24,800.00		
HUNGO	$27,215.90		$16,197.90		$11,018.00
PARIS	$11,918.70				$11,120.80
PICCO	$23,225.50	$4,010.00	$14,000.00		$5,215.50
PRINI	$3,794.85	$341.90		$3,452.95	

chapter
twelve

| Step 7 | *Close* | qryCustomers Served_Crosstab |

Now that you created a crosstab query for Alan, he wants you to create a query to calculate new prices for products in a certain category.

12.c Creating a Calculated Field

Using calculations in Access gives you information such as the total amount of the orders from a given customer. To calculate data, you add extra fields that perform calculations on the other fields in the query. To create a field that calculates values, enter an expression in an open Field cell in a query's design grid. If the expression includes a field name, include brackets around it. After you create a calculated field, you can set properties for it, because it doesn't inherit properties from the underlying table.

Alan wants to find out how much Dynamic would charge for housewares products if they raised the prices by 25 percent. You can provide this information by adding a calculated value to qryProducts.

To add a calculated field to a query:

Step 1	*Open*	qryProducts in Design view
Step 2	*Click*	in the Criteria: cell for the Category Name field
Step 3	*Key*	Housewares
Step 4	*Click*	the first open Field cell

Now you enter the calculation you want Access to perform. Start by entering the name of the new field followed by a colon (:). In brackets, enter the name of the field containing the current price followed by the multiplication operator (*) and the amount you want to multiply by.

| Step 5 | *Key* | New Price:[UnitPrice]*1.25 and press Enter key |

Your screen should look similar to Figure 12-6.

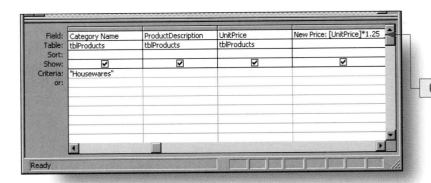

FIGURE 12-6
Calculation Entered in
Design View

Calculated field

| Step 6 | *Switch* | to Datasheet view |

You see the new column. Because it's a calculated value, it doesn't inherit the properties from the underlying table. Alan wants to display the data in this field as currency. You can do so by changing its Format property in Design view.

To change a format property:

Step 1	*Switch*	to Design view
Step 2	*Click*	in the New Price field, if necessary
Step 3	*Click*	View
Step 4	*Click*	Properties

You see the Property list for this field.

Step 5	*Click*	in the Format field and then click the list arrow in the Format field
Step 6	*Click*	Currency
Step 7	*Close*	the Field Properties Dialog box
Step 8	*Switch*	to Datasheet view

Your screen should look similar to Figure 12-7.

QUICK TIP

You can also add a calculated field when you create a query using the Simple Query Wizard. To start the Simple Query Wizard, click Queries on the Objects bar, click the New button on the Database toolbar, and then click Simple Query Wizard.

When you display the results of a calculation in a field, the results aren't actually entered in the underlying table. Instead, Access performs the calculation each time you run the query so you see the most current results.

MOUSE TIP

You can also click the Properties button on the Query Design toolbar to see the property list.

chapter
twelve

FIGURE 12-7
Reformatted Calculated
Field

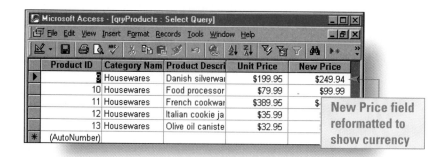

Product ID	Category Nam	Product Descri	Unit Price	New Price
9	Housewares	Danish silverwar	$199.95	$249.94
10	Housewares	Food processor	$79.99	$99.99
11	Housewares	French cookwar	$389.95	$
12	Housewares	Italian cookie ja	$35.99	
13	Housewares	Olive oil caniste	$32.95	
* (AutoNumber)				

New Price field reformatted to show currency

Step 9	*Close*	qryProducts, saving your changes

You used a numeric expression in a calculated field. You can also use text expressions to concatenate fields.

12.d Using Concatenation in Queries

Concatenate means to connect or link in a series. You can use a calculated text field to concatenate two text fields into a single field. Alan wants to combine the FirstName and LastName fields in qryCustomer Orders to show one full name in a single field. Start by deleting one of the fields you want to combine—the FirstName field. Then convert the other field—the LastName field—to a calculated field that concatenates two text fields.

To concatenate two text fields:

Step 1	*Open*	qryCustomer Orders in Design view
Step 2	*Click*	the selection bar above the FirstName field
Step 3	*Press*	the DELETE key
Step 4	*Click*	in the LastName Field cell, if necessary, to highlight the field name

You are now ready to concatenate the fields. Use this general format: *NewFieldName*: [Field1]& " " &[Field2]. Be sure to include a space between the quotation marks—this adds the space between the first and last names.

| Step 5 | *Key* | Employee:[FirstName]& " " &[LastName] |
| Step 6 | *Switch* | to Datasheet view |

Your screen should look similar to Figure 12-8.

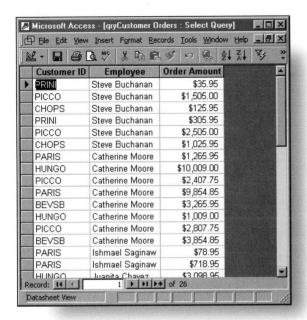

FIGURE 12-8
Concatenated Field

| Step 7 | *Close* | qryCustomer Orders, saving your changes |
| Step 8 | *Exit* | Access |

You have created several advanced queries to provide information from the Dynamic database. Giang and Alan appreciate your help.

chapter
twelve

Summary

▶ You can create a multiple table query to join tables and then query them to find the information you want.

▶ The relationships you establish by adding joins in the Query Design window remain established until you remove the join.

▶ Crosstab queries take a large amount of complex data and summarize some or all of the information into a row-and-column format. This format helps you make comparisons and see trends in your data. You can also use a crosstab query as the basis for a report.

▶ Using calculations in Access gives you information such as the total amount of the orders from a given customer.

▶ After you create a calculated field, you can set properties for it. This is necessary because it doesn't inherit properties from the underlying table.

▶ Concatenate means to connect or link in a series. You can use a calculated text field to concatenate two text fields into a single field.

Commands Review

Action	Menu Bar	Shortcut Menu	Toolbar	Keyboard
Create a query	Insert, Query		New	ALT + I, Q
Open a query			Open	
Show a table in Design view	View, Show Table	Show Table		ALT + V, H

Concepts Review

SCANS

Circle the correct answer.

1. Use a multiple table query to:
[a] remove joins in a query.
[b] query more than one joined table.
[c] query more than one table even if they're not joined.
[d] make more than one table in your database.

2. Joining tables shows Access:
[a] which tables you want to use in your query.
[b] how to sort the records the query retrieves.
[c] how to connect the information in the tables.
[d] how to combine two fields into one column.

3. Use a crosstab query to:
[a] summarize a large amount of data into a compact format.
[b] query more than one table.
[c] build a summary query.
[d] concatenate fields in different tables.

4. One use of a crosstab query is to:
[a] combine two fields into a single column.
[b] improve the appearance of query reports.
[c] perform calculations on a number of fields.
[d] help you compare data and see trends.

5. To create a calculated field:
[a] you must include brackets around it.
[b] enter an expression in an open Field cell.
[c] use the Calculated Fields Wizard.
[d] first delete unnecessary fields.

6. If the expression in a calculated field includes a field name:
[a] include brackets around it.
[b] you must include the expression in a new field.

[c] you cannot create the query.
[d] you can use it to create a summary query.

7. Set properties after you create a calculated field because:
[a] the field does not calculate correctly if you don't.
[b] you must join any calculated field to one in another table.
[c] the wizard doesn't ask you for this information.
[d] it doesn't inherit properties from the underlying table.

8. Concatenate means to:
[a] cut off or shorten.
[b] connect or link in a series.
[c] join two tables with join lines.
[d] perform an action query.

9. To combine two text fields into a single field:
[a] use a calculated number field.
[b] use a calculated text field.
[c] choose a text field as the field you want to use for row headings.
[d] create an action query first.

10. Specifying row and column headings is part of creating a:
[a] crosstab query.
[b] multiple table query.
[c] concatenation query.
[d] calculated field.

chapter twelve

Circle **T** if the statement is true or **F** if the statement is false.

T F   1. Create a crosstab query to set up a cross-reference.

T F   2. Build a summary query to summarize complex data in a simple format.

T F   3. You can use a multiple table query to query more than one table even if they are not related.

T F   4. You must use the Relationships window to join tables.

T F   5. You can specify a function and a field to calculate using the Crosstab Wizard.

T F   6. To add more tables to your query, you click the Show Table button on the Query Design toolbar.

T F   7. Concatenation is one example of a calculated text field.

T F   8. Summary is one example of a calculated number field.

T F   9. The way a crosstab query formats your data can help you make comparisons and see trends in your data.

T F   10. You can concatenate two numeric fields to calculate their total.

Skills Review

Exercise 1

1. If necessary, open the *mdbDynamicInc12* database.

2. Create a multiple table query using tblOrders and tblOrder Details.

3. Join the OrderID fields in both tables, unless Access does it for you automatically.

4. Add the following fields from tblOrders: OrderID, CustomerID, OrderDate, and Order Amount. Add the following fields from tblOrder Details: ProductID, Quantity.

5. Save the query as qryOrders With Details.

6. Run and close the query.

Exercise 2

1. If necessary, open the *mdbDynamicInc12* database.

2. Open qryOrders With Details you created in Exercise 1 in Design view.

3. Remove the joins in the query. Remove tblOrder Details from the query.

4. Save and close the query.

Exercise 3

1. If necessary, open the *mdbDynamicInc12* database.

2. Use the Crosstab Query Wizard to create a crosstab query based on qryProducts.

3. Choose the Category Name field as the row heading. Choose Product Description as the column heading. Choose Unit Price as the field to calculate. Choose Avg as the function.

4. Save the query as qryProducts_Crosstab.

5. View and close the query.

Exercise 4 [C]

1. If necessary, open the *mdbDynamicInc12* database.

2. Use the Crosstab Query Wizard to create a crosstab query based on qryProducts.

3. Choose the ProductDescription field as the row heading. Choose Category Name as the column heading. Choose Unit Price as the field to calculate. Choose Avg as the function.

4. Save the query as qryProducts_Crosstab1.

5. View the query and compare it to qryProducts_Crosstab, and then close both queries.

Exercise 5 [C]

1. If necessary, open the *mdbDynamicInc12* database.

2. Open qryOrders With Details you modified in Exercise 2 and create a calculated query to show the shipping amount in a calculated column called Shipping. Do so by multiplying the amount in the Order Amount field by .25.

3. Run the query and view the results.

4. In Design view, format the Shipping field to show currency, and then run the query again.

5. Save the query as qryOrders with Details2 and then close the query.

Exercise 6

1. If necessary, open the mdbDynamicInc12 database.

2. Open the qryCustomers Served query in Design view and concatenate the FirstName and LastName fields. Use "Name" as the new field name.

3. Run the query to test it.

4. Save the query as qryCustomers Served 1 and then close the query.

Exercise 7 [C]

1. If necessary, open the *mdbDynamicInc12* database.

2. Open the qryCustomers Served 1 query you created in Exercise 6 in Design view and add a calculated field named Discounted Order Amount to show the order amount if customers pay early—Dynamic gives a 25 percent discount. (*Hint:* Multiply by .75.)

3. Format the new field to show currency.

4. Run, save, and close the query.

Exercise 8

1. If necessary, open the *mdbDynamicInc12* database.

2. Open qryProducts in Design view and change the criteria to retrieve products in the Automotive and Electronics categories. Show the new price if Dynamic raised the unit price from 25 percent to 30 percent.

3. Run, save, and close the query.

chapter twelve

Case Projects

Project 1

Using the Office on the Web command on the Help menu, open the Microsoft home page and then link to pages that provide information about the types of queries covered in this chapter. Print at least two of the Web pages.

Project 2

Connect to your ISP and load the home page for a search engine. Search for an online computer dictionary or encyclopedia and find definitions for terms covered in this chapter, such as *concatenate, crosstab,* and *expression.* Print at least two definitions or explanations. Close the browser and disconnect from your ISP.

Project 3

Alan Golden wants to change the properties of the join in qryOrder Details to include all records from tblOrders and only those records from tblOrder Details where the joined fields are equal. Search the Access online Help for information on join properties and instructions on changing them. Then follow these instructions to change the property of the join in qryOrder Details according to Alan's request.

Project 4

Alan wants to include a calculated field that shows the unit price of an order. Create a calculated field in the qryOrder Details you modified in Case Project 3 that shows the unit price by dividing the Order Amount by the Quantity. Format the new field to show currency amounts.

Project 5

Now Alan wants to create a query to prepare for his year-end sales report for the previous year. He wants to create a query that shows only the year

"1998" instead of the full order date. You can use the DatePart function to extract part of a date from qryOrders Query. Search the Access online Help for instructions on using the DatePart function. Then follow these instructions to create a query to provide the information Alan wants.

Project 6

In qryOrders Query, Alan wants to see only the IDs for companies who ordered from Dynamic. You can do this for him by creating a query that selects only unique values. Search the Access online Help for instructions on the UniqueValues property. Then follow these instructions to create a query to meet Alan's request.

Project 7

Alan wants to create a query to find Dynamic orders placed after 12/25/98, including the employee who made the sale and the customer who placed the order. The fields he wants come from the tblOrders, tblEmployees, and tblCustomers tables. Create a query that contains three tables. Join the appropriate fields. Then create the query to find the information Alan wants. Search the Access online Help for instructions on creating a query that contains three tables, if necessary.

Project 8

Alan wants to find Dynamic customers whose names start with "P" and any orders they placed. He wants to list customers even if they didn't place any orders yet. You can do this by creating an outer join between tblCustomers and tblOrders. Search the Access online Help for more information, if necessary. Then create a query that provides the information Alan wants.

Advanced Report Features

Chapter Overview

In this chapter, you create a grouped report from a query, modify report properties, include calculations in reports, add custom pages, customize a footer, and present and modify information in a chart.

LEARNING OBJECTIVES

▶ Create a grouped report from a query
▶ Modify report properties
▶ Use a calculated control in a report
▶ Customize a report footer
▶ Present information in a chart
▶ Modify a chart

Case profile

You create first-draft monthly reports for Dynamic's department managers. Reviewing your work, you discover several changes that you want to make to some of the reports. For example, you decide to include a calculation and a chart. To make these modifications, you can use some of Access' advanced report features.

**chapter
thirteen**

13.a Creating a Grouped Report from a Query

A **grouped report** allows you to separate groups of records visually and to display introductory and summary information for each group. A **group** is a collection of records, and includes a group header, detail records, and a group footer. For Dynamic, this means you can show all the orders shipped in a particular week, and then display a subtotal. The entire report has four groups—one for each week in the month.

Alan Golden, Dynamic's sales manager, wants you to create a monthly report showing Dynamic's orders per month. For this report, you use qryOrders Query as the basis. You group the data by month, so that Alan can easily see the difference between each month's sales.

To create a grouped report:

Step 1	*Open*	*mdbDynamicInc13*
Step 2	*Click*	Reports 🖼 on the Objects bar
Step 3	*Double-click*	Create report by using wizard
Step 4	*Click*	Query: qryOrders Query in the Tables/Queries list
Step 5	*Move*	all the fields to the Selected Fields: list
Step 6	*Click*	Next >

You can now group the data. Because you want to show the difference between each month's sales, group the data by month.

Step 7	*Double-click*	OrderDate

Your screen should now look similar to Figure 13-1.

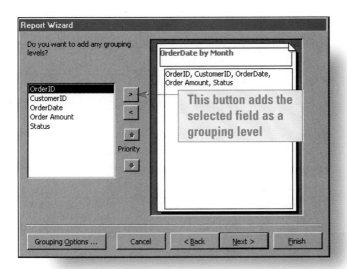

FIGURE 13-1
Adding a Grouping Level in
the Report Wizard

You can also change the field on which the data is grouped by clicking the > button. You can specify the grouping intervals by clicking the Grouping Options button on this page of the wizard. For example, instead of grouping the data by month, you can group by quarter, by week, or by some other interval.

| Step 8 | *Click* | Next > |

Now you can choose how you want to sort the data. Alan wants to sort the records by customer.

| Step 9 | *Click* | CustomerID in the list box |

You also want some summary information on the total amount of orders that were filled for the month.

| Step 10 | *Click* | the Summary Options button |

chapter
thirteen

The Summary Options dialog box on your screen should look similar to Figure 13-2.

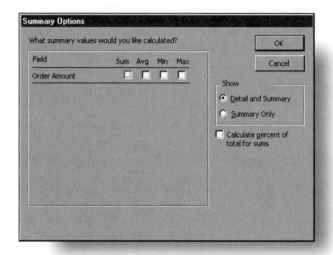

This dialog box asks what summary values you want to calculate. You can calculate the sum, average, minimum, and maximum values in the Order Amount field. You can also calculate the percent of total for sums. Alan wants to calculate the sum and the percent of total of the order amount.

To specify summary values and complete the Report Wizard:

Step 1	*Click*	the Sum check box
Step 2	*Click*	the Calculate percent of total for sums check box
Step 3	*Click*	OK
Step 4	*Click*	Next >

Now you see the layout of the page. Click Layout option to see a preview. You and Alan think Stepped, the default option, is fine.

Step 5	*Click*	Next >
Step 6	*Click*	Corporate as the style, if necessary
Step 7	*Click*	Next >
Step 8	*Key*	rptMonthly Orders as the report title
Step 9	*Click*	Finish

Your report should look similar to Figure 13-3.

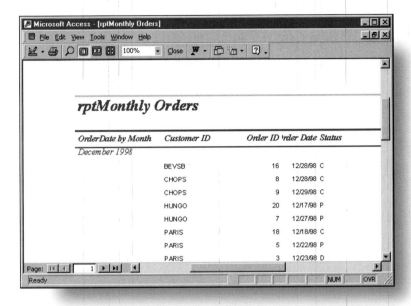

FIGURE 13-3
rptMonthly Orders Report

Access automatically saves the report when you create it. If you make changes to a report, Access reminds you to save it.

Looking at the report, you decide you want it to print only one month's data per page. To do this, you can use the Properties tool.

13.b Modifying Report Properties

Everything in Access has properties, including the report, the report sections, and the report controls. To set up the report to print only one month's data per page, change the report properties. You can do so using the Properties tool.

To modify the report using the Properties tool:

Step 1	*Switch*	to Design view
Step 2	*Close*	the Field List, if necessary
Step 3	*Right-click*	a blank spot in the Order Date Footer section to display the shortcut menu
Step 4	*Click*	Properties
Step 5	*Click*	the All tab, if necessary

M OUSE TIP

You can also click the Order Date Footer bar and then click the Properties button to see the footer's properties.

chapter
thirteen

The Group Footer Section properties on your screen should look similar to Figure 13-4.

FIGURE 13-4
Group Footer Section
Properties

| Step 6 | *Click* | in the Force New Page field |

A list arrow appears in the field.

| Step 7 | *Click* | After Section in the list |

Clicking After Section inserts a page break after each section of the report. Because you grouped by date, each section is also a new month, so this option sets a page break after the data for each month.

| Step 8 | *Close* | the Properties dialog box |

Now Alan wants to modify the sum field so it shows currency amounts. To modify the Sum field properties:

Step 1	*Click*	in the Sum text box in the Report Footer section
Step 2	*Click*	the Properties button on the Report Design toolbar
Step 3	*Click*	the All tab, if necessary
Step 4	*Click*	in the Format field
Step 5	*Click*	Currency in the list box, if necessary
Step 6	*Close*	the Properties dialog box
Step 7	*Verify*	the Format properties for the SUM and STANDARD fields in the Order Date Footer are Currency and Percent, respectively

| Step 8 | *Click* | the Print Preview button on the Report Design toolbar |

You and Alan notice sizing and spacing problems with the Order ID, Order Date, Status, and Order Amount labels and fields.

| Step 9 | *Switch* | to Design view and modify the size and spacing of the labels and fields to present an attractive report |
| Step 10 | *Close* | rptMonthly Orders, saving your changes |

Now that you modified rptMonthly Orders' properties, you decide to add a control—an element such as a label, text box, or image box—to make a calculation on another report.

13.c   Using a Calculated Control in a Report

C

To make a calculation on a report, you create and insert a calculated text box into a report. You then type a formula in the text box. Access automatically performs the calculation that you specified in the text box.

When entering formulas, you must use standard mathematical operators, such as (+) add, (–) subtract, (*) multiply, and (/) divide. Further, all formulas must begin with the equals sign (=) and all field names must appear in parentheses.

Alan created a report called rptCustomer Orders, which summarizes customer information as well as some order details. He now wants to calculate a 9 percent freight charge on the report.

To create a calculated text box:

Step 1	*Open*	rptCustomer Orders in Design view and display the Toolbox, if necessary
Step 2	*Click*	the Text Box button ab| on the Toolbox
Step 3	*Click*	in the Detail section of the report below the Order ID field
Step 4	*Click*	in the label, which contains placeholder text similar to "Text25:" and then select the placeholder text
Step 5	*Key*	Freight Charge
Step 6	*Select*	the text box
Step 7	*Click*	in the text box

chapter thirteen

Step 8	*Key*	=(Quantity)*(UnitPrice)*.09
Step 9	*Click*	outside the text box when finished
Step 10	*Size*	and reposition the label and text box to view the entire contents
Step 11	*Change*	the format to Currency in the text box Properties dialog box

Your screen should look similar to Figure 13-5.

FIGURE 13-5
rptCustomer Orders with Calculated Text Box

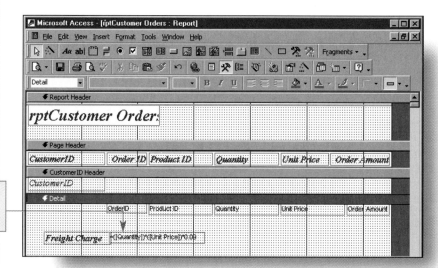

Calculated text box for calculating freight charge

Step 12	*Click*	the Print Preview button on the Report Design toolbar

Viewing the report, you see that Access made the calculations. Now Alan wants to add the Dynamic motto to the last page of the report. You can do this by customizing the report footer.

C 13.d Customizing a Report Footer

A report footer appears at the end of a report, at the end of the last page. Often, any group totals appear in the report footer. However, you can customize the footer by adding any element that suits your needs. You can do the same for the page footer, which appears at the bottom of every page.

To customize the report footer:

| Step 1 | *Switch* | to Design view |

The report footer now shows the Grand Total. You need to make space for the motto.

Step 2	*Drag*	the bottom edge of the Report Footer section down approximately ½ inch
Step 3	*Click*	the Label button [Aa] on the Toolbox
Step 4	*Click*	in the Report Footer section of the report below Grand Total
Step 5	*Key*	Dynamic Inc.: Meeting the Needs of Millions
Step 6	*Adjust*	the text box so that it is centered in the footer section and all of the text is visible
Step 7	*Click*	the Print Preview button [🔍] on the Report Design toolbar
Step 8	*Click*	the navigation buttons to go to the last page in the report

You see the motto at the end of the report.

| Step 9 | *Close* | the report, saving your changes |

Alan decides he also wants to include a graph to show how many orders each customer made in relation to other customers. You can present this information in a chart.

13.e Presenting Information in a Chart

Most people understand numeric information better if it is presented visually. When you want to compare numeric information, consider creating a chart report. A **chart report** shows information in the form of a graph, such as a bar chart, pie chart, or line graph. To create a chart report, you use the Chart Wizard.

Alan asks you to add a chart to accompany the rptMonthly Orders report.

CAUTION TIP

If you want a footer to appear at the bottom of every page, click in the Page Footer section. If you want it to appear only at the end of the report, click in the Report Footer section.

chapter thirteen

To create a chart report:

Step 1	*Click*	Reports 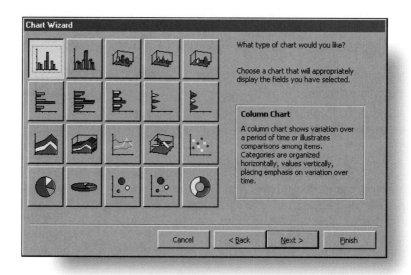 on the Objects bar, if necessary
Step 2	*Click*	the New button on the Database toolbar
Step 3	*Click*	Chart Wizard in the New Report dialog box
Step 4	*Select*	qryCustomer Orders in the Choose a table or query where the object's data comes from: list box
Step 5	*Click*	OK
Step 6	*Double-click*	the CustomerID and Order Amount fields to move them to the Fields for Chart: list
Step 7	*Click*	Next >

You are now given several chart options from which to choose. Your screen should look similar to Figure 13-6.

FIGURE 13-6
Chart Type Options in the
Chart Wizard

QUICK TIP

To find out what each chart displays, click the icon and the description appears in the lower right portion of the window.

You decide to use the pie chart.

| Step 8 | *Click* | the pie chart icon in the first column, fourth row |
| Step 9 | *Click* | Next > |

You are now asked about the data layout. Access shows you the default setting for this type of chart, which you decide is fine.

To complete the Chart Wizard:

Step 1	*Click*	<u>N</u>ext >
Step 2	*Key*	chtCustomer Orders as the chart title
Step 3	*Click*	<u>F</u>inish

The chart Access creates should look similar to Figure 13-7.

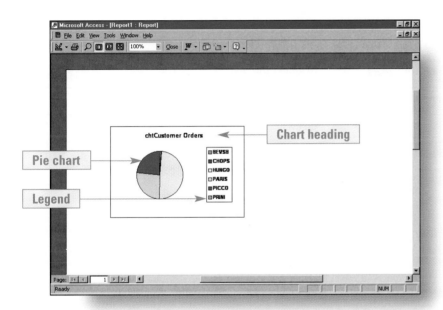

FIGURE 13-7
Pie Chart of Customer
Orders

Looking at the chart, you and Alan decide to make some changes to improve its appearance. You can modify the chart next.

13.f Modifying a Chart

Once you create a chart, you can modify it to make sure it presents the visual information effectively. All of its elements, such as its heading, legend, size, and colors, should be easy to read and understand.

Alan wants to improve the chtCustomer Orders chart by changing the heading, enlarging the chart area, and adding a title. Your first task is to modify the heading.

To modify the heading:

Step 1	**Switch**	to Design view
Step 2	**Right-click**	the chart
Step 3	**Point to**	Chart Object
Step 4	**Click**	Open

You see the chart in Microsoft Graph.

Step 5	**Click**	the Chart Title
Step 6	**Drag**	to select the text
Step 7	**Key**	Dynamic Customer Orders
Step 8	**Click**	elsewhere to deselect the heading text
Step 9	**Click**	in the report area to close Microsoft Graph
Step 10	**Switch**	to Print Preview to view the chart and then switch back to Design view to resize chart

Now you can resize the chart.
To resize the chart:

Step 1	**Click**	the chart to see the selection handles
Step 2	**Drag**	the center-right handle to increase the size of the chart area

Now you're ready to resize the chart itself.

Step 3	**Right-click**	the chart
Step 4	**Point to**	Chart Object
Step 5	**Click**	Edit

You see the chart's datasheet and a selection box around the Dynamic Customer Orders graph.

Step 6	**Close**	the datasheet
Step 7	**Drag**	the bottom-right selection handle to resize the chart to fit the chart area
Step 8	**Click**	in the report area to deselect the chart object

Now that you resized the chart, you can add a title to the chart report. To add a title to a chart report:

Step 1	*Click*	the Label button  on the toolbox
Step 2	*Click*	in the Page Header section of the report
Step 3	*Key*	Customer Monthly Orders Chart in the text box
Step 4	*Click*	outside the title
Step 5	*Click*	the title label again to select it
Step 6	*Click*	18 in the Font Size list on the Formatting toolbar
Step 7	*Resize*	the Page Header area, if necessary
Step 8	*Drag*	the bottom right selection handle to resize the label
Step 9	*Reposition*	the label attractively in the heading, if necessary
Step 10	*Click*	the Print Preview button on the Report Design toolbar

Your screen should look similar to Figure 13-8.

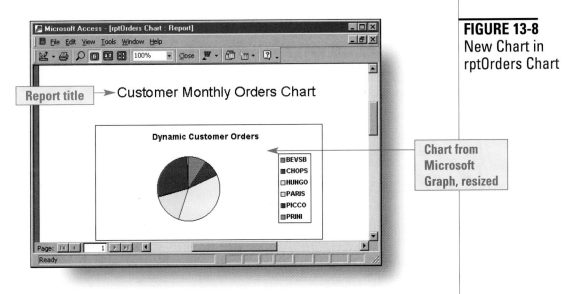

FIGURE 13-8
New Chart in rptOrders Chart

Step 11	*Save*	the chart as rptOrders Chart and close the report
Step 12	*Exit*	Access

The rptMonthly Orders report is much more effective with the revised chart.

Summary

▶ A grouped report allows you to separate groups of records visually and display introductory and summary information for each group.

▶ Everything in a report has properties, including the report itself, the report sections, and the report controls. You can modify report properties using the Properties tool.

▶ To make a calculation on a report, you create and insert a calculated text box, and then type a formula in the text box. Access then automatically performs the specified calculation.

▶ When entering formulas, you must use standard mathematical controls. All formulas must begin with the equal sign (=) and all field names must appear in parentheses.

▶ You can customize a report footer, which appears at the end of a report, at the end of the last page, by adding any element that suits your needs.

▶ A chart report shows information in the form of a graph, such as a bar chart, pie chart, or line graph. To create a chart report, you use the Chart Wizard.

▶ Once you create a chart, you can modify it to make sure it is easy to read and understand.

Commands Review

Action	Menu Bar	Shortcut Menu	Toolbar	Keyboard
Display the property sheet	View, Properties	Properties		ALT + V, P
Select multiple controls	Edit, Select All		Click selection boxes to the left of section headers	CTRL + A ALT + E, A
Create a new report	Insert, Report	New		CTRL + N ALT + I, R
Insert a new control into a report	Insert, ActiveX Control			ALT + I, C
Create a chart report			New	
Modify chart properties		Chart Object, Edit		

Concepts Review

Circle the correct answer.

1. To include a chart or graph in your report, use the:
[a] Chart Wizard.
[b] Pivot Table Wizard.
[c] AutoReport:Columnar option.
[d] AutoReport:Tabular layout.

2. Use a grouped report to:
[a] customize a footer.
[b] logically separate groups of records.
[c] present information in a chart.
[d] insert information into a report.

3. How many properties can you set in a report?
[a] one
[b] two
[c] several
[d] none

4. You can change the grouping of the report in:
[a] the Report Wizard.
[b] Print Preview.
[c] the Chart Wizard.
[d] the Summary Options dialog box.

5. Calculation fields use:
[a] advanced mathematical formulas.
[b] basic mathematical formulas.
[c] presorted fields.
[d] the results of a query.

6. To create a calculated field in a report:
[a] insert a chart from Microsoft Graph.
[b] change the properties of any control.
[c] include a calculated field in the underlying query.
[d] insert a calculated text box.

7. One of the properties you can set for a footer section is:
[a] Force New Page.
[b] Currency.
[c] Decimal Place.
[d] Chart Type.

8. To customize a footer, you must:
[a] be in the footer section of the report.
[b] create a custom report.
[c] delete all footer information.
[d] use a calculated field.

9. To create a chart report, you:
[a] use the AutoReport feature.
[b] use the Chart Wizard.
[c] enter the data that you want to use in the chart.
[d] draw the chart.

10. To modify a chart report, you:
[a] use the AutoReport feature.
[b] use the Chart Wizard.
[c] select Edit from the menu bar.
[d] right-click and select Chart Object, then Edit.

chapter thirteen

Circle **T** if the statement is true or **F** if the statement is false.

T F   1. Grouped reports are always based on queries.

T F   2. A grouped report separates the information into sections.

T F   3. Each control has its own properties tool.

T F   4. You can set different properties for each section of a report.

T F   5. When entering formulas in a calculated field, you must use standard mathematical operators.

T F   6. All formulas must begin with the equal sign (=) and all field names must appear in parentheses.

T F   7. A chart report shows information in the form of a Word table.

T F   8. You create a customized footer in the Detail section of the report.

T F   9. Once you create a chart, you can modify its elements, such as its heading, legend, size, and colors.

T F   10. A group is a collection of records, and includes a group header, detail records, and a group footer.

Skills Review

Exercise 1

1. If necessary, open the *mdbDynamicInc13* database.

2. Create a grouped report based on all the fields in qryCustomers Served.

3. Group the data by employee ID.

4. Show the sum for the order amount and calculate the percent of total for the sum. Use the Stepped layout and the Corporate style.

5. Save the report as rptCustomers Served.

6. Preview the report.

Exercise 2

1. If necessary, open the *mdbDynamicInc13* database.

2. In Design view, change the properties of the EmployeeID Footer in rptCustomers Served that you created in Exercise 1 in order to print one employee's data per page.

3. Save and print the report.

Exercise 3

1. If necessary, open the *mdbDynamicInc13* database.

2. In Design view, change the properties of the Grand Total control in the Report Footer of rptCustomers Served that you modified in Exercise 2 in order to boldface the total and display it in Arial instead of Times New Roman.

3. Rearrange and size the report labels and fields as necessary.

4. Save and print the report.

Exercise 4   ⓒ

1. If necessary, open the *mdbDynamicInc13* database.

2. In Design view, add a calculated text box to rptCustomers Served that you modified in Exercise 3 in order to calculate the average order amount for each employee. (*Hint:* Use =Avg as the function.) Format the calculated field for Currency. Modify label and field sizes and reposition them as necessary.

3. Save and print the report.

Exercise 5   ⓒ

1. If necessary, open the *mdbDynamicInc13* database.

2. In Design view, customize the page footer in rptCustomers Served that you modified in Exercise 4 in order to print *Dynamic Inc.* at the bottom of every page.

3. Save and print the report.

Exercise 6

1. If necessary, open the *mdbDynamicInc13* database.

2. Use the Chart Wizard to create a chart report based on qryCustomers Served. Use the Employee ID and Order Amount fields in the chart.

3. Choose the Column chart type.

4. Delete the suggested chart name, if necessary.

5. Save the chart as chtCustomers Served and close it.

Exercise 7

1. If necessary, open the *mdbDynamicInc13* database.

2. Open the chtCustomers Served report in Design view. Double-click the chart to open Microsoft Graph.

3. Add the title "Dynamic Customers" to chtCustomers Served using the Chart Options command on the Chart menu.

4. Format the title with 12 pt font using the Font Size button on the Formatting toolbar.

5. Close Microsoft Graph.

6. Save and print the chtCustomers Served report.

Exercise 8

1. If necessary, open the *mdbDynamicInc13* database.

2. Open the chtCustomers Served report in Design view.

3. Change the heading of the chtCustomers Served to Dynamic Inc. and format the label with 18 pt font. Size and position the label appropriately.

4. Save and print the chtCustomers Served report.

Case Projects

Project 1

Using the Office on the <u>W</u>eb command on the <u>H</u>elp menu, open the Microsoft home page and then link to pages that provide information about the topics covered in this chapter, such as grouped reports and charts. Print at least two of the Web pages.

Project 2

Using the Office on the <u>W</u>eb command on the <u>H</u>elp menu, open the Microsoft home page and then link to pages that provide information about Microsoft Graph. Print at least three or four pages that explain what Graph can do and how to use it.

Project 3

Alan Golden wants to display the Grand Total in rptMonthly Orders in blue if the number is positive, or in red if it is negative. You can do this by applying conditional formatting. Search the Access online Help for information on conditional formatting in reports. Then follow these instructions to format the Grand Total field to meet Alan's needs.

Project 4

Alan wants to add a background picture to rptCustomers Served modified in Exercise 5 so it looks like a watermark. Search the Access online Help for instructions on adding a background picture. Then use the *Watermark.bmp* file on the Data Disk to add a background picture to rptCustomers Served.

Project 5

Alan wants to set properties in rptMonthly Orders modified in Case Project 3 so that the information in a group always prints together, instead of possibly splitting across a page. You can set this property in the Sorting and Grouping box. Search the Access online Help for information about specifying how a group prints on a page. Then follow these instructions to set a property that keeps group information together in rptMonthly Orders.

Project 6

Alan wants to combine text values in rptCustomers Served modified in Case Project 4 so that the first and last name appear in one field. Search the Access online Help for instructions on combining text fields. Then follow these instructions to combine the first and last name fields in rptCustomers Served. (*Hint:* Don't delete the existing fields—hide them by changing their Visible property.)

Project 7

Apply what you learned in Project 2 about Microsoft Graph to the chart in rptOrders Chart. For example, change its format, the legend, colors, or the data on which the chart is based.

Project 8

Alan wants to print mailing labels with customer name and address. You can do this using the Label Wizard. Search the Access online Help for information about the Label Wizard. Then use it to print a report of mailing labels for customers based on tblCustomers.

Creating and Using Macros and Other Access Tools

Chapter Overview

In this chapter, you learn about macros, including when to create and use them. You create a simple macro, and then create a command button on a form and assign a macro to it. You also create a conditional macro to improve accuracy in forms. Finally, you protect your data with passwords and encryption.

Case profile

Dynamic Inc.'s managers have some ideas for working with the database more efficiently. Maria Moreno, Dynamic's owner, wants to display a welcome message to database users. Alan Golden, the sales manager, wants to make it easy for his staff to open a new form from the one they currently use. He also wants to display a reminder message so his staff doesn't forget to include crucial information. You can do all of this with macros. Finally, Maria asks you to protect the database's contents by setting a password and encrypting it.

LEARNING OBJECTIVES

- ► Understand macros
- ► Create a macro using the Macro Builder
- ► Create a command button
- ► Run macros using controls
- ► Create a conditional macro
- ► Set and modify a database password
- ► Encrypt and decrypt a database

chapter fourteen

14.a Understanding Macros

A **macro** is a set of one or more actions performing one or more operations. Macros help to make a database simpler and faster to manage because they automatically carry out tasks for you. Each task that you want Access to perform is called an **action**. When you create a macro in the Macro Design window, you select the actions you want Access to perform from a list. When you run the macro, Access performs these actions in the order you list them.

A macro can have many uses in Access. You can use a macro to open any table, send a report to the printer, or execute a select query or an action query. Other examples of macro uses include displaying informative messages or sounding a warning noise if you enter invalid data.

Maria wants to display a message welcoming users to the Dynamic database. You can do so by creating a macro to open a message box.

C 14.b Creating a Macro Using the Macro Builder

Create a simple macro in the Macro Design window and then test it to see how it runs. Start by creating a simple macro to open a message box displaying welcome text when you open the Dynamic database. Your first step is to open the macro window.

To open the macro window:

Step 1	*Open*	mdbDynamicInc14
Step 2	*Click*	Macros on the Objects bar
Step 3	*Click*	the New button ⏃ New on the Database toolbar

Your screen should look similar to Figure 14-1.

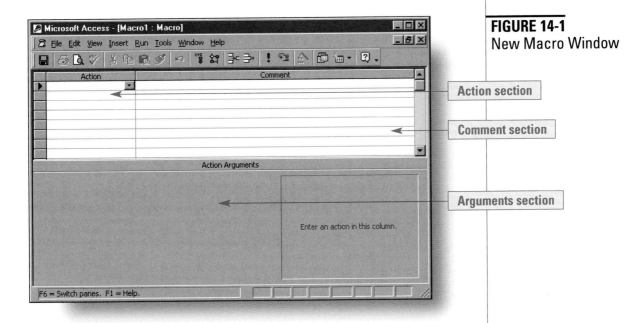

FIGURE 14-1
New Macro Window

Action section

Comment section

Arguments section

Notice the Macro window has three sections: Action, Comment, and Action Arguments. In the Action section, select the actions you want the macro to perform. Add notes about the action in the Comment section so others can understand the design and purpose of your macro. Enter settings, called **arguments**, in the Action Arguments section. Arguments give Access additional information on how to carry out an action, such as which object or data to use. Notice also the Help message box in the lower-right corner, which describes the action or action argument you choose.

Access includes many predefined macros that provide the basis for your own customized macros. To create the macro to display a message, use the MsgBox macro.

To begin creating a macro:

| Step 1 | *Click* | the list arrow in the first Action box |
| Step 2 | *Click* | MsgBox in the Action list |

As the Help message box indicates, use this action to display a warning or informational message. Notice that the Action Arguments section now displays text boxes. First, though, you want to describe your macro in the Comment section. It is always a good idea to be as specific as possible when inserting comments.

QUICK TIP

You can press the F6 key to move between the Action and Action Arguments sections.

chapter
fourteen

Step 3	*Click*	in the Comment text box
Step 4	*Key*	Greeting message
Step 5	*Click*	in the Message text box in the Action Arguments section
Step 6	*Key*	Welcome to the Dynamic Inc. Database

In the Beep text box, you can set a sound to play when the message is shown on the screen. In the Type text box, you can choose the type of message you want to display—a critical message, warning, or information. Maria wants a beep to sound, but doesn't want to restrict the message to a particular type, so you can keep the default options. Now you can name and save your macro.

To complete the macro:

Step 1	*Click*	File
Step 2	*Click*	Save As

Now you are prompted to name the macro.

Step 3	*Key*	mcrGreetingMessage in the Save Macro 'Macro1' To: text box
Step 4	*Click*	OK

After you save a macro, test it to see if it works correctly. Access lets you check each step of the macro process and helps you catch any errors.

Step 5	*Click*	Run on the menu bar
Step 6	*Click*	Single Step
Step 7	*Click*	the Run button [!] on the Macro Design toolbar

The Macro Single Step dialog box on your screen should look similar to Figure 14-2.

Step 8	*Click*	Step

MOUSE TIP

You can test a macro step-by-step by clicking the Single Step button on the Macro Design toolbar.

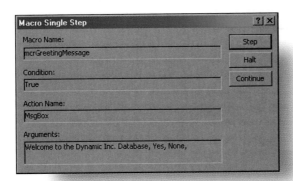

FIGURE 14-2
Macro Single Step
Dialog Box

You should now see the message box with the message "Welcome to the Dynamic Inc. Database" on your screen. The macro works.

Step 9	*Click*	OK

This closes the message box. If you defined more than one action in your macro, you return to the Macro Single Step dialog box for additional testing.

If you make an error in your macro, Access displays the Action Failed dialog box, which informs you which action caused the problem.

Step 10	*Click*	the Single Step button on the Macro Design toolbar to turn off the single step process
Step 11	*Close*	the Macro window

Now that you created a simple macro, you can create another, more complex one that runs when you click a button in a form.

14.c Creating a Command Button

A **command button** is a button that carries out a macro action or event procedure. An **event procedure** is a Visual Basic procedure that runs when an event occurs on a form. You can use the Command Button Wizard to guide you through the steps of creating a command button and using an event procedure. You can also use the Command Button Wizard to create a command button to which you later assign to a macro.

Alan and his sales staff want to make the database easier to navigate. In particular, they want to be able to click a button on the frmCustomers form to open the frmOrder Details form. You can do this by adding a command button to the frmCustomers form and then assigning a macro to it.

**chapter
fourteen**

To begin creating a command button:

Step 1	**Click**	Forms ⊞ on the Objects bar
Step 2	**Double-click**	frmCustomers
Step 3	**Switch**	to Design view
Step 4	**Click**	the Control Wizard button ⬚ on the Toolbox, if necessary, to select it
Step 5	**Click**	the Command Button ⬚ on the Toolbox
Step 6	**Click**	an open area in the Detail section

You can move the command button later, after you create it. The Command Button Wizard dialog box on your screen should look similar to Figure 14-3.

FIGURE 14-3
Command Button Wizard
Dialog Box

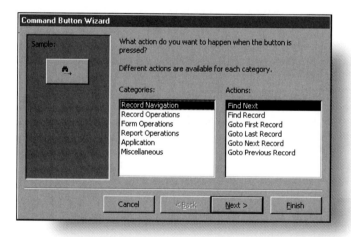

The **Command Button Wizard** guides you through the steps of creating a command button and the action you want it to perform. In the first dialog box, you want to select the Forms Operations category because you want to perform an action involving a form.

To use the Command Button Wizard:

Step 1	**Click**	Form Operations in the Categories: list box
Step 2	**Click**	Open Form in the Actions: list box
Step 3	**Click**	Next >
Step 4	**Click**	frmOrder Details to select it as the form the command button opens

Step 5	*Click*	N̲ext >

Now you need to determine if you want the form to open showing all records or only specific data. You want the form to show all records, the default option.

Step 6	*Click*	N̲ext >

Now you can specify the text or picture you want to show on the button. Alan doesn't want to use a picture for this command button, but he does want text to appear on the button.

Step 7	*Click*	in the Text: text box
Step 8	*Delete*	the existing text
Step 9	*Key*	Order Details
Step 10	*Click*	N̲ext >

You are now prompted to name the button. It is always a good idea to provide a meaningful name to the button for future reference.

Step 11	*Key*	New Customer Order
Step 12	*Click*	F̲inish

Your screen should now look similar to Figure 14-4.

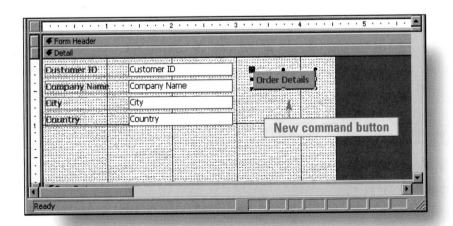

FIGURE 14-4
Form with Command Button

Now that you created the command button, you can assign a macro to it. Then, when you click the command button, frmOrder Details opens.

chapter
fourteen

14.d Running Macros Using Controls

You can run macros using controls, such as a command button. Alan created the open order form macro, called mcrOpen Orders. You now need to assign this macro to the command button you added to frmCustomers.

To assign a macro to a command button:

Step 1	*Right-click*	the Order Details command button
Step 2	*Click*	<u>P</u>roperties
Step 3	*Click*	the Event tab

Your screen should look similar to Figure 14-5.

FIGURE 14-5
Command Button
Properties

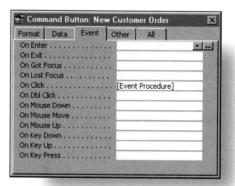

You want the macro to be activated by clicking the command button. You therefore need to select the mcrOpen Orders macro in the On Click text box.

Step 4	*Click*	in the On Click field
Step 5	*Click*	mcrOpen Orders from the list
Step 6	*Close*	the Properties dialog box

You can now test the command button and macro.

Step 7	*Switch*	to Form view

| Step 8 | *Click* | the Order Details command button |

Your screen should look similar to Figure 14-6.

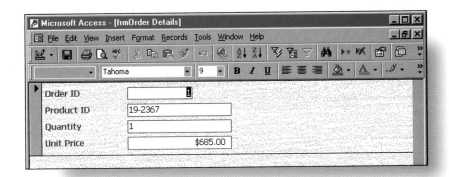

FIGURE 14-6
frmOrder Details

| Step 9 | *Close* | frmOrder Details |
| Step 10 | *Close* | frmCustomers, saving your changes |

Now Alan wants to create a macro that displays a reminder message if his staff forgets to add Product ID information. You can do this by creating a conditional macro.

14.e Creating a Conditional Macro

At times, you may want to create a **conditional macro**, in which the action takes place only if certain conditions apply. Alan finds that his staff often bypasses the Product ID field in the frmOrders form. He wants to display a message reminding them to enter the Product ID code. To do so, create a conditional macro, where the macro action takes place if certain conditions are met.

To create a conditional macro:

| Step 1 | *Click* | Macros 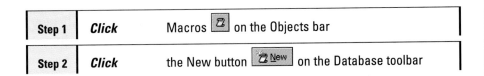 on the Objects bar |
| Step 2 | *Click* | the New button on the Database toolbar |

You see the Macro Design window.

| Step 3 | *Click* | the Conditions button 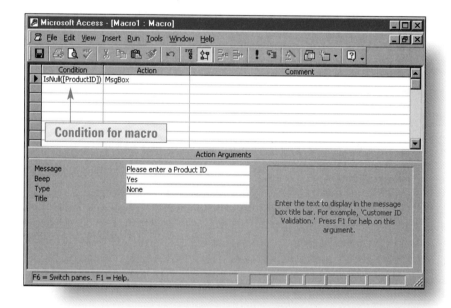 on the Macro Design toolbar |
| Step 4 | *Key* | IsNull([ProductID]) in the first Conditions field |

This condition means that if the value in the ProductID field is null—if there's no value in the field—then Access should run the actions you specify.

Step 5	*Click*	the list arrow in the first Action field
Step 6	*Click*	MsgBox from the list
Step 7	*Click*	in the Message field in the Action Arguments section
Step 8	*Key*	Please enter a Product ID

Your screen should look similar to Figure 14-7.

FIGURE 14-7
Conditional Macro in
Macro Design Window

If the value in the ProductID field is null, Access should now display the message "Please enter a Product ID." You now need to save the conditional macro.

To save the conditional macro:

| Step 1 | *Click* | File |

Step 2	*Click*	Save <u>A</u>s
Step 3	*Key*	mcrProduct ID Reminder
Step 4	*Click*	OK to close the Save As dialog box
Step 5	*Close*	the Macro Design window

Now you need to assign the macro and then test it.
To assign and run the macro:

Step 1	*Click*	Forms ▣ on the Objects bar
Step 2	*Double-click*	frmOrders
Step 3	*Switch*	to Design view
Step 4	*Right-click*	the ProductID field
Step 5	*Click*	Properties
Step 6	*Click*	the Event tab, if necessary
Step 7	*Click*	in the On Exit field and click the list arrow
Step 8	*Click*	mcrProduct ID Reminder

This means that when the user exits the Product ID field, if they
have not entered a value, Access runs mcrProduct ID Reminder.

Step 9	*Close*	the Properties dialog box
Step 10	*Switch*	to Form view
Step 11	*Press*	the TAB key until you exit from the Product ID field without entering a value

You see a message reminding you to enter a Product ID.

| Step 12 | *Click* | OK to clear the message |
| Step 13 | *Close* | frmOrders, saving your changes |

Now that the Dynamic database is working effectively, Maria wants
to protect its data with passwords and encryption.

**chapter
fourteen**

14.f Setting and Modifying a Database Password

You can protect the data in your database by adding a database password. That way, when you try to open a database, Access first asks you for the password. If you enter the password correctly, Access opens the database. If you enter an invalid password, the database remains closed. Be sure to make a backup copy of the database before you set a password. Also write down your password and store it in a safe place—if you lose or forget your password, it can't be recovered, and you won't be able to open your database.

Maria wants to protect the data in the Dynamic database by adding a password. She wants to use a password that's easy to remember, but that no one outside of Dynamic could guess. She chooses "Vanhise," the name of Dynamic's founder. Maria also wants you to show her how to modify and remove a password, if necessary.

Before you add a database password, you must open it exclusively so that Access knows you are the only one using the database.

To open a database exclusively:

Step 1	*Close*	*mdbDynamicInc14*
Step 2	*Click*	File
Step 3	*Click*	Open

You see the Open dialog box. Look for the Open button in the lower-right corner of the dialog box. You need to choose an option from its drop-down list.

Step 4	*Click*	*mdbDynamicInc14*
Step 5	*Click*	the list arrow next to the Open button
Step 6	*Click*	Open Exclusive

The *mdbDynamicInc14* database opens.

Step 7	*Click*	Tools on the menu bar
Step 8	*Point to*	Security
Step 9	*Click*	Set Database Password

The Set Database Password dialog box on your screen should look similar to Figure 14-8.

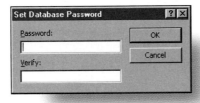

FIGURE 14-8
Set Database Password
Dialog Box

You are now ready to set the password.
To set a database password:

Step 1	*Key*	Vanhise in the <u>P</u>assword: text box
Step 2	*Key*	Vanhise in the <u>V</u>erify: box
Step 3	*Click*	OK
Step 4	*Close*	the database

This sets the password to "Vanhise." The next time you or any other user opens the database, you see a dialog box requesting the password.

Step 1	*Open*	*mdbDynamicInc14* exclusively

You see the Password Required dialog box.

Step 2	*Key*	Vanhise in the <u>P</u>assword: text box
Step 3	*Click*	OK

Now that the password is set, Maria wants you to show her how to remove it. Remember that you must open a database exclusively before you work with passwords. The *mdbDynamicInc14* database is still open exclusively, so you are now able to remove the password.

CAUTION TIP

Passwords are **case sensitive**, meaning users must enter upper- and lowercase letters exactly as you do when you set the password.

QUICK TIP

C You can use Access's Replication commands to create replicas of your database as well as synchronize them on demand. For example, you can create anonymous replicas for Internet applications, which will maintain the security of the original database.

chapter
fourteen

To remove a database password:

Step 1	*Click*	Tools on the menu bar
Step 2	*Point to*	Security
Step 3	*Click*	Unset Database Password

You see the Unset Database Password dialog box.

Step 4	*Key*	Vanhise
Step 5	*Click*	OK

This removes the database password. After considering the password, Maria decides it may be too easy for an outsider to guess. She wants to change it to "vanHiSe," which is harder to enter randomly.
To modify a database password:

Step 6	*Repeat*	the method learned earlier in this section to set and then remove the password "vanHISe"

After learning about passwords, Maria wants to encrypt the Dynamic database for extra protection.

14.g Encrypting and Decrypting a Database

When Access **encrypts** a database, it compacts the database file and makes it indecipherable by a utility program or word processor. This protects sensitive data, such as salary information, from anyone who tries to open the database without Access.

Maria wants to encrypt the Dynamic database to protect its data. Then she wants you to show her how to **decrypt** it by reversing the encryption.

To encrypt a database:

Step 1	*Close*	mdbDynamicInc14
Step 2	*Click*	Tools
Step 3	*Point to*	Security

Step 4	*Click*	Encrypt/Decrypt Database

You see the Encrypt/Decrypt Database dialog box, which looks much like a standard Open or Save dialog box.

Step 5	*Click*	mdbDynamicInc14 as the database you want to encrypt
Step 6	*Click*	OK

You see the Encrypt Database As dialog box.

Step 7	*Select*	mdbDynamicInc14 as the name for the encrypted database
Step 8	*Click*	Save
Step 9	*Click*	Yes to replace the existing file

Now Maria wants you to show her how to decrypt the database. You follow the same basic steps as you did when you encrypted it.

To decrypt a database:

Step 1	*Use*	Steps 1–9 above as your guide to decrypt the mdbDynamicInc14 database
Step 2	*Exit*	Access

You have completed modifying the Dynamic database so that the staff can use it more efficiently and accurately. Maria personally thanks you for your help.

CAUTION TIP

You can only encrypt or decrypt a database when it's closed.

If you specify the same name, drive, and folder as the original database, Access automatically replaces the original file with the encrypted one. You can create the encrypted file in another location or with a different name if you want to maintain your original, unencrypted copy.

**chapter
fourteen**

Summary

▶ A macro is a set of one or more actions performing one or more operations.

▶ The Macro window has three sections: Action, Comment, and Action Arguments. In the Action section, select the actions you want the macro to perform. Add notes about the action in the Comment section so others can understand the design and purpose of your macro. Enter settings, called arguments, in the Action Arguments section. Arguments give Access additional information on how to carry out an action, such as which object or data to use.

▶ Access includes many predefined macros that provide the basis for your own customized macros.

▶ After you save a macro, test it to see if it works correctly. Access lets you check each step of the macro process and helps you catch any errors using the Single Step feature.

▶ A command button is a button that carries out a macro action or event procedure. An event procedure is a Visual Basic procedure that runs when an event occurs on a form. You can use the Command Button Wizard to guide you through the steps of creating a command button and using an event procedure. You can also use the Command Button Wizard to create a command button to which you later assign a macro.

▶ You can create a conditional macro, in which the action takes place only if certain conditions apply.

▶ You can protect the data in your database by adding a database password. Be sure to make a backup copy of the database before you set a password and to write down your password and store it in a safe place—if you lose or forget your password, it can't be recovered, and you won't be able to open your database.

▶ Passwords are case sensitive, meaning users must enter upper and lowercase letters exactly as you do when you set the password.

▶ When Access encrypts a database, it compacts the database file and makes it indecipherable by a utility program or word processor. Decrypting reverses the encryption.

Commands Review

Action	Menu Bar	Shortcut Menu	Toolbar	Keyboard
Display the property sheet	View, Properties	Properties		ALT + V, P
Select multiple controls	Edit, Select All		Drag around all the controls you want to select	Shift + Click each control you want to select ALT + E, A

Concepts Review

SCANS

Circle the correct answer.

1. A macro is a:
[a] larger way of looking at the database.
[b] control you can add to a form.
[c] set of actions performing one or more operations.
[d] way to protect the data in your database.

2. Each task that you want Access to perform in a macro is called a(n):
[a] action.
[b] macro step.
[c] event procedure.
[d] command.

3. The advantage of using macros is that they:
[a] take the place of long queries.
[b] prevent unauthorized users from opening your database.
[c] provide a way to comment about the data in your database.
[d] automatically carry out tasks for you.

4. You can include arguments in a macro to:
[a] give Access additional information on how to carry out an action.
[b] describe the actions you choose.
[c] perform calculations.
[d] define the three sections of the Macro Design window.

5. Access provides many predefined macros so you can:
[a] perform calculations.
[b] customize your own macros.
[c] test an action.
[d] save them all in the Database window.

6. You can assign a macro to:
[a] any database objects except forms.
[b] a condition.
[c] a command button.
[d] a message box.

7. When you create a conditional macro:
[a] Access performs the action only if specified conditions apply.
[b] it creates a null value in a field.
[c] you can click a button on one form to open another form.
[d] Access retrieves only those records that meet the conditions.

8. Use a database password to:
[a] back up your data.
[b] protect your data.
[c] close your database.
[d] allow case-sensitive data.

9. Before you can assign a database password, you must:
[a] open the database exclusively.
[b] close the database.
[c] compact the database.
[d] encrypt the database.

10. When Access encrypts a database, it compacts the database and:
[a] assigns a password.
[b] archives the data.
[c] makes it indecipherable by another version of Access.
[d] makes it indecipherable by a utility program or word processor.

chapter fourteen

Circle **T** if the statement is true or **F** if the statement is false.

T   F   1. Once you encrypt a database, you cannot reverse the encryption.

T   F   2. If you lose or forget a password, Access provides another one for you.

T   F   3. You can use the Command Button Wizard to create a command button and set the action you want it to perform.

T   F   4. You can enter the password "PASS" as "pass" or as "Pass."

T   F   5. You can create macros to help users remember to enter data in fields.

T   F   6. If you test a macro before you save it, you may lose valuable data.

T   F   7. Macros automatically perform tasks for you.

T   F   8. You can use the Macro Wizard to create a macro.

T   F   9. You can use a macro to open a table or perform a query.

T   F   10. When you add a database password, you must enter it before you open a report or form.

Skills Review

SCANS

Exercise 1

1. If necessary, open the *mdbDynamicInc14* database.

2. Create a macro that displays a warning when someone opens the frmOrders form. The warning should say "Warning. Only authorized employees can use this form."

3. Save the macro as mcrOrders Warning, and then close the macro.

4. Open frmOrders in Design view. Choose mcrOrders Warning in the On Open property list box for the whole frmOrders form.

5. Save and close the form.

6. Open the frmOrders form to test the macro, and then close the form.

Exercise 2

1. If necessary, open the *mdbDynamicInc14* database.

2. Create a macro to open the frmCustomers form. Choose OpenForm as the action, and frmCustomers as the name of the form.

3. Save the macro as mcrOpen Customers, test the macro, and then close the macro.

4. Open *frmOrders* in Design view. Choose mcrOpen Customers in the On Close property list box for the whole frmOrders form.

5. Save and close the form.

6. Open the frmOrders form, and then exit from it to test the macro.

7. Close the frmCustomers form.

Exercise 3

1. If necessary, open the *mdbDynamicInc14* database.

2. Open frmOrders in Design view, and create a Form Operations command button to open the frmCustomers form and show all the records.

3. Add the text "Customer Form" to the button.

4. Assign the mcrOpen Customers macro to the command button.

5. Save the form and open it in Form view to test the command button.

6. Close all open forms.

Exercise 4

1. If necessary, open the *mdbDynamicInc14* database.

2. Create a macro named mcrPrint to print out all of the active database objects.

3. Open frmOrder Details in Design view. Use the Command Button Wizard to create a command button. Select the Form Operations and Print Current Form options in the Wizard step 1. Show a picture of a printer on the button. Name the button Print Form and assign the mcrPrint macro to the button.

4. Save the form and then open the form in Form view and test the button.

5. Close the frmOrder Details form.

Exercise 5 `C`

1. Open the *mdbDynamicInc14* database using the Open Exclusive option.

2. Add *access* as the database password.

3. Close *mdbDynamicInc14*.

4. Open the database again and enter the correct password.

Exercise 6 `C`

1. Open the *mdbDynamicInc14* database using the Open Exclusive option.

2. Remove the password from the database.

3. Close *mdbDynamicInc14*.

4. Open the database again without a password and then close it.

Exercise 7 `C`

1. Encrypt the *mdbDynamicInc14* database as *mdbDynamic14Encrypted*.

2. Open the *mdbDynamic14Encrypted* database and then close it.

chapter fourteen

Case Projects

Project 1

Using the Office on the <u>W</u>eb command on the <u>H</u>elp menu, open the Microsoft home page, and then link to pages that provide information about the topics covered in this chapter, such as macros and database security. Print at least two of the Web pages.

Project 2

Connect to your ISP and load the home page for a search engine. Search for an online computer dictionary or encyclopedia and find definitions for terms covered in this chapter, such as *macro, argument, encryption,* and *case sensitivity.* Print at least two definitions or explanations. Close the browser and disconnect from your ISP.

Project 3

Maria Moreno wants to activate certain options when users start Access. She wants to show *Dynamic Database* in the title bar of the Database window, and she wants frmCustomers to open automatically. Use the *mdbDynamicInc14Encrypted* database you created in Exercise 7. To set these startup options, click Startup on the Tools menu. In the Application Title box, enter *Dynamic Database*. In the Display Form/Page box, click frmCustomers.

Project 4

Maria also wants to know if the performance of *mdbDynamicInc14Encrypted* is optimal. To analyze all the tables in the database, use an Access Add-in called Analyzer. On the Tools menu, point to Analyze, and then click Performance. Click the Tables tab. Click the check box to select each table, and then click OK. Review all the recommendations and suggestions, and then close the Performance Analyzer.

Project 5

Alan Golden, the sales manager, often travels on business and wants to use the Dynamic database. You can replicate the database so Alan can take it with him. Open the *mdbDynamicInc14Encrypted* database you modified in Case Project 3. On the Tools menu, point to Replication, and then click Replica. Click Yes to close the database, and then click Yes again to make a backup of the database. Select location options, name the database *mdbDynamicInc14Replica,* and then click OK to replicate the database.

Project 6

Maria wants a diagram showing how the tables in *mdbDynamicInc14* are related. You can do this by printing the relationships. Search the Access online Help for instructions on printing database relationships. Then follow these instructions to do so.

Project 7

Maria is concerned that *mdbDynamicInc14* is taking up too much disk space. You can compact the database to save room. Search the Access online Help for instructions on compacting a database. Then follow these instructions to compact *mdbDynamicInc14*.

Project 8

Maria also wants general reference information about *mdbDynamicInc14*, including all the properties in the forms and their controls. You can provide this information by using the Documenter Analyzer. On the Tools menu, point to Analyze, and then click Documenter. Click the All Object Types tab, and then click Select All. Click OK to analyze the database.

Working with Windows 98

T Appendix Overview

The Windows 98 operating system creates a workspace on your computer screen, called the desktop. The desktop is a graphical environment that contains icons you click with the mouse pointer to access your computer system resources or to perform a task such as opening a software application. This appendix introduces you to the Windows 98 desktop by describing the default desktop icons and showing how to access your computer resources, use menu commands and toolbar buttons to perform a task, and select dialog box options.

LEARNING OBJECTIVES

- ► Review the Windows 98 desktop
- ► Access your computer system resources
- ► Use menu commands and toolbar buttons
- ► Use the Start menu
- ► Review dialog box options
- ► Use Windows 98 shortcuts
- ► Understand the Recycle Bin
- ► Shut down Windows 98

A appendix

A.a Reviewing the Windows 98 Desktop

Whenever you start your computer, the Windows 98 operating system automatically starts and the Windows 98 desktop appears on your screen. To view the Windows 98 desktop:

| Step 1 | **Turn on** | your computer and monitor |
| Step 2 | **Observe** | the Windows 98 desktop, as shown in Figure A-1 |

FIGURE A-1
Windows 98 Desktop

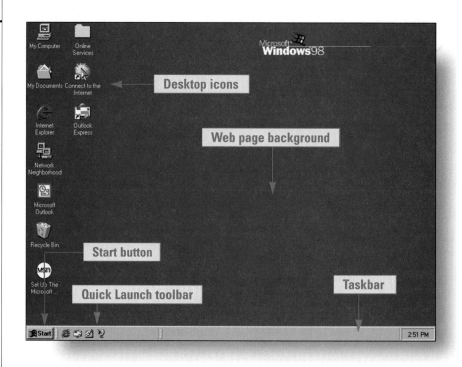

The Windows 98 desktop contains three elements: icons, background, and taskbar. The icons represent Windows objects and shortcuts to opening software applications or performing tasks. Table A-1 describes some of the default icons. By default, the background is Web-page style. The taskbar, at the bottom of the window, contains the Start button and the Quick Launch toolbar. The icon types and arrangement, desktop background, or Quick Launch toolbar on your screen might be different.

The Start button displays the Start menu, which you can use to perform tasks. By default, the taskbar also contains the **Quick Launch toolbar**, which has shortcuts to open Internet Explorer Web browser, Outlook Express e-mail software, and Internet channels, as well as to switch between the desktop and open application windows. You can customize the Quick Launch toolbar to include other toolbars.

Icon	Name	Description
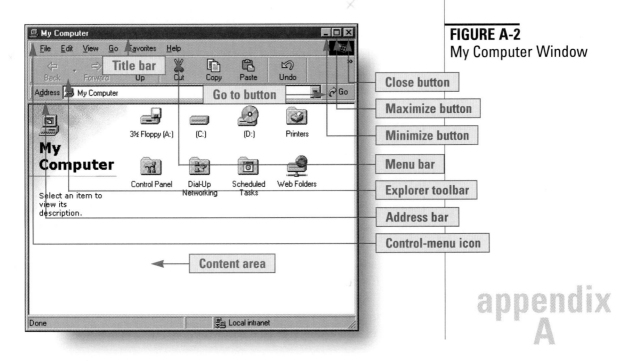	My Computer	Provides access to computer system resources
	My Documents	Stores Office 2000 documents (by default)
	Internet Explorer	Opens Internet Explorer Web browser
	Microsoft Outlook	Opens Outlook 2000 information manager software
	Recycle Bin	Temporarily stores folders and files deleted from the hard drive
	Network Neighborhood	Provides access to computers and printers networked in your workgroup

TABLE A-1
Common Desktop Icons

A.b Accessing Your Computer System Resources

The My Computer window provides access to your computer system resources. To open the My Computer window:

Step 1	**Point to**	the My Computer icon on the desktop
Step 2	**Observe**	a brief description of the icon in the ScreenTip
Step 3	**Double-click**	the My Computer icon to open the My Computer window shown in Figure A-2

FIGURE A-2
My Computer Window

appendix
A

A window is a rectangular area on your screen in which you view operating system options or a software application, such as Internet Explorer. Windows 98 has some common window elements. The **title bar**, at the top of the window, includes the window's Control-menu icon, the window name, and the Minimize, Restore (or Maximize), and Close buttons. The **Control-menu icon**, in the upper-left corner of the window, accesses the Control menu that contains commands for moving, restoring, sizing, minimizing, maximizing, and closing the window. The **Minimize** button, near the upper-right corner of the window, reduces the window to a taskbar button. The **Maximize** button, to the right of the Minimize button, enlarges the window to fill the entire screen viewing area above the taskbar. If the window is already maximized, the Restore button appears in its place. The **Restore** button reduces the window size. The **Close** button, in the upper-right corner, closes the window. To maximize the My Computer window:

| Step 1 | *Click* | the Maximize button ▣ on the My Computer window title bar |
| Step 2 | *Observe* | that the My Computer window completely covers the desktop |

When you want to leave a window open, but do not want to see it on the desktop, you can minimize it. To minimize the My Computer window:

| Step 1 | *Click* | the Minimize button ▬ on the My Computer window title bar |
| Step 2 | *Observe* | the My Computer button added to the taskbar |

The minimized window is still open but not occupying space on the desktop. To view the My Computer window and then restore it to a smaller size:

Step 1	*Click*	the My Computer button on the taskbar to view the window
Step 2	*Click*	the Restore button ▤ on the My Computer title bar
Step 3	*Observe*	that the My Computer window is reduced to a smaller window on the desktop

You can move and size a window with the mouse pointer. To move the My Computer window:

| Step 1 | *Position* | the mouse pointer on the My Computer title bar |

| Step 2 | *Drag* | the window down and to the right approximately ½ inch |
| Step 3 | *Drag* | the window back to the center of the screen |

Several Windows 98 windows—My Computer, My Documents, and Windows Explorer—have the same menu bar and toolbar features. These windows are sometimes called **Explorer-style windows**. When you size an Explorer-style window too small to view all its icons, a vertical or horizontal scroll bar may appear. A scroll bar includes scroll arrows and a scroll box for viewing different parts of the window contents.

To size the My Computer window:

Step 1	*Position*	the mouse pointer on the lower-right corner of the window
Step 2	*Observe*	that the mouse pointer becomes a black, double-headed sizing pointer
Step 3	*Drag*	the lower-right corner boundary diagonally up approximately ½ inch and release the mouse button
Step 4	*Click*	the right scroll arrow on the horizontal scroll bar to view hidden icons
Step 5	*Size*	the window twice as large to remove the horizontal scroll bar

You can open the window associated with any icon in the My Computer window by double-clicking it. Explorer-style windows open in the same window, not separate windows. To open the Control Panel Explorer-style window:

| Step 1 | *Double-click* the Control Panel icon |
| Step 2 | *Observe* | that the Address bar displays the Control Panel icon and name, and the content area displays the Control Panel icons for accessing computer system resources |

A.c Using Menu Commands and Toolbar Buttons

You can click a menu command or toolbar button to perform specific tasks in a window. The **menu bar** is a special toolbar located below the window title bar that contains the File, Edit, View, Go, Favorites, and Help menus. The **toolbar**, located below the menu bar, contains shortcut "buttons" you click with the mouse pointer to execute a variety of commands. You can use the Back and Forward

appendix
A

QUICK TIP

You can use Start menu commands to create or open Office 2000 documents, connect to the Microsoft Web site to download operating system updates, open software applications, open a favorite folder or file, or open one of the last fifteen documents you worked on. You can also change the Windows 98 settings, search for files, folders, and resources on the Internet, get online Help, run software applications, log off a network, and shut down Windows 98.

buttons on the Explorer toolbar or the <u>B</u>ack or <u>F</u>orward commands on the <u>G</u>o menu to switch between My Computer and the Control Panel. To view My Computer:

Step 1	*Click*	the Back button ⬅ on the Explorer toolbar to view My Computer
Step 2	*Click*	the Forward button ➡ on the Explorer toolbar to view the Control Panel
Step 3	*Click*	<u>G</u>o on the menu bar
Step 4	*Click*	the My <u>C</u>omputer command to view My Computer
Step 5	*Click*	the Close button ✕ on the My Computer window title bar

A.d Using the Start Menu

The **Start button** on the taskbar opens the Start menu. You use this menu to access several Windows 98 features and to open software applications, such as Word or Excel. To open the Start menu:

| Step 1 | *Click* | the Start button 🏁Start on the taskbar to open the Start menu (see Figure A-3) |

FIGURE A-3
Start Menu

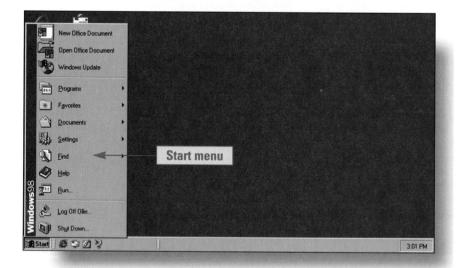

| Step 2 | *Point to* | <u>P</u>rograms to view the software applications installed on your computer |
| Step 3 | *Click* | the desktop outside the Start menu and <u>P</u>rograms menu to close them |

A.e Reviewing Dialog Box Options

A **dialog box** is a window that contains options you can select, turn on, or turn off to perform a task. To view a dialog box:

Step 1	*Click*	the Start button [Start] on the taskbar
Step 2	*Point to*	Settings
Step 3	*Point to*	Active Desktop
Step 4	*Click*	Customize my Desktop to open the Display Properties dialog box
Step 5	*Click*	the Effects tab (see Figure A-4)

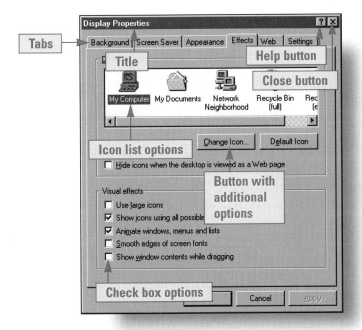

FIGURE A-4
Effects Tab in the Display Properties Dialog Box

Step 6	*Click*	each tab and observe the different options available *(do not change any options unless directed by your instructor)*
Step 7	*Right-click*	each option on each tab and then click What's This? to view its ScreenTip
Step 8	*Click*	Cancel to close the dialog box without changing any options

appendix
A

QUICK TIP

Many of the Windows 98 shortcuts are also available in Windows 95 and NT 4.0 if you have Internet Explorer 4.0 or later and Windows Desktop Update installed.

MOUSE TIP

One way to speed up tasks is to single-click (rather than double-click) a desktop icon just like you single-click a Web page hyperlink. You can create a Web-style, single-click environment by opening the Folder Options dialog box from the View menu in any Windows 98 Explorer-style window or from the Settings command on the Start menu. The Web Style option adds an underline to icon titles, similar to a hyperlink.

A.f Using Windows 98 Shortcuts

You can use the drag-and-drop method to reposition or remove Start menu commands. You can also right-drag a Start menu command to the desktop to create a desktop shortcut. To reposition the Windows Update item on the Start menu:

Step 1	*Click*	the Start button [Start] on the taskbar
Step 2	*Point to*	the Windows Update item
Step 3	*Drag*	the Windows Update item to the top of the Start menu

To remove the Windows Update shortcut from the Start menu and create a desktop shortcut:

Step 1	*Drag*	the Windows Update item to the desktop
Step 2	*Observe*	that the desktop shortcut appears after a few seconds
Step 3	*Verify*	that the Windows Update item no longer appears on the Start menu

To add a Windows Update shortcut back to the Start menu and delete the desktop shortcut:

Step 1	*Drag*	the Windows Update shortcut to the Start button [Start] on the taskbar and then back to its original position when the Start menu appears
Step 2	*Close*	the Start menu
Step 3	*Drag*	the Windows Update shortcut on the desktop to the Recycle Bin
Step 4	*Click*	Yes

You can close multiple application windows at one time from the taskbar using the CTRL key and a shortcut menu. To open two applications and then use the taskbar to close them:

| Step 1 | *Open* | the Word and Excel applications (in this order) from the Programs menu on the Start menu |

Step 2	*Observe*	the Word and Excel buttons on the taskbar (Excel is the selected, active button)
Step 3	*Press & Hold*	the CTRL key
Step 4	*Click*	the Word application taskbar button (the Excel application taskbar button is already selected)
Step 5	*Release*	the CTRL key
Step 6	*Right-click*	the Word or Excel taskbar button
Step 7	*Click*	Close to close both applications

You can use the drag-and-drop method to add a shortcut to the Quick Launch toolbar for folders and documents you have created. To create a new subfolder in the My Documents folder.

Step 1	*Click*	the My Documents icon on the desktop to open the window
Step 2	*Right-click*	the contents area (but not a file or folder)
Step 3	*Point to*	New
Step 4	*Click*	Folder
Step 5	*Key*	Example
Step 6	*Press*	the ENTER key to name the folder
Step 7	*Drag*	the Example folder to the end of the Quick Launch toolbar (a black vertical line indicates the drop position)
Step 8	*Observe*	the new icon on the toolbar
Step 9	*Close*	the My Documents window
Step 10	*Position*	the mouse pointer on the Example folder shortcut on the Quick Launch toolbar and observe the ScreenTip

You remove a shortcut from the Quick Launch toolbar by dragging it to the desktop and deleting it, or dragging it directly to the Recycle Bin. To remove the Example folder shortcut and delete the folder:

Step 1	*Drag*	the Example folder icon to the Recycle Bin
Step 2	*Click*	Yes
Step 3	*Open*	the My Documents window
Step 4	*Delete*	the Example folder icon using the shortcut menu
Step 5	*Close*	the My Documents window

CAUTION TIP

Selecting items in a single-click environment requires some practice. To **select** (or highlight) one item, simply point to the item. *Be careful not to click the item; clicking the item opens it.*

You can use the SHIFT + Click and CTRL + Click commands in the single-click environment. Simply *point to* the first item. Then press and hold the SHIFT or CTRL key and *point to* the last item or the next item to be selected.

MENU TIP

In the Windows environment, clicking the right mouse button displays a **shortcut menu** of the most commonly used commands for the item you right-clicked. For example, you can use a shortcut menu to open applications from the Programs submenu. You can right-drag to move, copy, or create desktop shortcuts from Start menu commands.

appendix
A

A.g Understanding the Recycle Bin

The **Recycle Bin** is an object that temporarily stores folders, files, and shortcuts you delete from your hard drive. If you accidentally delete an item, you can restore it to its original location on your hard drive if it is still in the Recycle Bin. Because the Recycle Bin takes up disk space you should review and empty it regularly. When you empty the Recycle Bin, its contents are removed from your hard drive and can no longer be restored.

A.h Shutting Down Windows 98

It is very important that you follow the proper procedures for shutting down the Windows 98 operating system when you are finished, to allow the operating system to complete its internal "housekeeping" properly. To shut down Windows 98 correctly:

| Step 1 | *Click* | the Start button [Start] on the taskbar |
| Step 2 | *Click* | Shut Down to open the Shut Down Windows dialog box shown in Figure A-5 |

FIGURE A-5
Shut Down Windows
Dialog Box

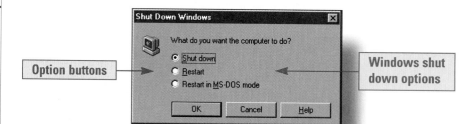

Option buttons

Windows shut down options

You can shut down completely, restart, and restart in MS-DOS mode from this dialog box. You want to shut down completely.

| Step 3 | *Click* | the Shut down option button to select it, if necessary |
| Step 4 | *Click* | OK |

Managing Your Folders and Files Using Windows Explorer

Appendix Overview

Windows Explorer provides tools for managing your folders and files. This appendix introduces the Windows Explorer options of expanding and collapsing the folder view, creating new folders, renaming folders and files, deleting folders and files, and creating desktop shortcuts.

appendix

notes The default Windows 98 Custom folder options are used in the hands-on activities and figures. If you are using the Windows 95 operating system, your instructor will modify the hands-on activities and your screen will look different.

B.a Opening Windows Explorer

You can open Windows Explorer from the Programs command on the Start menu or from a shortcut menu. To open Windows Explorer using a shortcut menu:

Step 1	*Right-Click*	the Start button [Start] on the taskbar
Step 2	*Click*	Explore
Step 3	*Maximize*	the Windows Explorer window, if necessary (see Figure B-1)

FIGURE B-1
Windows Explorer Window

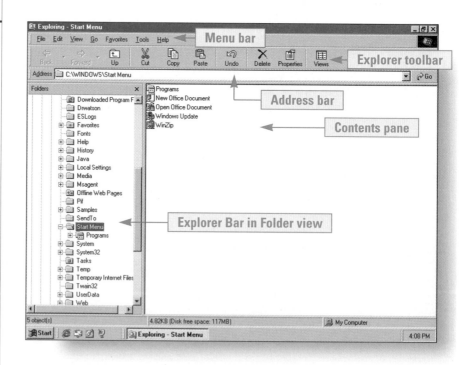

QUICK TIP

You can also use the My Computer Explorer-style window to manage your files and folders. If you are using Windows 95, the list of disk drives and folders is called the **Tree pane**.

The window below the menu bar, toolbar, and Address bar is divided into two panes: The **Explorer Bar** on the left shows the computer's organizational structure, including all desktop objects, My Computer objects, and the disk drive folders. The **Contents pane** on the right shows all subfolders and files for the folder selected in the Explorer Bar. The panes are divided by a **separator bar** that you drag left or right to resize the panes.

B.b Reviewing Windows Explorer Options

You can view disk drive icons, folders, and files (called **objects**) for your computer by selecting an item from the Address bar list or by clicking an object in the Explorer Bar. To view all your computer's disk drives and system folders:

Step 1	*Click*	the Address bar list arrow
Step 2	*Click*	My Computer to view a list of disk drives and system folders in the Contents pane
Step 3	*Click*	the (C:) disk drive object in the Explorer Bar to view a list of folders (stored on the C:\ drive) in the Contents pane

You can expand or collapse the view of folders and other objects in the Explorer Bar. To collapse the view of the C:\ drive in the Explorer Bar:

Step 1	*Click*	the minus sign (–) to the left of the (C:) disk drive object in the Explorer Bar
Step 2	*Observe*	that the C:\ drive folders list is hidden and the minus sign becomes a plus sign (+)
Step 3	*Click*	the plus sign (+) to the left of the (C:) disk drive object in the Explorer Bar
Step 4	*Observe*	that the list of folders stored on the C:\ drive is again visible

You can view a folder's contents by clicking the folder in the Explorer Bar or double-clicking the folder in the Contents pane. To view the contents of the folder that contains the Data Files:

| Step 1 | *Click* | the disk drive in the Explorer Bar where the Data Files are stored |

MOUSE TIP

Point means to place the mouse pointer on the command or item. **Click** means to press the left mouse button and release it. **Right-click** means to press the right mouse button and release it. **Double-click** means to press the left mouse button twice very rapidly. **Drag** means to hold down the left mouse button and then move the mouse pointer. **Right-drag** means to hold down the right mouse button and then move the mouse pointer. **Scroll** means to use the application scroll bar features or the IntelliMouse scrolling wheel.

MENU TIP

By default, the Explorer Bar shows your local and network folders. This is the Explorer Bar Folder view option. You can view Internet resources and a list of favorites by clicking View, pointing to Explorer Bar, and clicking Search, Favorites, or History.

appendix
B

| Step 2 | Double-click | the Data Files folder in the Contents pane (scroll, if necessary) to view a list of Data Files and folders |

You can resize and reposition folders and files in the Contents pane and add more details about the file size, type, and date modified. To change the size and position of the Data Files and folders:

Step 1	Click	the Views button list arrow ▦▾ on the Explorer toolbar
Step 2	Click	Large Icons to view horizontal rows of larger folder and file icons in the Contents pane
Step 3	Click	Small Icons on the Views button list to view horizontal rows of smaller folder and file icons in the Contents pane
Step 4	Click	Details on the Views button list to view a vertical list of folders and files names, sizes, types, and dates modified
Step 5	Click	List on the Views button list to view a simple list of the files and folders

B.c Creating a New Folder

You can create a new folder for an object in the Explorer Bar or the Contents pane. To add a folder to the My Documents folder in the C:\ drive folder list:

Step 1	Click	the My Documents folder in the Explorer Bar to select it (scroll, if necessary)
Step 2	Click	File
Step 3	Point to	New
Step 4	Click	Folder
Step 5	Observe	the newly created folder object in the Contents pane with the selected temporary name New Folder

To name the folder and refresh the Explorer Bar view:

Step 1	Key	Practice Folder
Step 2	Press	the ENTER key
Step 3	Observe	the new folder name in the Contents pane
Step 4	Click	View

Step 5	*Click*	R̲efresh
Step 6	*Observe*	that the My Documents folder has a plus sign, indicating that the folder list can be expanded

B.d Moving and Copying Folders and Files

You select folders and files by clicking them. You can then copy or move them with the Cut, C̲opy and P̲aste commands on the E̲dit menu or shortcut menu, the Copy and Paste buttons on the Explorer toolbar, or with the drag-and-drop or right-drag mouse methods. To copy a file from the Data Files folder to the Practice Folder using the right-drag method:

Step 1	*View*	the list of Data Files in the Contents pane
Step 2	*Right-drag*	any file to the My Documents folder in the Explorer Bar and pause until the My Documents folder expands to show the subfolders
Step 3	*Continue*	to right-drag the file to the Practice Folder subfolder under the My Documents folder in the Explorer Bar
Step 4	*Click*	C̲opy Here on the shortcut menu
Step 5	*Click*	the Practice Folder in the Explorer Bar to view the copied file's icon and filename in the Contents pane

B.e Renaming Folders and Files

Sometimes you want to change an existing file or folder name to a more descriptive name. To rename the copied file in the Practice Folder:

Step 1	*Verify*	the icon and filename for the copied file appears in the Contents pane
Step 2	*Right-click*	the copied file in the Contents pane
Step 3	*Click*	Rena̲me
Step 4	*Key*	Renamed File
Step 5	*Click*	the Contents area (not the filename) to accept the new filename

appendix
B

B.f Creating Desktop Shortcuts

You can add a shortcut for folders and files to the Windows desktop by restoring the Windows Explorer window to a smaller window and right-dragging a folder or file icon to the desktop. You can also right-drag a folder or file icon to the Desktop icon in the Explorer Bar inside the Windows Explorer window. To create a desktop shortcut to the Practice Folder using the Desktop icon:

Step 1	*Expand*	the My Documents folder in the Explorer Bar, if necessary, to view the Practice Folder subfolder
Step 2	*Right-drag*	the Practice Folder to the Desktop icon at the top of the Explorer Bar
Step 3	*Click*	Create Shortcut(s) Here
Step 4	*Minimize*	the Windows Explorer window to view the new shortcut on the desktop
Step 5	*Drag*	the Shortcut to Practice Folder desktop shortcut to the Recycle Bin to delete it
Step 6	*Click*	Yes
Step 7	*Click*	the Exploring-Practice Folder taskbar button to maximize the Windows Explorer window

B.g Deleting Folders and Files

When necessary, you can delete a folder and its contents or a file by selecting it and then clicking the Delete command on the File menu or shortcut menu, or pressing the DELETE key. You can also delete multiple selected folders and files at one time. To delete the Practice Folder and its contents:

Step 1	*Click*	the Practice Folder in the Explorer Bar to select it, if necessary
Step 2	*Press*	the DELETE key
Step 3	*Click*	Yes to send the folder and its contents to the Recycle Bin

Index